Ink marks 12/99

Saint Louis

LOUIS IX

Most Christian King of France

by the same author

SIMON DE MONTFORT

A BARONIAL HOUSEHOLD OF THE THIRTEENTH CENTURY

A detail from the statue of Louis at Mainneville (Eure)

Saint Louis

LOUIS IX

Most Christian King of France

by

MARGARET WADE LABARGE

with maps and illustrations

LITTLE, BROWN AND COMPANY BOSTON TORONTO

LIBRARY OF CONGRESS CATALOG CARD NO. 68-17271

FIRST AMERICAN EDITION

PRINTED IN THE UNITED STATES OF AMERICA

To R.C.L

Contents

Illustrations

PLATES

MAPS

Drawn by John Flower

Acknowledgements for the illustrations

The author and publishers are grateful to the following for permission to reproduce copyright material:

Archives Nationales for Plates 16a, 16b; Archives Photographiques for frontispiece and Plates 3, 4, 5, 13a, 13b, 14; the Bibliothèque Nationale for Plate 8, Ms. Fr. 13568, p. 83, from Joinville, *Vie de St Louis*, c. 1360, Plate 10a, Ms. Fr. 5716, 246, Plate 10b, Ms. Fr. 5716, p. 137, Plate 11a, Ms. Fr. 5716, f. 48, Plate 11b, Ms. Fr. 5716, p. 277, all from Guillaume de St Pathus, *Life and Miracles of St Louis*; the Trustees of the British Museum for Plate 6a, MS. Royal 16 G. VI, f. 395r, Plate 7a, MS. Royal 16 G. VI, f. 404v, both from the *Chroniques de St Denis* and Plate 9, MS. Cotton Titus A XVII, f. 43v; Photo Bulloz for Plate 7b from Bibliothèque Nationale, Ms. Fr. 5716, f. 40. Guillaume de St Pathus, *Vie et Miracles de St Louis*, Plates 12a, b, c, from B. de Montfaucon, *Monumens de la Monarchie française*, II, Paris 1730, LXXVIII–IX, Plate 15 an engraving from the edition of Joinville by Du Cange, 1668; the Master and Fellows of Corpus Christi College, Cambridge for Plate 16c from Corpus Christi College MS. 16 (Matthew Paris), f. iv a; Photo Giraudon for Plate 2 and Plate 6b, June from the *Très Riches Heures de Duc de Berry* in the Musée Condé, Chantilly; and the Trustees of the Pierpont Morgan Library for Plate 1, MS. 240, f. 8, *Moralised Bible*, c. 1250.

Preface

This study of St Louis, who has been surprisingly neglected in the English-speaking world, inevitably owes much to the kindness of many scholars and experts who patiently answered my questions and furthered my researches. I am particularly grateful to the Information Service of the French Embassy in Ottawa; to R. Millette, Cultural Attaché of the Canadian Embassy in Paris; and to Prof. J. R. Strayer, Prof. Thurman E. Philoon, and Rev. Michael Sheehan, C.S.B., but they share no responsibility for any errors. The Cercle Culturel de Royaumont kindly allowed me the use of their library and the opportunity to visit the remains of Louis's great abbey. I have received help and hospitality from many libraries in Canada and abroad, but I must acknowledge a special debt to the Library of Parliament, Ottawa; the Parliamentary Librarian, Erik Spicer; and the Assistant Librarian, Pamela Hardisty. They cheerfully tracked down rare and difficult books and efficiently demonstrated that the inherent problems of studying medieval France in present-day Canada could be overcome.

It has seemed essential to present French and Moslem names as simply and intelligibly as possible. Such terms as bailli, enquêteur, and Parlement, are easily recognizable but completely change meaning in translation, and have been used directly in the text without italics. French names have generally been translated into their English equivalents unless it seemed likely that misunderstanding might arise. The thorny question of the accurate rendering of Moslem names is still hotly debated by the experts. For convenience, I have adopted the style used by Sir Steven Runciman in his *History of the Crusades* as being both intelligible and acceptable.

Finally, my husband and children have given me unflagging support, encouragement, and useful criticism during the several years that the thirteenth century has invaded our home. This acknowledgement serves only as a token thank-you.

Margaret Wade Labarge

Saint Louis

LOUIS IX

Most Christian King of France

Louis IX seemed a prince destined to reform Europe, had it been capable of being reformed, to render France triumphant and civilized, and to be in every respect a model for the rest of mankind. His piety, which was that of an anchorite, did not deprive him of any of the virtues of a king; nor did his liberality break in upon the bounds of a prudent economy. He knew how to reconcile the profoundest politics with the strictest justice, and perhaps was the only sovereign who deserved this praise: in council he was prudent and firm, in battle intrepid but not rash, and compassionate, as if he had always been unhappy. In a word, it is not in the power of man to carry virtue to a greater height.

Voltaire, *Essay on the Manners and Spirit of Nations*

THE FAMILY OF LOUIS IX

PHILIP AUGUSTUS
King of France, 1180–1223
b. 1165 m. (1) Isabel of Hainault
(2) Ingeborg of Denmark
(3) Agnes of Meran

ALFONSO VIII the Noble
King of Castile 1158–1214
b. 1155 m. 1170 Eleanor dau. of
Henry II of England, d. 1214

Children of Philip Augustus:

- (3) Philip Hurepel, Count of Boulogne d. 1234
- (1) LOUIS VIII (1223–26) b. 1187 — m. 1200 — Blanche 1188–1252

Children of Alfonso VIII:

- Blanche 1188–1252
- Urraca d. 1220 m. Alfonso of Portugal
- Berengaria d. 1244 m. Alfonso IX of Leon

Children of Louis VIII and Blanche:

- 3 children d. young
- Philip 1209–18
- LOUIS IX (1226–70) b. 1214 m. 1234 Marguerite of Provence 1221–95
- Robert Count of Artois 1216–50 m. 1237 Mahaut of Brabant
- John 1219–c. 1227
- Alphonse Count of Poitiers 1220–71 m. 1237 Jeanne of Toulouse, d. 1271
- Philip Dagobert 1222–35
- Isabel 1223–69
- Stephen b. 1225 d. young
- Charles Count of Anjou King of Naples (1266–85) b. 1226 m. (1) 1246 Beatrice of Provence (2) 1268 Margaret of Burgundy

Children of Louis IX and Marguerite of Provence:

- Blanche 1240–43
- Isabel 1242–71 m. 1255 Theobald V of Champagne King of Navarre d. 1271
- Louis 1244–60
- PHILIP III the Bold (1270–85) b. 1245 m. (1) 1262 Isabella of Aragon, d. 1271 (2) 1274 Marie of Brabant, d. 1321
- John b. & d. 1248
- John Tristan Count of Nevers 1250–70 m. 1266 Yolande of Nevers d. 1280
- Peter Count of Alençon 1251–84 m. 1272 Jeanne of Châtillon d. 1291
- Blanche 1253–1323 m. 1269 Ferdinand of Castile d. 1275
- Marguerite 1254–71 m. 1270 John duke of Brabant d. 1294
- Robert Count of Clermont 1256–1318 m. 1277 Beatrice heiress of Bourbon d. 1310
- Agnes 1260–1327 m. 1279 Robert duke of Burgundy d. 1305

Son of Philip III:

- PHILIP IV the Fair (1285–1314)
  - last Capetian kings of France and the Valois kings of Navarre

Introduction

It is admittedly surprising to find a medieval saint enthusiastically praised by Voltaire, but the voice of the eighteenth century rationalist is only the most unexpected note in the general chorus of admiration for St Louis. Louis IX, Most Christian King of France, who lived from 1214 until 1270 and was therefore almost an exact contemporary of Henry III of England, earned the respect and approval of his contemporaries, both secular and religious, and has proved an almost inexhaustible topic for French biographers through the centuries. The approach of these writers has varied with the aspect of Louis's character they wished to emphasize. Devout believers, interested in hagiography, have been inspired by the charming stories told by Louis's clerical companions: they have praised the saint and his virtues, but have had little time for the king. Ardent patriots, on the other hand, have interpreted his achievements, even his unsuccessful crusades as the natural and inevitable result of peculiarly French virtues, designed to glorify the French monarchy. Unfortunately there have not been many historians among these biographers. In the seventeenth century Le Nain de Tillemont wrote an extremely valuable six-volume life of Louis, based on all the documents then available, but his work stands alone and is still unsurpassed. Several of the best-known medievalists of France have dealt with certain specialized aspects of the time or have given excellent, but very brief, summaries, but French scholarship has yet to provide the exhaustive biography which is so badly needed. The modern lives of Louis have been rapid surveys or special pleadings and have not taken into consideration the recent research. In fact, so little new work of synthesis has been attempted that the accepted French authority is still the life written by Henri Wallon, and published in 1876, while the sole biography written in English was published in 1901. This contemporary neglect of Louis is particularly unfortunate since he was one of the most important rulers of the Middle Ages, and a knowledge of his actions and motives is essential for an understanding of medieval history. But to look at Louis only through the glasses of national or religious chauvinism gives not only an incomplete but a misleading view. The resulting picture is as close to the reality of a thirteenth-century Christian monarch as the eighteenth-century portrait of St Louis which shows him as a fashionable fop in silk stockings and high-heeled shoes, daintily flourishing a silk handkerchief containing the Crown of Thorns.*

In the middle of the thirteenth century France was at the centre of the development of learning in Europe. The influence of the growing University of Paris was enhanced by the presence of such philosophers as Aquinas, Albert the Great, and Bonaventura. The vernacular was emerging as the medium for everything from poems to law treatises, from sermons to scurrilous stories. French was indeed the *lingua franca* not only of France but also of England, Sicily and Outremer. The cathedrals of Chartres, Paris, Rheims, and Amiens displayed the magnificent surge of French Gothic. This leadership in art and culture enhanced the prestige of the French king, while the peace and tranquillity established within his realm, so unlike the wranglings in England and in the Empire, reinforced his European position. Louis was the most respected monarch of his day and France a rich and ever more powerful kingdom. But even to his contemporaries, Louis was more than just a successful king. He symbolized the accepted ideals of his age, and, at the same time, he combined a firm belief in the older traditions with a skilful use of the newer methods.

The ancient title of Most Christian King, awarded to the French kings by an eleventh-century pope, was literally applicable to Louis IX. More than any other medieval ruler, he regarded his kingly duties as part of his Christian vocation. He believed that personal holiness was not enough for a king; he must also embody

*This particular portrait was painted in colonial Quebec in the early eighteenth century, but it was a recognized French convention to paint St Louis with the features and fashionable clothes of the reigning monarch – a heavy-handed compliment.

and put into practice the secular virtues of justice and peace, both within his realm and wherever else his influence allowed. A Christian king must, as far as it lay within his power, make it easy and even necessary for his people to live a Christian life. Naturally Louis understood this duty in thirteenth-century terms. There was, for example, an overwhelming emphasis on the safety of the community, rather than on the abstract rights of the individual conscience. The rulers of that time felt that tolerance for heretics, Moslems, Jews, or even usurers was a sign of weakness and lack of fervour, for all of them were considered dangerous to the state as well as to the church. Private morality, too, was regarded as a matter of public concern and a fit subject for legislative order. But Louis's moralistic outlook was combined with a thorough-going recognition of the rights, as well as the duties, of the king of France. The king's claims to rents, services, and lordships were continually put forward by the advocacy of the royal officials. The strength of the king's servants and the prestige of the royal justice contributed enormously to the centralization of the realm and opened the door to the despotism of less scrupulous rulers. For a brief golden period Louis IX blended the traditions of the old and the dynamism of the new in apparent harmony.

The Christian ideal of sanctity was generally admired and respected in the thirteenth century, even though most medieval men did not attempt to approach holiness. Brought up strictly and devoutly by his Spanish mother, Louis was taught from childhood to combine asceticism and piety with the justice, liberality, and strength demanded of a good ruler. His crusading experience reinforced and deepened his unwavering faith and encouraged his natural tendency to prayer, mortification, and charity. Nevertheless, Louis did not allow his devotions to interfere with his kingly duties or to weaken his control of his kingdom, so that his reign was soon looked back upon as the very symbol of 'the good old days'. Louis's canonization in 1297 marked the official recognition by the church of his heroic sanctity, but it merely added papal sanction to an existing legend which was constantly fed by French clerics. Their attitude was well summed up by the anonymous clerk who described the king's virtues in the liturgy of his feast:

Happy the realm whose king is foresighted,
Peaceful, pious, and virtuous,
Always intrepid in adversities.
Such was Saint Louis![1]

A study of Louis IX must also recognize that the extraordinary charm and personal influence of the man helped to enhance the position of the French monarchy. Louis's moral dignity and reputation for justice made him the favoured arbiter and peacemaker of all Europe. His enormous prestige with all classes of society created a reservoir of good will and affection within his own kingdom. This popularity, esteem, and above all sanctity make possible a more rounded study of Louis than is usual for a medieval subject. The Middle Ages were not normally concerned with the cult of an individual, unless he was a saint or a king, and even then official lives were usually written to an accepted pattern. The lives officially composed to celebrate Louis's virtues, the chronicles of the kingdom of France and its regions, and the official documents of his own administration and of his relations with popes and princess are all full of information. Most important is the memoir of John of Joinville, knight, seneschal of Champagne, and crusading companion. His vivid and human life of his sovereign and friend makes Louis a living personality, not a plaster saint or an unapproachable king. Louis embodied the highest ideals of his time in his interests, beliefs, and friendships, and his long reign reflected the enormous range of political, religious, and social life in thirteenth-century France.

The Young King's Inheritance

The future Louis IX was born on April 25, 1214, at Poissy, a quiet little town on the Seine a few miles west of Paris. His birthday was the feast of St Mark and a Rogation Day, the time when crosses veiled in black were carried in procession through the fields. John of Joinville suggests that this coincidence was an early warning of the number of people, including Louis himself, who were to die on the two crusades of his reign[1] – but no such forebodings or presages of future glory surrounded the baby's cradle. Louis already had an older brother, Philip; the second son was welcomed as insuring the line of succession. Soon after his birth Louis was baptised in the church of Poissy, which still proudly exhibits the baptismal font used for him. Poissy, for Louis, was more important even than Rheims. At Rheims, he said, he was crowned king of France, but at Poissy he had received the grace of baptism, 'a greater gift and incomparable dignity above all honours or worldly rewards'.[2]

The life of a younger son of the royal family was not to continue for long. When Louis was only four his elder brother Philip died and he stepped into the direct line of succession.

But Louis had always lived in the shadow of his overpowering grandfather, Philip Augustus, whom he greatly admired and whose methods and practices he was often to quote in his own policy. The old king's conscious and consistent exploitation of the royal power had been buttressed by his many conquests. When he died in 1223 he left his son Louis VIII a kingdom immensely enriched and strengthened and inspired by the beginning of a national consciousness. Louis VIII was a capable and ambitious prince, well educated and considered learned by his contemporaries. Gerald of Wales, the irascible archdeacon and vain literator, described him as the only prince in Europe to whom it might be worthwhile for an author to present his works. Gerald's reasons were characteristically ambiguous: he claimed that Louis 'had been imbued from his youth with letters and liberal studies . . . and also because he was notably generous'.[3] However, Louis IX had little real contact with his father, who had campaigned in England during his early childhood and whose reign of only three years was also mainly devoted to campaigning.

The strongest and most pervasive influence in the life of the young Louis was that of his mother, Blanche of Castile. She was perhaps the outstanding woman of the thirteenth century and both in her private and public life acted with force and judgment. Blanche had notable forebears: she was the daughter of Alfonso the Noble of Castile and Eleanor of England, and thus the granddaughter of Eleanor of Aquitaine and Henry II. In typical thirteenth-century fashion, Blanche first appears in French history as a useful counter in the inevitable bargaining over peace treaties. When Philip Augustus and King John of England were attempting to come to a peaceful settlement of their contest in Normandy, in January 1200, they decided on a marriage alliance between Philip's heir Louis and one of the daughters of Alfonso, at that time John's closest heirs. John was to abandon to his niece as dower the city and county of Evreux, as well as the strongholds that the French occupied in Normandy at the time of the death of Richard I, Cœur de Lion (1199): in addition, he was to give her 30,000 marks* of silver. King John sent a hasty message to his mother at Bordeaux, asking her to go to the court of Alfonso to bring back the desired bride. Queen Eleanor was almosty eighty, but she was still indomitable and undiscouraged by the proposed journey. Accompanied by a party of French ambassadors, she set off through the wintry weather and the rugged country of the Pyrenees and northern Spain. When the French and English emissaries arrived at the Castilian court, they found that they had two princesses from whom to choose. Berengaria, the oldest, had been married in 1197 to the king of Leon, but there remained Urraca and Blanche. No previous decision had been made between the two sisters, although Urraca at thirteen was a year older,

*A mark was worth two-thirds of an English pound.

usually a sufficient reason. The story goes that the French ambassadors looked at the two girls to make their choice and thought Urraca slightly more beautiful, but they were sure that their countrymen could never get used to the difficulty of her name.[4] They decided on Blanche who started almost immediately on the long journey to France, leaving Spain behind her forever. By the beginning of April Blanche and her grandmother had arrived in Bordeaux where Queen Eleanor, at last overcome with fatigue, handed over her charge to the care of the archbishop of Bordeaux and retired to the abbey of Fontevrault. This was one of the last public functions of the old queen, and it is a pity that there is no record of the journey which threw together in extraordinary circumstances the strong-willed woman who had influenced so much of the history of the twelfth century and the young girl who was similarly to influence the destinies of France during the first half of the thirteenth century.

After Easter the archbishop of Bordeaux conducted Blanche of Castile on the last leg of her journey to Normandy. The treaty of Le Goulet was signed on May 22, 1200, ratifying John's cession of Evreux and its district, most of the Norman Vexin, and some other fiefs. The following day, at Pontmort in English territory, Blanche was married to the thirteen-year-old Prince Louis. Since Philip Augustus was under papal interdict over the problems of his marriage, the ceremony could not be solemnized in his lands nor could he be present. The church chosen was barely inside the boundary of English Normandy, and the marriage was presided over by the archbishop of Bordeaux, of the English province of Aquitaine.

There is little doubt that the marriage so carefully arranged for dynastic and territorial purposes was a happy one. Blanche may have suffered from homesickness during the early months: there is a pleasant story of her young husband beseeching St Hugh of Lincoln, who was passing through Paris on a pilgrim's tour of notable shrines, to come and see his wife. The holy bishop found the bride very sad 'but a few words from him cheered her up so much that she immediately forgot the grief and depression under which she had laboured for some days, and her happiness was reflected in her face'.[5] Blanche certainly missed Spain and her relatives there: her continued Spanishness was one of the complaints that the French barons later laid against her. Although she never returned to Spain, once she vowed a pilgrimage to St James of Compostela, the pilgrimage shrine on the Galician coast of Spain, but William of Auvergne, the bishop of Paris, urged her to fulfil her vow by giving the money to St James in Paris, the home of the poverty-stricken Dominicans, and Blanche obeyed him.[6] She must have regretted the lost opportunity, for she allowed the groom in charge of her sumpters to go to Compostela in 1239 and gave him a generous gift of 60 sous.[7]

Blanche soon became rooted in the French court. She and Louis had twelve children, although four died before her husband came to the throne, and three more were to die before Louis IX came of age. Nevertheless constant childbearing did not stop Blanche showing her concern with affairs of state. When Prince Louis embarked on his ill-advised and unsuccessful invasion of England in 1216, Blanche consistently tried to rally men and material for his support. A contemporary story suggests the force of her personality. Blanche demanded help from her redoubtable father-in-law and was refused. She then swore that she would pawn her children if necessary to get some money for her husband, and Philip Augustus was sufficiently moved to offer her some assistance from his treasure.[8]

During Louis VIII's brief reign Blanche took no share in the affairs of the realm. She arranged for the education and upbringing of her children and even the future king was treated with salutary firmness. He was taught his letters, was occasionally beaten by his master, and early learned to share his mother's strict piety and devotion to the services of the church.[9] Blanche was a stern Christian although the most famous of all her remarks: 'Dearest son, I would rather you incur temporal death than by any mortal sin you should offend your Creator'[10] has been made more uncompromising than was actually intended. Nevertheless Blanche's training of the future king was rigorous and demanding; even when he was a child she insisted that he must hear all the hours of the Office – the daily prayer said by the monks at different times of day – and to listen to sermons on feast days.[11] Their quiet and essentially domestic life was to end abruptly.

Louis VIII made his will in 1225,[12] when no concern was felt over the possibility of his early death; and he was a vigorous man not yet forty when he embarked on a successful crusade against the Albigensians in the summer of 1226. But on his way back to Paris he was struck down at Montpensier in the Auvergne by a fatal attack of fever and dysentery. When the king realized that he was dying, he immediately did everything he could to provide for the peaceful accession of his son and the maintenance of the peace of the realm during its rule by a minor. He demonstrated his confidence in his wife's ability by naming her guardian of the kingdom, as well as of the royal children, and had the bishops of Sens, Beauvais, and Chartres swear that this had been done in their presence and while the king was still 'sane of mind'. Only a few days before his death on November 8, the king summoned all the bishops, lords and officials who had accompanied him to the south and made them solemnly swear that in the event of his death they would have his son crowned as soon as possible.[13] The need for speed and immediate action seems to have been uppermost in Louis's mind and perhaps was a further reason for the unprecedented naming of a woman to serve as regent of the kingdom. The dying king too may have been somewhat suspicious of his half-brother Philip Hurepel, the 'Shaggyhead', count of Boulogne. Philip was in his prime at twenty-eight and may well have harboured ambitions to dispossess his young nephew and mount the throne. Whatever the reasons, Blanche was left in full charge.

The sudden illness and death of Louis VIII after a reign of only three years, leaving an heir who was a minor and a kingdom ruled by a woman, seemed to presage the undoing of all Philip Augustus's work in enlarging and strengthening France and the royal domain. Many of the great feudal lords saw this as a heaven-sent opportunity to reassert their independence of the crown. The twelve-year-old Louis entered upon an inheritance encumbered with many pressing problems, but one which had some hidden and valuable assets.

First of all, the young king was heir to a tangled complex of royal powers and attributes. Kingship was still not fully defined in the beginning of the thirteenth century, although what had been an abstract concept was rapidly becoming more powerful under the twin stimuli of growing royal prestige and the expanding influence of Roman law. Even in the weakest days of the French monarchy the strong and often rebellious feudal lords recognized the theoretical supremacy of the king as their suzerain, and did him homage. The very weakness of the early Capetian kings had been a royal asset, since it temporarily blinded the great lords to the extent of the rights claimed as an integral part of the royal powers. Philip Augustus accelerated the transformation of these theoretical claims into actual enforceable rights, for his continued acquisition of territories for the royal domain gave him a substantial basis of support in his struggle against the independent feudal lords. The revival of Roman law, with its emphasis on the untrammelled superiority of the ruler, encouraged the royal drive towards more absolute power by providing a legal definition and precedent. Even the royal title in the thirteenth century illustrates the shift in interpretation of the idea of kingship from the Germanic to the Roman, from the personal link to the territorial one. Louis IX is the first king to be more commonly described in contemporary records as 'king of France', rather than 'king of the French'. The obvious fact of growing royal power in the thirteenth century, compared to the actual weakness of the Empire during the same period, helped to consolidate the theoretical as well as the practical supremacy of Europe's kings.

This enhancement of the position and powers of the king was much encouraged by the church, especially in France. The clergy saw the king's duty of maintaining justice and peace in purely religious terms: they interpreted his responsibility as a call to build the City of God here on earth, and proceeded to aid him with both temporal and spiritual weapons. The prestige of the monarchy was emphasized by this ecclesiastical support. Only the French ruler enjoyed the title of Most Christian King, a distinction supposedly conferred on Clovis, king of the Franks, by St Rémy. The mystical element which gradually developed in the ceremonial surrounding the royal coronation also testified to the quasi-religious position of the king. The act of crowning was the sign of the king's temporal sovereignty, but the anointing with holy oil had sacramental significance as the heavenly source of royal dignity and of such thaumaturgic powers as the king's touch for the healing of the sick. The holy oil used in the coronation of the French king was particularly revered, since it was reputed to have been brought by a dove directly from heaven at the time of the baptism of Clovis. The possession of this holy ampoule was the basis of the successful claim of Rheims to be the proper place of coronation, and the right of its archbishop to officiate at the ceremony.

Legends crystallized around this vague conviction of the specially holy nature of the Frankish king. One of the most popular, current from the tenth to the fourteenth centuries, described his special vocation claiming that the last and greatest of his line would unite Romans and Greeks, convert the Jews, and finally lay down his sceptre and crown on the Mount of Olives as tokens of the surrender of the earthly kingdom to the rule of Jesus Christ.[14] Such amorphous religious beliefs, with their strong emphasis on symbolism, are difficult for the present-day mind to grasp or to estimate at their contemporary value. For the men of the thirteenth century a symbol was merely one valid and conclusive way of expressing truth: they found no difficulty in accepting the special status of their king as part of their religious beliefs and of the natural order of the universe.

More than symbolism was required, however, to translate royal claims into actual power, and to insure general obedience to the royal commands. The moral authority of the thirteenth-century French kings was enforced and exercised by means of a closely knit household and appointed royal officials. The political theory of the time recognized the need for royal counsellors, although the exact status of these men was never fully defined. In administrative matters, the thirteenth century was an age of rapid change marked by an uneasy coexistence of old feudal practices with the newer manifestations of royal power. The great magnates, insistent on their feudal rights, felt that they were naturally entitled to be the closest advisers of their suzerain, the king. They laid particular emphasis on the rights of the peers of France, and their proper place in the *curia regis*, the king's court, which was at once the supreme seat of justice and the ceremonial centre of the realm. They argued with vigour, but with singular lack of success, that they were subject only to trial by their peers, not to the decisions in which the king was aided by the professional, but socially unequal, judges of the king's court.

These feudal claims were being constantly opposed by the growing royal power. From 1180 on the Capetian kings steadily reduced their dependence on the great lords. The major offices of the royal household, such as Seneschal, Constable, Steward, which had been in the hands of certain noble families as hereditary honours, were either not filled, or their functions were made purely honorary. Instead, the king gathered around himself a group of counsellors, both cleric and lay, who were chosen for competence and loyalty, not for their place in the feudal structure. This new professional class became increasingly important in the central government finding royal service an interesting and profitable career. They looked after their own material interests through gifts from the royal bounty. By the thirteenth century the most important local officials, too, the baillis and the seneschals, were appointed and paid by the king and held office at his pleasure. This nascent civil service, which both sprang *from* and added *to* the steady growth of the royal administrative system, was one of the main instruments of the royal power and a valuable part of young Louis's inheritance.

A very important part of the functions of these royal administrative officers was to make sure that all the moneys owed to the king were actually collected. The king's revenues in the thirteenth century were a mixture of feudal dues, payments in lieu of military service, profits from the sale of goods, profits from the exercise of justice, and various special levies, particularly those raised both from the church and the towns on the occasions of Louis IX's crusades. There was as yet no regular system of taxation but, except for the unusual years of the crusades, Louis's revenues seem to have been more than sufficient for his expenses. In fact, the revenues rose considerably faster than his obligations. Unlike his royal brother-in-law in England, Henry III, the French king was never forced by over-spending to bow to the will of his barons. Louis was not so much of a spendthrift, nor as extravagant a builder, and he never became personally embroiled in the expensive wild goose chase for the Sicilian throne. Apart from the crusades, his expenses were reasonable and, so far as we can tell from the fragmentary nature of the accounts, the king had ample revenue to 'live of his own', the medieval ideal for the self-sufficient monarch.

One of the reasons for this financial self-sufficiency was the great extension in the domain of France achieved by Louis's father and grandfather. The thirteenth-century map of France differed widely from the one we know: until the middle of the twelfth century 'France' referred only to the Ile-de-France, the original domain of the French monarchy. Working outwards from this small and unprotected core the twelfth-century kings had begun to add to their lands and increase their powers. Philip Augustus, above all, was spectacularly successful. He achieved territorial gains in several ways; by the accepted method of marriage alliances, by the exploitation of all possible feudal rights against his perennial enemies the Plantagenets and other important lords, and by an astuteness which profited by the wars and conquests of others.

The first wife of Philip Augustus was Isabel of Hainault, the niece of Philip of Alsace, the count of Flanders, and she brought as her dowry the county of Artois, that is, the southern part of the great county of Flanders. The details of the agreement and counter-agreement between the king and the count of Flanders and his heirs are unnecessary to follow in detail. By the time the king died in 1223 he had successfully asserted French influence in Flanders, and had acquired not only Artois but also Vermandois and Valois. The valleys of the three great rivers of the north, the Somme, the Aisne, and the Oise, were all in royal hands so that Paris was protected from the north and had a safe line of communication with Artois.

Philip's most extensive acquisitions of territory were made at the expense of the Plantagenets, who in the middle of the twelfth century had rejoiced in an Angevin empire which stretched from the English Channel to the Pyrenees, controlling Normandy, Maine, Touraine, Anjou, Poitou, and Aquitaine. Buttressed by his continental domains as well as the power and prestige of the English throne, Henry II, although nominally the vassal of the French king, bestrode Europe. His power did not even survive his death, as his jealous and warlike sons split the empire he had amassed. Philip Augustus cleverly used every opportunity to turn one brother against the other and to undermine the Angevin power. He succeeded by a complicated series of manœuvres in trapping John both legally and militarily. The French court pronounced the confiscation of the lands which John held from the French king because of John's refusal to answer the summons to his suzerain's court. Philip Augustus's army finally made the legal decision fact. The decisive victory of Bouvines in 1214, followed by the Treaty of Chinon, put the seal on the French king's gains at the expense of John. Normandy, Maine, Anjou, and much of Poitou came under the control of the French crown, although legal recognition of the conquest by the English only came after another forty-five years.

Louis VIII continued the policy of expansion. He fought one campaign in Poitou to subdue its lords who were always in rebellion, and ensured French control of La Rochelle and the Ile d'Oléron, further isolating the English lands in Aquitaine. Louis's most important contribution to the territorial growth of France was his successful move towards the acquisition of the county of Toulouse and the territory of the Albigeois. The Albigensian Crusade* against the Catharist heretics of Languedoc had been inaugurated by Pope Innocent III during the reign of Philip Augustus. The French king refused to join it, but he allowed many of his northern barons to go south and fight in a war which was partly a genuine struggle against the widespread heresy threatening the whole religious and to a lesser extent the social structure of the South, but also a licence to obtain new lands and rich booty. Simon de Montfort,† the leader of the crusade, was from the minor

*The Catharists, or Albigensians – so named from their concentration at Albi, were dualists, inheritors of the ancient Manichean heresy. They believed that the world was ruled by two equal principles of good and evil, spirit and matter. This belief entailed an abhorrence for all the material side of man, since it was essentially evil. From this sprang a particular detestation for marriage and procreation which perpetuated man's physical nature. The sect was divided into two classes: a small group of Perfect, who lived a most rigorous and ascetic life; and the great majority of Believers, who were subject to few restraints except to endeavour to join the Perfect before death. The heresy spread very widely in twelfth-century Languedoc where the holy lives of the Perfect contrasted most favourably with the decadence and luxury of many of the leading ecclesiastics.

†Simon the Crusader, father of Simon de Montfort, earl of Leicester.

nobility of the Ile-de-France: pious, brutally harsh and enormously ambitious, he was a remarkably competent leader of the papal forces. The war raged through the south of France for ten years while the northern armies devastated the rich lands of Languedoc and the cities in which the arts flourished. Despite the military successes of the crusaders and the brutal massacre of many of the Albigensian heretics and their frequently innocent supporters, no final peace had been reached when Simon de Montfort was killed in 1219 during the siege of the city of Toulouse.

The struggle continued intermittently but the count of Toulouse, a secret supporter of the heretics, anxious to uphold his position against the northern French, began to regain his influence. Simon de Montfort's eldest son Amaury was quite incapable of bringing the war to a satisfactory conclusion. He attempted to surrender to the French king the claims to the county of Toulouse, the duchy of Narbonne, and the viscounty of Carcassone which he had inherited from his father. Philip Augustus refused the offer but in 1224 Louis VIII accepted the cession. After his success in Poitou, and encouraged by a church council at Bourges, Louis mounted a further crusade against the Albigensians. He had successfully besieged Avignon and marched on to subdue many further strongholds in the south, before he died, on his way back to Paris. Toulouse and many of the lordships subject to it had not yet become part of the French domain by the accession of Louis IX, but the way had been prepared and St Louis's reign was to see the triumph of French administration and orthodox religion in Languedoc.

Louis IX came to the throne of a France much increased in geographical extent, but still ringed by major and potentially dangerous lordships. Here too, the work of his ancestors in taming and attaching the great feudatories to the throne by threads of relationship and self-interest simplified his problems. The great county of Flanders in the north had been almost powerless since the capture of Count Ferrand at Bouvines. In 1226 Countess Jeanne was still trying to achieve her husband's release. The country of Boulogne had been given by King Louis VIII to his brother Philip Hurepel in 1224, and Philip safeguarded the royal interests. The great houses of Blois and Champagne had been linked to the Capetians by marriage alliances at the time of Louis VII, and Count Theobald IV of Champagne, although not wholly reliable, was still generally to be found on the royal side. After his defeat at Bouvines John Lackland had also been forced to cede the suzerainty of the county of Brittany to the French king. Philip Augustus attempted to safeguard the Capetian interests by marrying Alix, the countess of Brittany, to his cousin Peter of Dreux, the great-grandson of Louis VI. Peter of Dreux, better known as Mauclerc, the 'scourge of the clergy', swore liege homage to Philip Augustus but took every opportunity to play off the French against the English king. Among the other great feudal lords, the dukes of Burgundy were faithful vassals, and the counts of Toulouse were enfeebled by the continuing war in the south. Two lands now considered as French were outside France's suzerainty in the thirteenth century. The county of Provence, including the city of Marseilles, was officially a fief of the Empire. Louis IX's marriage to the oldest daughter of the count of Provence began the slow process of French infiltration into the affairs of the county. Gascony, or Aquitaine, was the last great fief left in France of the Angevin empire. It recognized the English king as overlord, though the Gascons were always turbulent and restless vassals. Nevertheless, ties of trade, particularly the massive export of wine, bound them more closely to the English market than to the French mainland.

Louis IX was also left a legacy of possible great danger. When Louis VIII drew up his will he left detailed provision for his younger sons in the form of appanages, that is, grants of land given for their maintenance which actually detached parts of the royal domain from the king's hand and could have been the beginning of new and independent lordships. Robert was left the county of Artois; Alphonse, the county of Poitou and Auvergne; and Charles, the youngest, received Anjou and Maine because of the death of his brother John for whom they were originally intended. It is amusing to speculate on what would have happened if John had survived long enough to inherit this appanage. Louis VIII's will specifically ordered that any subsequent sons not provided for should become clerks.[15] Charles was one of the most able and ambitious men of the thirteenth century; as an ecclesiastic he would have been satisfied with nothing less than the papacy.

The territorial, governmental, and personal elements of the inheritance of Louis IX therefore brought advantages and disadvantages. Most immediately important for the future of France was the character of Blanche of Castile. From the moment the messengers brought her the news of her husband's fatal illness until her own death twenty-six years later, the queen's every effort was directed to one end – the maintenance and strengthening of the royal authority in France.

II

Blanche of Castile and the Regency 1226–1234

Queen Blanche might mourn the premature death of her husband, but the maintenance of order, and the need to have the young Louis crowned quickly, gave her little time to indulge her grief. The arrangements for the coronation began immediately so that as many of the important nobles as possible should be rallied to the side of the king. The barons were given no time to group against the legitimate heir; the coronation was set for Rheims on November 29, the first Sunday of Advent, and letters to this effect were sent out to the leading bishops and nobles.[1]

It is hard to over-estimate the importance of the rite of coronation at this period, since it put the seal of divine approval and recognition on the new king and enhanced him with a quasi-religious aura. The swift accomplishment of the coronation with its accompanying oaths of homage was all the more necessary in the case of a king as young as Louis IX since open revolt against a crowned and properly acknowledged king was regarded very seriously, even by rebellious feudal vassals.

Blanche and Louis set out for Rheims a few days before the date set. On their way they stopped at Soissons, where Louis was knighted. To save the boy's strength he made much of the trip in a carriage, but his formal entrance into Rheims was on a great warhorse. On Sunday morning the long and complicated ceremony took place in the cathedral of Rheims, still under construction after a disastrous fire some fifteen years before. Although it was the cherished and jealously maintained right of the archbishop of Rheims to preside at the king's coronation the see was vacant in 1226, and the archbishop's place was taken by his suffragan Jacques Bazoches, bishop of Soissons.

The established *ordo* for the rite of coronation was made at

Rheims at the end of St Louis's reign but it undoubtedly enshrines the main elements of his own coronation. Surrounded by those peers of France whom loyalty or the hope of future benefits had brought to his side, the young king was anointed with the holy oil and attired in the magnificent coronation regalia. These had been brought for the ceremony, according to custom, by the abbot of St Denis in whose abbey near Paris they were kept. The peers put their hands on the king's crown to support it and then saw the great sword of Charlemagne carried unsheathed before the king by the count of Boulogne. As the procession made its way from the cathedral to the palace Queen Blanche was probably too concerned with the many problems which lay ahead to encourage more than the minimum courtesies. The usual long-drawn out and brilliant feasts and celebrations were not provided, but the penitential season of Advent may have served as an excuse. Although a great number of prelates were present, many of the powerful nobles had stayed away. Flanders and Champagne were represented only by their countesses, and the count of Brittany and Hugh count of La Marche and leader of the Poitevin lords, did not appear at all.

Once Louis had been properly acknowledged and crowned as lawful king of France, Blanche moved quickly to forestall the rising tide of revolt among the nobles. Philip Hurepel, the count of Boulogne, was rewarded for his initial fidelity with the castles of Mortain and Lillebonne, and the right to the homage of the county of St Pol, while the Candlemas accounts of 1227 show that he was also given 1,000 pounds.*[2] Countess Jeanne of Flanders, who had been trying for some time to win the freedom of her husband, Ferrand of Portugal, imprisoned after opposing Philip Augustus at the battle of Bouvines, was able to improve the conditions of the treaty worked out with Louis VIII in April 1226. Even before Louis's coronation Jeanne had sent emissaries to the

*Medieval French currency, like that of England, was nominally based on the weight of a pound of silver. Each pound, or *livre*, was made up of twenty shillings or *sous* of twelve pennies each. Only the penny, or *denier*, was an actual coin; the others were merely moneys of account. However, the currency had depreciated unequally over the centuries. In thirteenth-century France two types of royal money were current; the pound Paris, official money of all the royal accounts, and the more popular pound *tournois* (minted at Tours), which was worth about four-fifths of the pound Paris.

king's council armed, as the chronicle puts it, with 'marks and pounds' to buy the count's deliverance. The council replied that all decision had to be put off until after the king was crowned.[3] Their decision came soon after, however, for before December 6 two members of the king's household were sent to Flanders to receive the pledges and oaths of fidelity from the knights and towns of Flanders, according to the agreement reached between the king and the Countess Jeanne.[4] By the terms of the agreement the king was to hold the great fortress of Douai for ten years, the costs being borne by the count and countess of Flanders; the towns and knights were to give pledges to the king; and the count and countess promised to keep the peace made at Melun in 1226, not to wage war against the king or his men, and not to make new fortresses in Flanders.[5] The provision against the building of fortresses was considered particularly important in an era when warfare consisted mostly of sieges, and the possession of strong fortified castles could overawe a whole countryside. The regent continued to watch the building activities of the royal vassals very carefully, although certain concessions were given for good behaviour and continued fidelity. In August 1229, for example, Ferrand was allowed to build a moat and palisade at his manor of Gravelines and to reconstruct the city gate of Lille. Even this permission was grudging, for the act carefully specified that only the foundations could be in stone; the superstructure had to be in wood and the ditches could only be of a limited depth.[6]

By acting quickly Queen Blanche safeguarded the royal power in the north of the kingdom. Trouble was still ready to flare in the west and south-west. The absence of the counts of Brittany and La Marche from the coronation ceremonies was a bad omen. Both lords were independent and ambitious, both felt that they could count on active assistance from England in any intrigues against the French throne. Peter Mauclerc, count of Brittany, was a particularly brusque and ambitious man who served as count only during the minority of his son, but took all possible advantage of the strategic position of Brittany. Hugh of La Marche, the head of the notorious Lusignan family, was married to Isabel of Angoulême, the vain widow of King John of England. Hugh's power in Poitou had been lessened by the successful campaigns of

Louis VIII and the count of La Marche was anxious to seize any opportunity to reassert his independence. The two counts were joined in their alliance against the king by Count Theobald of Champagne, a potentially dangerous rebel whose lands marched along the eastern frontier of the Ile-de-France. Count Peter seized the strongholds of Bellême and St James-de-Beuvron, on the border between Brittany and Normandy, and the rebellious nobles gathered their forces.

A show of royal strength was essential if the rebellion was not to spread. The queen regent was assisted by the count of Boulogne and Robert, count of Dreux and brother of Peter Mauclerc, and by the advice and spiritual encouragement of the papal legate, Cardinal Romanus of St Angelo, who was in France from 1225 to 1229. Accompanied by a large army the royal forces set out for the south-west in the middle of winter. They were at Tours by February 20, 1227, at Chinon the following day, and from there pressed on towards Loudun. As was usual in medieval warfare the armies, having both shown their strength, then paused while negotiations went on to settle the affair without a pitched battle. The count of Champagne was the first to break from the conspiracy. He returned to the king, was greeted cheerfully, and restored to the royal friendship. Blanche also attempted to rivet his loyalties more firmly by the payment of 4,000 pounds.[7]

With the departure of the count of Champagne the rebellion lost much of its strength, especially as the English aid upon which the conspirators had been counting was not forthcoming. Peter Mauclerc and Hugh of La Marche refused to answer two of the royal summons but finally appeared reluctantly at Vendôme on March 16, 1227, and made their submission. In the presence of the legate they did homage to the young king and agreed to the conditions laid down by the regent. The settlement known as the Treaty of Vendôme, was in fact mild, since Queen Blanche was not yet in a position to lay down ultimatums. Its provisions were designed to bring the counts of Brittany and La Marche closer to the king of France through various marriage alliances. In addition, Richard of Cornwall, the brother of the king of England and who had been in Gascony during the plans for the revolt, agreed to the prolongation of the truce between England and France.[8]

The rebellious barons were not to be so easily intimidated and plans for rebellion continued to simmer beneath the surface, waiting only for a propitious moment to sputter into the open once more. One of the weapons the barons used in their struggle against Blanche was the accusation that royal policy was determined by the queen's improper love for Count Theobald and the papal legate. The count apparently wrote certain of his poems for the queen, but a liaison between the devout and arrogant widow of forty who had borne twelve children – the youngest within the last few months – and the gay but ineffectual count, thirteen years her junior, seems utterly implausible. The rumour about the legate, spread by popular and scurrilous political songs, many by aggrieved students, was equally unfounded. There were compelling reasons of policy for Blanche's actions; no furtive love affair was needed as a motive. The barons muttered too that the queen was a stranger, a Spaniard, and a woman: 'Queen Blanche ought not to govern so great a thing as the kingdom of France, and it did not pertain to a woman to do such a thing'.[9]

In an attempt to put their complaints into action the barons conspired together at Corbeil. They felt they could enforce their will if only they could gain control of the king's person. When Louis heard of the barons' plot he was riding in the Orléanais. Unable to reach the safety of Paris, Louis found refuge with his mother in the tower of Montlhéry, the strong fortress which guarded the highway from Orléans to Paris. Many years later the king told Joinville that he was delivered from the barons by the citizens of Paris who came out to rescue him. He returned in triumph to his capital, some twenty miles away, along a road lined by armed and unarmed men who had come out to escort their king safely home and who greeted him with shouts and prayers for his long life and safety.[10] It was an illuminating and unforgettable experience for the boy king.

The escape of the king discouraged the conspirators for the time being. William of Nangis put it in thirteenth-century terms when he remarked that divine providence kept the barons from attempting anything further against the king for the remainder of the year, 'seeing that the hand of God was with him'.[11] However, divine intervention was assisted by the firm policies of the regent and the royal counsellors. From 1228 to 1231 the feudal lords continually experimented with revolt and uprising, testing to their limits the fortitude and strategy of Queen Blanche.

The disaffection in the north was concentrated in two main sectors; the recurrent private war of the barons against the count of Champagne, and indirectly the king; and the efforts of Peter Mauclerc to detach Brittany from the overlordship of the French king. In the south the queen attempted to carry on, or at least maintain, the conquests of her husband against the spasmodic revolts of the count of Toulouse and his restless vassals. The rebellious barons co-ordinated their efforts so successfully that the royal army was continuously forced to turn from its eastern border on Champagne to its western flank in Brittany, while still maintaining a sufficient force in the Albigeois. The barons' moves against the count of Champagne were inspired by his shift to the royal party which they felt had deprived them of victory in 1227. As an additional weapon against Theobald they espoused the claims of Alix, queen of Cyprus, to the county of Champagne: the inheritance of this county was more than usually involved, but Alix's claims were bargaining counters rather than a serious threat to Theobald's possession. The regent was further weakened by the count of Boulogne's defection to the party of revolt – and because, after the expiration of the truce in July, 1229, war with England was likely.

Despite the continuing skirmishes in Champagne, the queen and her advisers determined to deal with Peter Mauclerc before he had a chance to gain English reinforcements, and summoned the count to the king's court at Melun for December 31, 1228. When he did not appear, the queen gathered an army and set off with her son to attack Count Peter. To do this in the dead of winter was so contrary to usual practice that the count had felt himself safe in his domains until spring opened the normal campaigning season. It was particularly cold in January 1229 when the royal army besieged Mauclerc's strong castle of Bellême. The queen was not satisfied merely to lend the encouragement of her presence to the royal soldiers. She worried about the effects of the cold on both men and horses, gave orders for great fires to be lit, trees to be cut down, and all kinds of firewood to be gathered and brought into the camp.[12] The need for wood, both for the fires and for the siege engines, was so desperate that nearly twenty years later the inhabitants of the local villages were still complaining about the destruction of their houses it had involved.[13] The royal army was successful in a short, sharp siege, using both its miners* and stone-throwers most efficiently.

Peter Mauclerc had had a serious but not fatal setback. To encourage English support he crossed to England in the autumn of 1229, claiming that the English troops would defeat the French easily and that the local barons would be glad to throw off the French yoke. He succeeded without much difficulty in convincing Henry III though others at the court had little trust in him. Matthew Paris, for example, described Peter as 'a man nourishing sedition in his soul'.[14] However Henry's promised invasion force never left the English coast.

When the royal army gathered at Portsmouth at Michaelmas the king discovered that he did not have sufficient ships to transport his men and supplies, and the invasion was put off till the following spring.

The spring of 1230 brought more acute problems to Queen Blanche. The endemic conflict between the count of Champagne and the other barons continued and at Easter Henry III and his army sailed for France. They landed at St Malo on May 3, to be greeted by Peter Mauclerc and some of the dissident Breton and Norman nobles who proceeded to do homage to the English king. This show of strength by the rebels however, did not prove effective. Louis and his mother had been enabled by the arrival of the English invasion army to demand military service from his recalcitrant vassals, who were busily engaged in their personal quarrel with the count of Champagne. They obeyed the summons reluctantly and in a meagre way – many came supported only by two knights, the minimum. But the count of Champagne, who was still grateful for the royal support against his fellow barons, sent a large contingent.

During June the French forces advanced into Anjou, making

*Miners were specially skilled men employed to tunnel under the foundations of a besieged castle or town wall in order to open a gap which would make entry possible.

their headquarters at Angers and capturing the strongholds of Oudon and Champtoceaux. Louis went on to Ancenis where he called a meeting of barons to display his strength before the invaders. The assembled magnates stripped Peter Mauclerc of his rights in Brittany and his Breton vassals were free of their obligations of fidelity and homage. Certain Breton lords, such as Andrew of Vitry, immediately turned to the French king.[15] Despite the provocation Henry made no attempt to give battle, merely looking on at the French advance from the safety of Nantes. He was encouraged by the fact that the forty-day term of feudal military service expired on July 1; most of the French barons immediately recalled their contingents and embarked once more on their civil war with the count of Champagne.

The French withdrew towards Paris, and Henry crossed to Poitou and on into Gascony, courting the fickle Poitevin lords. Henry's almost ceremonial march across south-west France achieved little. He captured the stronghold of Mirambeau and re-occupied the Ile-d'Oléron, taken by Louis VIII, but these were minor and inconclusive victories. When Henry set sail for England in October he left behind William Marshal and Earl Ranulf of Chester: they had valuable fiefs in Normandy and Brittany which they hoped to keep and thus were willing to help Peter Mauclerc. Although the English king had spent large sums he had achieved little more than a string of polite words and hollow promises. Henry had probably thought that the mere sight of the English king and his army was sufficient to encourage the barons of Brittany and Poitou to immediate and prolonged revolt. The assembly at Ancenis proved the inherent strength of the French king, for it was carried on under the noses of the English army and mustered most of the important barons. As was so often the case, Henry III had been the victim of wishful thinking and self-interested counsellors. The lords of Brittany and Poitou had no more desire for an active English king as their suzerain than they had for a powerful French king: their controlling desire was to find the best method to ensure their own power and independence.

The barons often found choice of loyalties difficult. Henry of Avaugour, a Breton lord from Mortain, later complained that he had lost lands in England worth 350 pounds sterling when he entered the service of the French king. His fidelity to Louis had also cost him the inheritance of his uncle's lands at Laigle, worth more than 3,750 pounds sterling. To these losses were added the damages caused by the wars and truces between the king and the count of Brittany, and yet Henry had never been recompensed by the French king.[16] The barons' indecisiveness between fidelity to the English or the French king was equally true in Normandy, where many were also being forced to choose between their lands in England and their lands in Normandy. The old carefree practice of holding fiefs on both sides of the Channel became impossible after the English loss of Normandy and the hostilities it caused. The consequent slow growth of a national consciousness was at first incomprehensible to those who had always thought in purely feudal terms and found it difficult to adjust to the changed order. For example, a Norman widow complained in 1247 that her husband had been unfairly treated at the time of the siege of St James-de-Beuvron. The royal bailli had unjustly accused him of aiding the enemy and denied him his rights. His lands were seized and turned over to the local royal castellan. Although the knight had fled to England and died there, his widow begged for justice at the hands of the French king.[17]

The campaign of 1230 was indecisive. Its most lasting result was perhaps Queen Blanche's construction of the great castle of Angers, the only piece of secular building still remaining which owes its start to her. Although Angers had been the headquarters of the French army in 1230 it was still an advance post, and Queen Blanche thought it essential to make it an important centre for the overawing of the neighbouring Bretons and their English allies. The old castle of the counts of Anjou was entirely transformed into a new and redoubtable fortress on the left bank of the river Maine. Town clearance was difficult even in the thirteenth century; Queen Blanche had to destroy churches, clear cemeteries, and cut down vines to make the necessary space. In addition, the bishop and canons of Angers complained bitterly that the royal agents had even taken for the castle ramparts the stones, plaster and lime destined for the cathedral.[18]

After the barons' swift return from the reluctant expedition to Brittany in the summer of 1230, their coalition against Theobald of Champagne appeared within sight of success. The barons invaded Champagne from three sides, putting Theobald to flight and even forcing him to burn some of his own towns for fear that his strongholds and their provisions might fall into his enemies' hands. At this crucial moment the royal army, led by Blanche and Louis, moved to within four leagues of Theobald's city of Troyes, near the rebels' camp. The king and the queen regent ordered the count of Boulogne and his allies to cease their attacks on the count of Champagne and to come to the king's court to plead their cause. Although the barons had continued to murmur against Blanche, they did not want to fight against the king in person. In an attempt to achieve their aim they offered the queen various minor concessions and begged that the king should retire from the army. Louis firmly refused, and Blanche insisted that the barons should evacuate Champagne before there could be any peace. The queen's firmness and prompt marshalling of the royal power succeeded in neutralizing the coalition. The count of Boulogne was the first to capitulate: he withdrew from the league, insisting on his duty to the king. The queen let him off lightly, concluding a truce with him in September. His departure effectively broke the back of the rebellion. During the autumn the various members of the league came to terms with the count of Champagne and by December 1230 peace had returned to the eastern section of the kingdom.

The settlement achieved in Champagne made Peter Mauclerc's situation in Brittany still more uneasy, since Queen Blanche could now concentrate the full weight of the royal strength against him. When the French forces again set out for Brittany in the early summer of 1231 their victory was predictable despite some limited successes of Earl Ranulf of Chester. The accounts for 1231 indicate the large royal army collected for this expedition – about 24,000 pounds Paris were paid out in wages to knights, mounted sergeants, footsoldiers, and the carters whose humble wagons were the baggage train of the army. The accounts also include gifts of up to 500 pounds to the most important knights of the region, ready proof that it was more profitable to recognize the king of France than oppose him.*[19]

*The money cart was such an important part of the royal baggage train that

The representatives of the English and French kings agreed to a preliminary truce at St Aubin-du-Cormier on July 4, 1231, to run until June 24, 1234.[20] Later in July Peter Mauclerc made his own truce with the queen regent. He promised not to enter castles or strongholds of the king, not to re-enter France for three years, not to spend a night in the towns of the royal domain, and – most important of all – not to put a foot in the domains of the count of La Marche.[21] This was a truce, not a permanent peace, but for the time being it separated the two arch-conspirators and encouraged peace in the west and south-west.

While Queen Blanche had been occupied with the rebellious lords of the north and west, the royal interests had also been upheld in the south, that continued focus of disaffection and revolt. Louis VIII in his brief campaign in the Albigeois before his death, had made good many of the royal claims to the lands conquered by Simon de Montfort and ravaged by the Albigensian Crusade. With the removal of his strong hand, the lords of the south, led by the restless and unstable Raymond VII of Toulouse, continued the struggle against the unwelcome invaders from the north. The queen put Humbert of Beaujeu, capable soldier and devoted royal adherent, in charge of the royal armies in the south. The cardinal legate also assisted by marshalling as much financial aid as possible from a reluctant clergy. Humbert of Beaujeu was faced with a difficult situation since the rebel lords of the south had seized on the king's minority and the regent's other preoccupations to rally as many of their disaffected followers as possible. Queen Blanche sent what aid she could and Humbert used his forces to the best advantage, laying waste much of the country around Toulouse in a campaign of planned destruction. Gregory IX, who succeeded Pope Honorius III in 1227, supported the French effort by pressing the legate Cardinal Romanus to negotiate a treaty which would provide a final peace in Languedoc. The negotiations began at Méaux in the autumn of 1228 and were finally concluded at Paris where the treaty was proclaimed on April 21, 1229.[22]

---

it had its own account and personnel. The clerk in charge was aided by a groom for counting the money – all in pennies – and the heavy cart, pulled by five horses, was accompanied by four armed guards and twelve foot soldiers.

The peace of Paris is a long and sweeping document, making enormous concessions to the French king. Raymond swore to be loyal to the king, to obey the church, to pay large indemnities, to do penance by going on crusade for five years, to keep the peace and expel mercenaries. His nine-year-old daughter and heir Jeanne was to be married to one of the king's brothers (actually Alphonse of Poitiers) with the right to inherit her father's lands. In fact, the city of Toulouse and its diocese could descend only to the king's brother or his heirs by Jeanne: if these failed, it was to fall to the king. The other lands of the count of Toulouse – roughly the western and northern sections of his original county – were to descend to Jeanne if Raymond died without a legitimate son. As well, Count Raymond had to do homage to the king for his remaining lands, to destroy the fortifications of the city of Toulouse and of thirty other towns, and to allow the king to garrison nine of his chief strongholds for ten years. Raymond also renounced forever any claims to the duchy of Narbonne and the viscounties of Nîmes, Beaucaire, and Carcassonne – the lands conquered by Simon de Montfort. In simple terms, the king received all the lands of the count of Toulouse west of the Rhône and south of the Tarn. Another article provided for the setting up of a fund with which to pay for ten years the salaries of fourteen teachers, who were to provide the nucleus of the new papally inspired university of Toulouse. The university of Toulouse was much needed to provide training and prestige for the orthodox clergy, but it may have been difficult to wean students and teachers away from the better-known charms of Paris. There exists a piece of propaganda, perhaps written by John of Garland, the English grammarian and Paris teacher who spent some time in Toulouse, which sings the charms of the southern city – easily available servants, scholastic liberty, cheap food and, above all, the courtesy of the people.[23]

In addition, Count Raymond agreed to join the king in the hunting down of heretics by the civil power. An ordinance, made in the name of Louis IX in 1229 and usually known as *Cupientes*, laid down the provisions for the search and punishment of heretics. The civil penalties were extreme: no heretic could make a will or inherit, and all his goods were to be confiscated with no possible reversion to his heirs. Even those who only sheltered heretics were not to be accepted as witnesses nor to receive any dignity.[24] The ecclesiastical council of Toulouse, in November 1229, was even more specific in its description of the measures to be taken in rooting out heresy.[25] Provision was made for the search for heretics and their ecclesiastical trial, but the specific weapon of the inquisition was only devised in the following decade.

The scene of Count Raymond's reconciliation to the church was one of those occasions full of the symbolism in which the Middle Ages delighted. On Good Friday, April 13, 1229, the count entered Notre Dame bare-foot and wearing only a shirt. Before the high altar his sentence of excommunication was lifted and he received the cross, symbol of his crusading vow, from the hands of the legate: at the same time he did homage to King Louis for his county. It was a dramatic moment of humiliation for Raymond; indeed, William of Puylaurens, the chronicler most favourable to the southern cause, expressed his shame and despair that the count should have so meekly surrendered so much to the French king. William felt that the count could not have lost much more by fighting to the very end.[26] Count Raymond was a brave man, but an unstable one, and he had felt keenly the enormous drain on his resources from the long years of fighting against the northern invaders. Nevertheless, he spent most of his remaining years trying to circumvent the most onerous provisions of the Treaty of Paris. He made several efforts to contract a marriage which would give him a son to inherit his remaining territories in Toulouse; he attempted to build an alliance of the lords of Languedoc against the French king; and he struggled to rehabilitate his father's name and to have his corpse buried in consecrated ground: in all these efforts he failed.

Peace was not completely restored in Languedoc by the settlement of 1229, but its foundations were laid. The assertion of French control and the extension of French administration were to increase slowly throughout St Louis's reign despite occasional murmurs of rebellion and two full-fledged revolts. This success was due to the treaty and to Alphonse of Poitiers who brought a period of good and careful government, helping to heal the wounds of the many years of civil war and political crusade.

The struggles of Queen Blanche with the count of Toulouse and with the rebellious barons occupied most of her time and thought. Nevertheless, she also felt the need of asserting the royal rights vis-à-vis the ecclesiastical lords, and was in no way inhibited in her dealing with the clergy by the valuable assistance she had received from the cardinal legate. The French monarchy had developed a tradition of dealing very firmly with bishops who intruded on secular jurisdiction, and Queen Blanche responded quickly to any such threat. In the thirteenth century there was a great mingling of secular and spiritual jurisdictions and powers and it was exceedingly difficult to draw a line of demarcation. The issue of excommunication and interdict was one of the thorniest of these problems. To exclude a baptised person from the sacraments and services of the church or to forbid the saying of Mass or the administration of the sacraments in certain localities were certainly spiritual punishments, but they also had important temporal results in a Christian society. The spiritual authorities further aggravated the difficulty by frequently using the weapon of excommunication to protect their own temporal goods and rights. At the same time, they insisted that their ecclesiastical censures should be enforced by the coercion of the temporal power but without any examination of the reasons for the original decree. This claim Queen Blanche, and later Louis himself, always opposed whenever it was a case of enforcing temporal rights of ecclesiastics by the use of excommunication or interdict without a review of the validity of the excommunication. Friction particularly occurred over the excommunication of royal officials, without consultation with the king, for actions which some bishop or abbot felt impinged on his rights. It was this issue which triggered the conflict between Queen Blanche and the archbishop of Rouen in which both sides refused to recognize the competence of the other's court and retaliated with the weapons at their command – the archbishop excommunicated and interdicted the king's officials and his chapels and cemeteries in the royal domain in the archdiocese of Rouen and Queen Blanche had the temporal goods of the archbishop seized. The final settlement in 1234, after seven years of intermittent conflict and uneasy truce, solved nothing but merely marked a retreat by both the archbishop and the royal power to their previous position.[27]

At Beauvais the conflict between the bishop and king illustrated even more clearly the intermingling of the spiritual and temporal jurisdiction. The bishop of Beauvais was also count of the town and the king was only overlord. One night in January 1223 trouble erupted in the town between the burgesses and the poorer classes over the choice of a new mayor. Queen Blanche and Louis were not far away, probably at Compiègne, and they moved very quickly to restore order in the city, perhaps to try to forestall the bishop. The king himself exercised justice and handed out stiff sentences. Milon of Nanteuil, the bishop, objected to the king's unwarranted intrusion on his rights. Milon, no doubt, expected greater consideration for he had been a faithful servant of Philip Augustus, having accompanied him to the Holy Land and spent some years there as a prisoner. In 1222 Milon had been consecrated by the pope for the see of Beauvais, to which he had been elected while in the Holy Land, and had resumed his place as a good friend of Louis VIII and one of the executors of his will.

The young king's justice was not only heavy-handed; he also demanded 800 pounds of *gîte** for his stay at Beauvais and left his officials to guard the bishop's palace. The sequel was to be expected: the king's officials were excommunicated and the bishop's temporalities were seized. Milon complained at a provincial synod and, despite lack of support from his fellow bishops, imposed an interdict on Beauvais. The case dragged on and the king remained immovable despite papal intervention and the naming of a papal mediator. Bishop Milon died while on the way to Rome to appeal his case and his successor Geoffrey 'spent few days and those full of affliction, in the episcopacy'.[28] The issue of Beauvais, and the further case dealing with Rheims which developed soon after, were not settled until after Louis had taken over personal control of the government. There is, perhaps, a slight difference in tone between Queen Blanche's and Louis's manner of dealing with ecclesiastical claims, but little difference in substance.[29]

**Gîte* was the right of the king and some great lords to visit certain towns and principal places once a year, to sleep there with his entourage for three days, and to have all his expenses defrayed by the lord or the inhabitants of the place. *Gîte* was also often levied at an agreed upon sum, payable yearly.

1. The young Louis and Blanche with Scribes from a Moralised Bible of *c.* 1250

2. Louis at the time of his majority – one of the keystones from the royal chapel of St Germain-en-Laye built *c.* 1230–38 thought to represent members of the royal family

The regent also had a long-drawn out struggle with the university of Paris, always jealous for its privileges. The clerks and masters of the schools of Paris were already, by the early part of the thirteenth century, an important element of the city of Paris and they cherished the extensive rights and privileges granted them by Innocent III and the charter of Philip Augustus. Paris was gaining great repute as the centre of learning, and the city reaped a commercial profit as well, but the students were, as students often are, addicted to riots over minor issues. In 1229 on the Shrove Monday and Tuesday before the beginning of Lent, which were days of holiday and celebration, the clerks went out, as usual, to amuse themselves at St Marcel outside the city walls. At the taverns the more they drank the more quarrelsome they became and they disputed the price with the tavernkeepers. Fights erupted and slaps and hair-pulling developed into more violent battles. The citizens got the best of it on Monday, but on Tuesday the students returned, armed with clubs and swords. They entered the house of the wine merchant, broke all his pots, and beat up the citizens.

The prior of St Marcel brought the case before the cardinal legate and William of Auvergne, the bishop of Paris. Neither of these men was inclined to be sympathetic towards the students. The ecclesiastical authorities resented their loss of jurisdiction over the university, and would have liked to have seen the chancellor of the university stripped of some of his powers. Queen Blanche was especially annoyed with the disorder and acted with high-handed dispatch. She sent soldiers to quiet the town and some of the scholars were killed. In retaliation, the masters of the university closed down all lectures and at the end of March declared that, if they did not receive satisfaction within a week from Easter, no master or student would be authorized to reside within the city or diocese of Paris, nor would they return until the injuries done to the university had been settled. Neither the queen nor the masters would budge from their positions, and the students dispersed to Rheims, Orléans, Angers and Toulouse, and even to Oxford and Bologna. As they travelled along the roads they told scurrilous tales of the queen and the legate who had driven them from Paris.[30] Ultimately the interests both of the students and of the king and the people of Paris called for a compromise. It took almost two years, but in 1231 the king settled the quarrels and agreed to ensure the students' privileges. The university then returned to Paris.

Queen Blanche and Louis also laid down regulations for another special group within the realm, the Jews. One of the first actions taken by Louis VIII, after his accession, had been to pass an ordinance on the Jews in which a large number of the barons concurred. This order illustrates vividly the secular difficulties of the Jews who were systematically exploited by the lords to whom they were presumed to belong as chattels. After November 1223 no further interest was to be charged on debts. This provision may have sprung from a pious desire to avoid usury, so deplored by the medieval church, but undoubtedly some of the royal advisers must have realized that it would also make borrowing cheaper. The Jews had to present to their lords a list of their debts, which then had to be paid through their lords. In addition, Jews were no longer allowed to have a seal, then the indispensable proof of authenticity on any document, and had to go to their lord with each bill and have him seal it, for a price. With the Jews' activities so sharply curtailed and strictly channelled towards the enrichment of their lord, a further provision was essential to protect these valuable sources of income: the king would not accept Jews from his barons' domains, or vice versa.[31] But the desired control could not have been achieved, for at Melun in December 1230 the king with the consent of the barons re-enacted its main provisions.[32] Queen Blanche looked at the matter primarily from the point of view of administrative benefits, for she did not share her son's rigid intolerance. All during Louis's reign harsh measures were taken against the Jews. These sprang both from a widespread current of anti-Semitism which swept much of thirteenth-century Europe and from Louis's own strong feelings against the Jews, whom he detested for their religion and for their practice of usury. The confiscation and burning of the Talmud in France were papal orders, enthusiastically carried out by the theologians of Paris, although agreed to by the king. Nevertheless, Queen Blanche showed considerable sympathy for the rabbis who came to plead for their scriptures in the king's court, and followed the debate with great interest.[33] Louis's attitude continued to harden throughout his reign, particularly after the crusade. Although he made genuine efforts to convert the Jews, and gave generous alms to those who did become Christians, he had no understanding and no sympathy for those who clung to their ancient faith.

Even before the regent had been able to solve many of her pressing problems she and her son put into effect Louis VIII's last request. In his will Louis had ordered all his precious stones and jewellery to be sold to provide funds for the founding of a new abbey dedicated to the Blessed Virgin. Although Louis VIII had originally specified that the new abbey was to be confided to the order of St Victor, it was given to Queen Blanche's favourites, the Cistercians, and in August 1228 the foundation of Royaumont was begun. Louis IX bought the land of Cuimont from the priory of St Martin-de-Boran, only a few miles from the royal castle at Asnières-sur-Oise, a favourite hunting retreat. Little is now left of the great church and the thirteenth-century buildings of the abbey; one lonely tower and the foundations of the ancient pillars suggest the extent and height of the original church. The monastic buildings have been much restored and changed over the centuries, but enough of the cloister, refectory and monks' kitchen remain to give us some idea of its thirteenth-century plan. Even now the abbey rests in solitude, in the well-watered and quiet valley that originally recommended it to the Cistercians.

The 1228 charter of foundation gave promise of continuing royal generosity to the abbey. The twenty Cistercian monks – later sixty – were to have extensive lands and generous provision in rents for their upkeep. The brothers were also to have free passage by land and water in all the royal domain for themselves and their purchases: they were to be free of all imposts and specially protected by the royal officials, as well as accountable only at the royal court in Paris.[34] The building of the abbey proceeded rapidly and no expense was spared: the church alone cost 100,000 pounds Paris and was consecrated on October 19, 1235. It was beautiful and elegant, one of the first brilliant examples of the style of Paris which was to influence all Europe during the century.

The young king was intimately concerned with the building of the abbey from the very beginning. William of St Pathus tells of Louis coming over from his castle at Asnières to find the monks at Royaumont building a wall. He immediately joined in the work with the monks, carrying stones and mortar as they did. Like many other older brothers, he insisted that his brothers should do the same and he scolded them when they did not carry out the duties which he had imposed on them, with what he felt was the required gravity and wholeheartedness.[35] The abbey filled an important place in Louis's life. It was always one of his favourite refuges, a spiritual home where he joined the monks in their exercise of piety. At Royaumont he happily cast off the responsibilities and ceremonies of kingship to serve the monks with his own hands. One of the favourite stories of his biographers, and the later illustrators, deals with his especial kindness to Brother Léger of Royaumont, who suffered from a grievous skin disease, generally considered to be leprosy. The sick monk was kept in a separate house away from his brethren who avoided him. The king not only insisted on visiting him but cut and served his meat with his own hand, bringing him special delicacies from the royal kitchen. Louis's humility with the sick startled his contemporaries. William of St Pathus, who tells the story, adds that the king knelt to serve the monk in the manner of a well-trained squire, at which the shocked abbot was forced to his knees because of the king.[36]

Several of Louis's brothers and his own children were buried at Royaumont and the king ordered magnificent tombs which were made in the abbey church. Even when the king was at Damietta in the first flush of his one crusading victory, he thought about and gave further grants to Royaumont.[37] His passion for the adornment of the great church brought the monks a censure from the Cistercian general chapter in 1253. The chapter considered the church to be too ornamented to suit the proper severity of their order and ordered the abbot to remove 'the pictures, images, sculptures, curtains, and columns with angels recently built near the high altar',[38] but the royal tombs could remain.

The building of Royaumont was one of the few happy events of the early years of the reign. It marked an oasis of peace and constructive achievement far removed from the turmoil of the barons' revolts and intrigues and from the energetic regent's insistent efforts to assert the royal power and to hand over to her son on his majority a peaceful kingdom where the royal authority was respected. The years from 1226 to 1234 were difficult and taxing for Queen Blanche, but she succeeded magnificently in her main objectives. Because of her strength and firmness, Louis was able, when he began to exercise personal power, to temper justice with mercy.

III

The King comes of Age 1234–1240

The reign of Louis IX is extremely well documented, therefore it is all the more remarkable that there is no official reference, no specific statement by a chronicler to mark the exact date on which Louis took over the reins of government from his mother. The lesser occasions of the knighting of his younger brothers and their enfeoffment with the appanages willed them by their father are described in the chronicles and the accounts. Since the influence of Queen Blanche remained so strong, the chroniclers saw no dividing lines between mother and son. Until after Blanche's death many secret reports on political intrigues and the conduct of war against the rebellious barons, as well as special requests from the pope and other rulers, were addressed to her only, not to Louis. But most French historians have agreed to regard 1234, the year in which Louis was twenty-one and married Marguerite of Provence, as marking the end of his minority, and the beginning of his personal rule.

The county of Provence, the strategic land which lay between the Rhône and the Alps, was on the frontier of the recently acquired French territories in Languedoc. Its count, Raymond Berenger IV, owed allegiance to the empire, but his position of independence was precarious. He espoused the cause of the pope and resisted the efforts of the Emperor Frederic II to revive the old imperial kingdom of Arles. Raymond Berenger and his wife, Beatrice of Savoy, had four beautiful daughters, all of whom were to marry kings – an extraordinary success story by medieval standards. Queen Blanche saw great advantages for France in closer relations with this neighbour. In 1233 Giles of Flagiac, a knight of the king's household, while on his way to deal with trouble in Toulouse was told to visit Provence to inspect the count's eldest daughter, Marguerite. He returned to the court with an encouraging report on the possible bride: 'a girl of pretty face but prettier faith'.[1] The following year Walter Cornut, the archbishop of Sens, and John of Nesle, a royal knight, were dispatched to Raymond Berenger as official ambassadors armed with the formal request for Marguerite as wife for Louis. The count was delighted and promised Marguerite a large dowry of 10,000 marks; unfortunately, the sum was not fully paid before the count's death and caused trouble for many years. Marguerite was brought back to Sens by the French ambassadors and the marriage took place in the cathedral of St Etienne on May 27, 1234.

Sens nowadays is a small sleepy town nestling on the bank of the river Yonne, and only the imposing mass of its cathedral and the great thirteenth-century synodal palace are reminders of its former glory. During the Middle Ages Sens was one of the important centres of Christianity, with one of the earliest Gothic cathedrals. It played host for eighteen months to Pope Alexander III during his struggle with the schismatic pope put forward by Frederick Barbarossa; it harboured Thomas Becket when he fled from Canterbury and Henry II's wrath. Sens also has remarkable links with some other archbishops of Canterbury and still displays a considerable devotion, not only to Becket, but also to Stephen Langton and Edmund Rich, who spent part of their exile at the Cistercian abbey of Pontigny, only forty miles away. It was, also, an architect from Sens who designed the new Canterbury Cathedral after the fire of 1174. Until the seventeenth century the archbishop of Sens was the head of an ecclesiastical province which included the dioceses of Paris, Chartres, Méaux, Auxerre, Orléans, Nevers, and Troyes. Obviously he was one of the leading churchmen of France and often served as a royal adviser. Sens was the first important town within the royal domain on the journey back from Provence. It was natural that Louis should come here to solemnize his marriage and the coronation of Marguerite in the cathedral.

The chroniclers do not give the ceremony much space but fortunately the accounts of the period from Candlemas to Ascension (February 2 – June 1) of 1234 survive and provide some idea of the splendour of the occasion. The normal expenses for the royal household when on journeys ran from 100 to 120 pounds a day, for the three days of the wedding and coronation they amounted to over 2,500 pounds, although this included over 1,000 pounds for robes and other special articles. The king's party was dressed most elegantly in robes of purple, scarlet and green trimmed with miniver and ermine: the king's younger brothers, Robert and Alphonse, had enamelled gold girdles, and fifteen gold buttons. Queen Blanche made sure that her nephew, Alfonso of Portugal, was also properly dressed and had given him sixteen pounds for linens and purple. Marguerite's gold crown cost fifty-eight pounds and a specially large and handsome gold cup cost over sixty pounds. The wedding of the king of France was a great event and was very properly celebrated with many trumpeters and minstrels.[2] The solemnities completed, the colourful procession headed slowly back towards Paris through all the springtime beauty of the great forest of Fontainebleau, pausing at the king's lodge there and at Corbeil.

The elegant trappings of a royal marriage could not hide the very real problems that lay ahead. At thirteen Marguerite was still a young girl and she had a most formidable mother-in-law. Queen Blanche had for so long dominated and controlled all of her son's life, undoubtedly in the belief that this was essential for the glory of the kingdom, that she resented any possible diminution of her influence. One of her stratagems was to try and keep the young couple apart except at night. Blanche obviously felt that the only function of the young queen was to ensure the succession, but Louis and Marguerite did not see matters in the same light. Joinville paints the charming picture of the young couple's special fondness for the royal lodging at Pontoise where their rooms were connected by a winding staircase on which they could meet and talk. Ushers posted at the doors would knock when they heard Queen Blanche coming so that Louis and Marguerite could quickly regain their own rooms.[3]

Marguerite and Louis had eleven children, including three born during Louis's first crusade. Marguerite was a brave and determined woman and she longed to play an important role in the kingdom as Blanche had done, but this Louis would never allow. He was as untouched by his wife's influence as he had been guided by his mother's. As early as 1238 Richard of Cornwall was recommending Louis's example to Henry III, who had recently married Marguerite's sister Eleanor. The French king, he said, did not give gifts to all the relatives and hangers-on of his wife,[4] not at all like the weak-willed and amiable Henry. In later years Marguerite constantly tried to involve Louis in various political manœuvres – against Charles of Anjou, who had married her youngest sister and inherited the county of Provence which she felt was rightfully hers; against the English barons because of their insults to her sister – but she was always unsuccessful. Marguerite was never regent, was never given political power, to her sorrow. Nevertheless, she gave Louis a background of happy family life and struggled to obey him. An ardent and pious Christian, she made no claims to being a saint and undoubtedly found her husband's ascetic habits something of a trial. For example, Robert of Sorbon tells a story of Marguerite's struggle to make her husband wear more elegant and ostentatious clothes. Finally Louis tired of her complaints and deftly turned the tables on her. He asked the queen if it would please her if he wore luxurious garments and she agreed quickly and wholeheartedly. The king said that he must consent, as the law of marriage urges a man to seek to please his wife, but in exchange she should conform to his wish that she wear the most humble robes. At this suggestion the queen became unaccountably deaf, and the matter was quickly dropped.[5]

Marguerite was a little frightened of her husband. When their first child was born in 1240 she did not dare to tell Louis that it was a daughter. She called in William of Auvergne, the bishop of Paris, and asked him to break the news. William reconciled the king to his disappointment by reminding him that a daughter could bring in valuable lands by a marriage, thus enriching France, while a son would have to be given lands as an appanage.[6] In later years Marguerite overcame some of her timidity. The evidence suggests that she loved Louis deeply and she even found it possible to weep for the death of Blanche of Castile because it caused Louis so much sorrow. The young queen was a vivid, lively and generally aggressive personality, typical of the women of her time and class.

The revolts of the feudal baronage had gradually become less dangerous but had never fully subsided. Theobald of Champagne continued to try the royal patience. In 1232 he had planned to marry Yolande of Dreux, the daughter of Peter Mauclerc. This union, with all its many possibilities for the upheaval of the realm, was immediately forbidden by both the pope and Louis. The king warned Theobald by special messenger that such a marriage would cost the count all his lands in the kingdom of France since 'the count of Brittany has done more harm to the king than any living man'.[7] Dissuaded by the threats, Theobald married Marguerite, daughter of Archambaud of Bourbon, a loyal vassal of the king.

During much of 1233 and 1234 Theobald was caught up in the litigation caused by the arrival of Alix, queen of Cyprus, who had come to plead her case for the county of Champagne, a claim in which she was championed by the barons who were Theobald's enemies. The proceedings dragged through the papal court, to test the matter of Alix's legitimacy, and then came before the royal court of France. But by 1234 the barons' coalition against Theobald had lost much of its strength because of the death of its most powerful members. Ferrand, count of Flanders, had died in July 1233; Philip Hurepel, count of Boulogne and Alix's strongest backer, died in January 1234, and Count Robert of Dreux a few months later. Theobald's position also changed, for on April 7, 1234 his uncle Sancho VII of Navarre died without direct heirs and Theobald became king of Navarre by right of his mother, Sancho's sister. Since Theobald had achieved his kingdom with some assistance from the French king he left the care of his lands in Champagne to Louis who quickly settled outstanding questions. In September 1234 Alix renounced all her claims to rights in Champagne and Brie in return for 2,000 pounds in rents and a lump sum of 40,000 pounds *tournois*. Louis paid the money for Theobald, but in return the king received the suzerainty of the counties of Blois, Chartres and Sancerre, and the viscounty of Châteaudun. The king did not delay in his share of the bargain: Alix gave her final quittance acknowledging that the money had been paid by November 11, 1234.[8] The years of Blanche's anxious diplomacy and her support of the count of Champagne against his enemies had proved successful. Since Theobald was more concerned with his position as king of Navarre than as a French baron, the county of Champagne was no longer his main interest or a focus of discontent. The king was steadily able to increase the royal supervision over the county and his acquisition of the immediate overlordship of Blois, Chartres and Sancerre added wealthy and important central lands to the royal domain.

Characteristically, Theobald did not allow peace to reign immediately: perhaps it was his poetic nature which led him so often into impulsive and quickly abandoned revolt. After taking the cross in 1235 Theobald returned to Champagne from Navarre and claimed that he had not renounced his suzerainty, but had only pawned it temporarily. He renewed his friendship and alliance with the counts of Brittany and La Marche, who were now related through the marriage of Hugh of La Marche's daughter to Count Peter of Brittany. Theobald also arranged the marriage of his daughter Blanche to John the Red, son of Peter Mauclerc, who was to become count of Brittany as soon as he reached his majority.[9] This action was particularly provocative as Theobald had done this and guaranteed his daughter's husband the right of succession to Champagne without the knowledge or consent of the French king, who as overlord had a recognized right to be consulted and to approve such decisions. Theobald was apparently counting on the papal protection due to him as a crusader to shield him from the results of his rashness. He also took the precaution of signing another treaty of alliance with the count of La Marche in April 1236.[10] Louis was not to be deterred. He called together his soldiers and made ready to march against the recalcitrant count, only to find that once again Theobald's display of boldness had no real substance and the count soon submitted. The terms of settlement were not unduly harsh, but Louis forced Theobald to give up completely his pretensions to Blois, Chartres and Sancerre, and also to surrender three fortresses in Champagne itself which had been left in the king's hand as a pledge of Theobald's good behaviour. As well, the count promised to remain away from France for seven years, either in Navarre or in Outremer.[11]

One of the later chroniclers gives a delightful, although

certainly apocryphal, account of the final interview between Queen Blanche and Count Theobald. She reproved him for his ingratitude, for she felt that he should have remembered how much he owed the king for the royal support when all the barons attacked him:

> The count looked at the queen who was so wise and so beautiful that he was completely overcome by her beauty. 'By my faith, Madam, my heart, my body and all my land are at your command. There is nothing that would please you which I would not willingly do, and never, if God pleases, will I go against you or yours.' He left pensively and often remembered the queen and her fair countenance.

According to the chronicler, the count was so overcome by love and depressed by the great and unbridgeable chasm between them that he turned to the composition of 'the most beautiful and melodious songs that have ever been heard' and had them painted on the walls of his hall at Provins and also at Troyes.[12] Although Theobald had a well-deserved reputation as a romantic poet, Queen Blanche was too virtuous, and too deeply absorbed in the practical problems of the realm, to be anything more than a remote figure of inspiration created by the poet's own enthusiasm.

A final settlement was also made with that other constant rebel, the count of Brittany. The truce made in 1231 after the useless expedition of Henry III to Brittany and Poitou was due to expire in June 1234. Louis was anxious to settle the struggle while Peter Mauclerc wanted an extension of the truce in hopes that he might get further aid from the English king. Henry provided only token help and in November 1234 Count Peter capitulated to Louis without even consulting the English king. Peter recognized the suzerainty of the French king over Brittany, surrendered the fortresses of Bellême and St James-de-Beuvron, and was stripped of any royal gifts in Maine and Anjou.[13] Henry, angry at this settlement, retaliated by depriving Peter of his English lands.[14] In 1237 Mauclerc's son, John the Red, came of age and took over the rule of Brittany. The young count arrived at Pontoise to ratify his father's cessions and to recognize King Louis's suzerainty over his county.[15] Peter Mauclerc was left with little scope for his energies and warlike spirit so he took the cross and shared with his old ally, Theobald of Champagne, in the crusade of 1239, and also joined Louis in the crusade of 1248. In the thirteenth century the crusades were an acceptable and sufficient outlet for Peter's irrepressible fighting urge, and the indulgences accorded to crusaders were certainly badly needed by one who was described by his contemporaries as 'the scourge of the clergy'. Peter's departure from Brittany and from France left the kingdom a more peaceful place.

The years between 1235 and 1240 were marked by several glittering ceremonial occasions. In October 1235 the great abbey church of Royaumont was consecrated and both Louis and Queen Blanche attended the ceremony. The king had also ordered the building of the Sainte Chapelle at his castle of St-Germain-en-Laye. It illustrates the tentative beginnings of the style that was to come to such magnificent flowering in another decade in the Sainte Chapelle at Paris. St Germain also gives us the earliest representations of the young Louis and Blanche, for their heads were carved at the crossing of the vaults, but the sculptures were rough and unflattering.

In June 1237 Robert of Artois, Louis's much loved younger brother, attained his majority, was knighted at Compiègne and given his appanage of Artois. A few months before he had married Mahaut, the daughter of the duke of Brabant, whose lands lay close to his own. The king was suitably generous to his brother and the young nobles knighted with him, providing them with both robes and horses. These horses cost Louis over 1,500 pounds, as well as an additional 271 pounds for the necessary sumpters, or baggage horses, for his brother's belongings.[16]

The festivities were extensive. Since Pentecost fell on June 7 in 1237 it was an ideal time for an outdoor celebration. The royal tents were carried from Paris to Compiègne and put up there to protect the guests while garden houses adorned with leaves were constructed within the enclosure of the royal palace. The king and his brother were splendidly dressed; the king in red samite with fur of ermine and sable and Robert in violet scarlet and satin with fur of miniver and vair, while both had caps of peacock feathers.

The younger brothers, Alphonse and Charles, wore striped scarlet. Great crowds must have been welcome at the feast as the accounts show the consumption of 70,000 loaves of bread, as well as a further 2,300 loaves of 'king's bread'. Adam the Cook had been forced to buy an extra supply of pots and pans to be able to prepare the food for all the guests and his expenses in the kitchen were over 1,000 pounds. The company was entertained by a great number of minstrels, trumpeters, and even by the piper of the Emperor Baldwin, the young Frenchman who struggled to maintain a shaky grip on the Latin Empire of Constantinople. It was a most elegant and colourful occasion.[17]

The rejoicing in the long days of early summer and the demonstration of the king's wealth and largesse were doubly welcome after the grim season just past. The winter of 1236–7 had been particularly rainy and by the middle of January the Seine had begun to overflow in the worst flood Paris had had for twenty years. Much damage was done to the bridges, the mills and the livestock, as well as to the houses. The citizens of Paris had been so upset that they finally decided to call on St Genevieve, and they felt sure that it was the procession in her honour that caused the water to recede.[18] Such natural catastrophes were particularly burdensome in the Middle Ages when the greater part of the population lived at all times on the borderline of starvation. A crop failure in one district brought great hardship, for the transport of items as bulky as grain was difficult and expensive. In 1235, for example, when famine was rife in Poitou and Aquitaine, the sester of wheat rose in price to 100 shillings and the poor were forced to eat the field grasses like animals. So many died from starvation and the accompanying pestilence that the bodies had to be cremated in a great fire.[19]

What really roused the enthusiasm and religious fervour of King Louis during the early years of his personal rule was his acquisition of the Crown of Thorns* and other relics of the Passion of Christ.

*The first mention of the Crown of Thorns is made by Paulinus of Nola in 409. It was venerated for centuries at the basilica of Mt Sion in Jerusalem, but after Saladin's victories it was transferred to Constantinople in the middle of the eleventh century. The Crown, still at Paris and now in the treasury of Notre Dame Cathedral, is a simple plait of rush; it may originally have been

The manœuvering behind these transactions was not edifying. Walter Cornut, the archbishop of Sens, in his sermon preached on the anniversary of the reception of the relics, gives the most detailed account of the bargaining required.[21] In the 1230s the Latin emperors of Constantinople were finding it difficult to maintain their precarious position against the dethroned but ever-active Greeks. They needed men and money, so in 1236 the young Emperor Baldwin, whose father-in-law John of Brienne was still the actual ruler of the empire, came to the west to try and gain spiritual and financial support. Baldwin also hoped to make good his claims to his inheritance of Courtenai and Namur. At the papal court, Gregory IX, always a strong ally of the Latin Empire, gave as much help as he could. From Rome Baldwin went on to France, where he relied on his ties of relationship – his wife, Mary of Brienne, was the grand-niece of Blanche of Castile – to gain him a sympathetic hearing. Louis and his mother gave him what help they could, lent him money, and encouraged Countess Jeanne of Flanders to give him Namur. They also agreed to take care of Baldwin's three young brothers-in-law, the sons of John of Brienne, who were generally known as the children of Acre. The children were brought up in the French court and at the king's expense. The situation in Constantinople became even more perilous with the death of John of Brienne in 1237. Baldwin's attempt to send to his wife's aid part of the army that he had been collecting was frustrated by Frederic II who refused the soldiers passage across the lands of the Empire.

According to Walter Cornut, Baldwin had already decided to offer the Crown of Thorns to Louis as a gift, no doubt knowing that he could rely on the generosity of the pious king to make a suitable return. In 1238 Louis sent two Dominican friars, one of whom was familiar with the Crown and could vouch for the genuineness of the relic, to Constantinople for the transactions. Baldwin also sent a special messenger ordering his barons to deliver the relic to the French messengers. When the French

---

surrounded by thorny branches. A possible explanation for the amazing number of thorns supposed to have come from the Crown may be found in the accepted convention which regarded a thorn which had been touched *to* the Crown as an authentic relic, and later described it as a thorn *from* the Crown.[20]

arrived at Constantinople they discovered that the imperial barons had been so hard-pressed for money that they had already pledged the Crown to the Venetian merchants as surety for a large loan. One of the conditions made by the Venetians was that the Crown was to become their possession if it had not been redeemed by the repayment of the loan before June 19, 1239, and that, in any case, it was to be transferred to Venice for the time being. The Latin barons of the east were delighted to see a possible way out of their financial embarrassment which would also checkmate the avariciousness of the Venetians. The royal messengers accompanied the Crown to Venice, a perilous and dreaded journey in the stormy seas of winter, and while Brother Andrew of Longjumeau stayed to guard the relic, deposited for safety in the treasury of St Mark, Brother James hurried back to France to get the necessary financial support from the king. The money was quickly obtained, the final formalities arranged, and by the beginning of August 1239 the messengers and their precious burden arrived at Troyes in Champagne. Louis, his mother and his brothers, Walter Cornut and other hastily summoned barons and knights, went to meet them at Villeneuve-l'Archêvéque, just inside the borders of France. Everything possible had been done to insure the authenticity of the relic and its safe arrival. Inside the wooden travelling box was a silver box sealed with the seals of the Latin barons of Constantinople. The royal party carefully compared these to the seals on the letters patent in which the barons surrendered the Crown to the French king. The seal of the doge of Venice had also been attached to this case for greater security. When the validity of these seals had been proved they too were broken and the silver box opened to disclose a reliquary of pure gold which enshrined the relic. The assembly examined it with great devotion, then the chests were closed and resealed with the king's seal. The following day the treasure was carried to Sens where it was met with great ceremony and rejoicing. The king and Robert of Artois, barefoot and wearing only their tunics, carried the chest on their shoulders while a procession, singing and praying, wound its way through the streets of Sens, which had been decorated with hangings and carpets. The bells rang and great candles burned everywhere. The relic was left overnight in

3. The refectory of the Cistercian abbey of Royaumont built by Blanche of Castile at the request of Louis VIII. Completed in 1235, the abbey was a favourite refuge of Louis

4. The interior of the Tower of Constance – built as Louis's own headquarters in 1248 at Aigues-Mortes, the port of embarkation for the Crusades

the cathedral of St Etienne and then was taken by boat from Sens to Paris under the guardianship of Brother James,[22] where it was finally deposited for safekeeping in the king's chapel of St Nicholas.

Other relics, also purchased from Baldwin of Constantinople for large sums, were added to the Crown of Thorns in 1241. They included part of the True Cross, as well as a large number of other items of most dubious authenticity. Some more secular pieces also came, among them the great Roman cameo of the triumph of Germanicus and a sardonyx bust of a Roman emperor which was later used to top the staff of the precentor of the chapel.*

Louis decided to replace the royal chapel of St Nicholas with a new chapel more fittingly designed for the treasures it enshrined. The Sainte Chapelle is the greatest architectural achievement of Louis's reign, and one of the lasting glories of French art. The illustration for June in the *Très Riches Heures* of the Duc de Berry, although done in the fifteenth century, gives a good idea of its appearance and situation in the courtyard of the king's palace. Art historians are still debating the identity of the architect, but whoever it was he succeeded beyond all dreams in making of the Sainte Chapelle a church which was itself a magnificent reliquary, glowing with gilding and sculpture and bathed in the ever-changing light from the great stained-glass windows. His work seems to embody the comment made by the monk Theophilus in the twelfth century when he talked about the practical application of techniques to the arts, and the effects to be sought in the embellishment of churches.

> You have approached the House of God with confidence, and have adorned it with so much beauty; you have embellished the ceilings or walls with varied work in different colours, and have, in some measure, shown to beholders the paradise of God, glowing with varied flowers, verdant with herbs and foliage. . . . For the human eye is not able to consider on what work first to fix its gaze; if it beholds the ceilings they glow like brocades; if it considers the windows they are a kind of paradise; if it regards the profusion of the light from the windows it marvels at the

*The cameo is a large and finely carved piece which has survived the vicissitudes of devastation and revolution and now rests in the Cabinet de Medailles of the Bibliothêque Nationale, as does the sardonyx bust.

inestimable beauty of the glass and the infinitely rich and various workmanship.[23]

From its completion and consecration just before Louis left on crusade in 1248, the Sainte Chapelle became one of the essential sights for the visitor to Paris. When John of Jandun wrote the praises of Paris at the beginning of the fourteenth century he spared no adjectives to describe this 'most beautiful of chapels'.[24] The relics within the Sainte Chapelle were kept in valuable and highly ornamented reliquaries of gold and silver, enshrined over the altar in the upper chapel. Twice a year, in August and September, the anniversaries of the relics' arrival were commemorated. On special occasions they were taken in procession to Notre Dame for the benefit of the people of Paris. All this religious ceremony satisfied one of the deepest needs of Louis's nature. But the king could not submerge his royal duties in private devotions.

A major expenditure for the king at this time was his purchase of the county of Mâcon to augment the royal domain. Countess Alix held the county by right of inheritance and was married to John of Dreux, younger brother of Peter Mauclerc. The couple were childless and the countess wanted to take the veil: she did, in fact, become the first abbess of the Cistercian convent of Lys, near Melun. In February 1239, the countess and her husband arranged to sell the country to Louis for the sum of 10,000 pounds *tournois*, and an annuity of a further 1,000 pounds.[25] The king's acquisition of the county gave him a useful foothold in the east, on the right bank of the Saône.

The household accounts from May-September 1239 also clearly show the many-sided interests of the king. There were, as might be expected, generous gifts to the poor and to lepers, to Jewish and Saracen converts, to retired servants and to crusaders of all ranks, from Amaury de Montfort, the Constable of France, to a groom of the harness cart. These donations were balanced by major expenditures on much more secular items. A gold cup was reworked and redecorated for Queen Marguerite and she also was given gold brooches, four gold rings, and two silver ornaments. Adam of Meulan, who was charged with the buying of cloth, purchased elegant and expensive materials for Louis's own use: capes and tunics of scarlet lined with silk, silk tunics, red and vermeil samite for making painted hangings, and caps of peacock feathers as well as cotton and felt. Several expensive horses were bought for the king, three hunters and three dappled grey palfreys for his travels. Other typical amusements of seigneurial society in the thirteenth century have also left their traces in the accounts. There are numerous entries for the expenses of falcons and falconers, huntsmen and their dogs, food for the royal menagerie – which included lions and a porcupine, and many payments to minstrels, singers, and harpers. From this evidence it is obvious that during the early years of his reign Louis was indeed pious and charitable but he maintained – and seems to have enjoyed – the proper state of his royal position, displaying elegance in dress and interest in the seigneurial pastimes.[26]

Many serious problems faced the king in the early part of his reign, and one, rendered even more pressing by his own devout faith, was the struggle with heresy. The Albigensian Crusade had attempted to stifle the widespread heresy in the south by the indiscriminate use of the sword. Although the policy had brought rich territorial rewards to France it had failed to enforce orthodoxy. Heretics were not confined to Languedoc. During the twelfth century northern Italy, and especially Milan, had become a stronghold of the Catharist faith. From this centre the free movement of merchants and weavers, probably the most peripatetic of all medieval workers, spread heretics, and those sympathetic to heresy, along the trade routes north to Burgundy, to the fairs of Champagne, and to the textile centres of Flanders. The town of La Charité-sur-Loire, in the county of Nevers, was one of the main centres of heresy despite the fact that the prior of the monastery was its temporal overlord.

In 1232 an extraordinary Dominican, Robert le Petit better known as Robert le Bougre,* appeared at La Charité to preach

*Bougre, or Bulgarian, was often used in thirteenth century France as another name for a Catharist. The prevalent belief that these heretics indulged in sexual orgies and perversions explains the double meaning of 'bougre', and also 'bugger' which derives from it.

against the heretics. Brother Robert was himself a converted heretic (the reason for his nickname) and he pursued his old brethren with extraordinary and terrifying zeal. However, it seemed to Pope Gregory IX, much concerned with the dangers of heresy, that Robert was attacking the problem not only with more fervour but with more success than the bishops had been able to muster in their continued efforts against heresy over the last fifty years. In February 1233 the pope gave Robert le Bougre and the Dominicans extensive powers against the heretics in northern France – a move which is generally regarded as the beginning of the Inquisition there. Robert exploited this commission and his own extraordinary magnetic power over the poor and humble. The climax of his career was an appalling *auto-da-fé* at Mont-Aimé in May 1239 when he had more than one hundred and eighty Cathars burnt. Robert had overstepped both his papal powers and the commands of his own superiors, and he then disappeared from view, ending his life in disgrace or prison. Although his activities did not come under immediate royal supervision Louis seems to have supported Pope Gregory in this use of the Dominicans, and certainly the royal power did nothing to intervene.[27]

Heresy in the north was still essentially a religious matter, but heresy in the south was fatally intertwined with major questions of politics and the establishment of French rule. The count of Toulouse had solemnly promised in the Treaty of Paris to assist the clergy in the rooting out of heretics within his lands. The prior of the Dominicans in Provence had become bishop of Toulouse in 1232 and he struggled vigorously against the heretics, making the count join him in night-time excursions to the mountains in search of them. According to William of Puylaurens, the count became much less zealous after these expeditions had caught some nineteen heretics, including a local lord. The papal legate and some of the local bishops then travelled to Melun to complain to the French king about the count's delay in carrying out the provisions of the treaty. In 1233 Giles of Flagiac, a knight of the royal household, was sent by the king to investigate the situation. He exerted further pressure on the count of Toulouse until Count Raymond formulated and published statutes deemed to be satisfactory to the king and the bishop.[28] Nevertheless Languedoc continued unsettled. The pope's decision to set up the inquisition there aroused much opposition and caused further upheaval. The Dominicans who attempted to carry out their papal commission in such cities as Toulouse found themselves consistently hindered and all the Dominican friars were finally ejected from the city after some three weeks of siege.[29]

Despite the continued incidents of local conflict and upheaval no major fighting broke out until 1240. In this year the count of Toulouse, encouraged by the Emperor Frederic, was again causing trouble with the count of Provence. The two counts had for some time disputed the control of Marseilles, the flourishing seaport and trading centre. The count of Provence was properly overlord of Marseilles, but its citizens had fought with him and with their bishop, and they turned instead to the count of Toulouse. Raymond was naturally delighted at the opportunity to extend his power and maintained a vicar in the city who took as much in rents as the inhabitants wanted to pay.[30] The count of Toulouse then began to devastate the Camargue, the marshy region at the mouth of the Rhône, which was also under the suzerainty of the count of Provence. Count Raymond Berenger naturally sought protection and aid from his son-in-law, the king of France. The chroniclers suggest that Louis dispatched seven hundred knights and many sergeants, under the command of John of Beaumont, to help repel the enemies of Provence.[31] The estimate of forces is, as usual, inflated, but a royal army was sent.

More trouble had already erupted, for Languedoc seemed to one exile to provide an ideal opportunity for the furtherance of his own ambition. After the Treaty of Paris, Raymond Trencavel, son of Raymond Roger, the dispossessed viscount of Carcassonne and Beziers, had retired to the court of the sympathetic James of Aragon. In 1240 Trencavel reappeared with a troop of Aragonese knights to try and re-establish a claim to his inheritance which had been forfeited to the French king. James of Aragon was delighted to help as he was particularly interested in curbing the power of the French king because of his own interests in the area. James controlled Roussillon and Catalonia and was suzerain, through his mother, of the thriving port and city of Montpellier.

Trencavel captured the fortresses of Montréal and Limoux,* and by the end of the summer had started to besiege the city and fortress of Carcassonne. William of Ormes, the royal seneschal in charge of its defence, sought aid from Raymond of Toulouse but the count claimed he was quite unable to assist. The defence of Carcassonne was complicated by its dual nature. The old city, enclosed by its ramparts, is on the hill overlooking the river Aude and quite separate from the new town, or burg, only established in the thirteenth century and much more open to attack. By September 8 Trencavel had had himself smuggled into the new town by his partisans among the townspeople. Many of the most important clerics, including the archbishop of Narbonne and the bishop of Toulouse, had fled to the Old City for refuge. Other clerics had remained in the New Town and when Trencavel and his supporters entered they fled to a church for sanctuary. Although the clerics had been given safe conduct, they were treacherously massacred by the rebels when they left the church. Trencavel and his men laid siege to the Old Town from September 17 to October 11 without success, until the arrival of the royal army under John of Beaumont heralded the raising of the siege and the recapture of the New Town by the royal forces. The king's army then went on to besiege Montréal to which Trencavel and his army had fled. This, too, soon surrendered and the counts of Toulouse and Foix recognized the royal power and capitulated while Trencavel fled once more to his safe retreat in Spain.[33] The smouldering fires of rebellion had been damped down again but the respite was not to last for long. Before Louis could end the conflicts of the rebellious barons and provide real peace in the realm he had to prove his supremacy by personal force of arms and win decisive military victory in the south and west.

*The vicissitudes of the town of Limoux illustrate the continuous state of unrest and warfare in the south in these years. The town on the hill was first destroyed and rebuilt on the plain by de Montfort. Constructed again on the mountainside by the strongly rebellious inhabitants, it was destroyed again by Louis VIII and once more removed to the plain. Nevertheless it continued to rise again in each rebellion and to take refuge in its old mountain stronghold. After the successes of John of Beaumont it finally accepted the new location and ultimately claimed compensation from the king for the fields of the townsmen on which the new city had been built.[32]

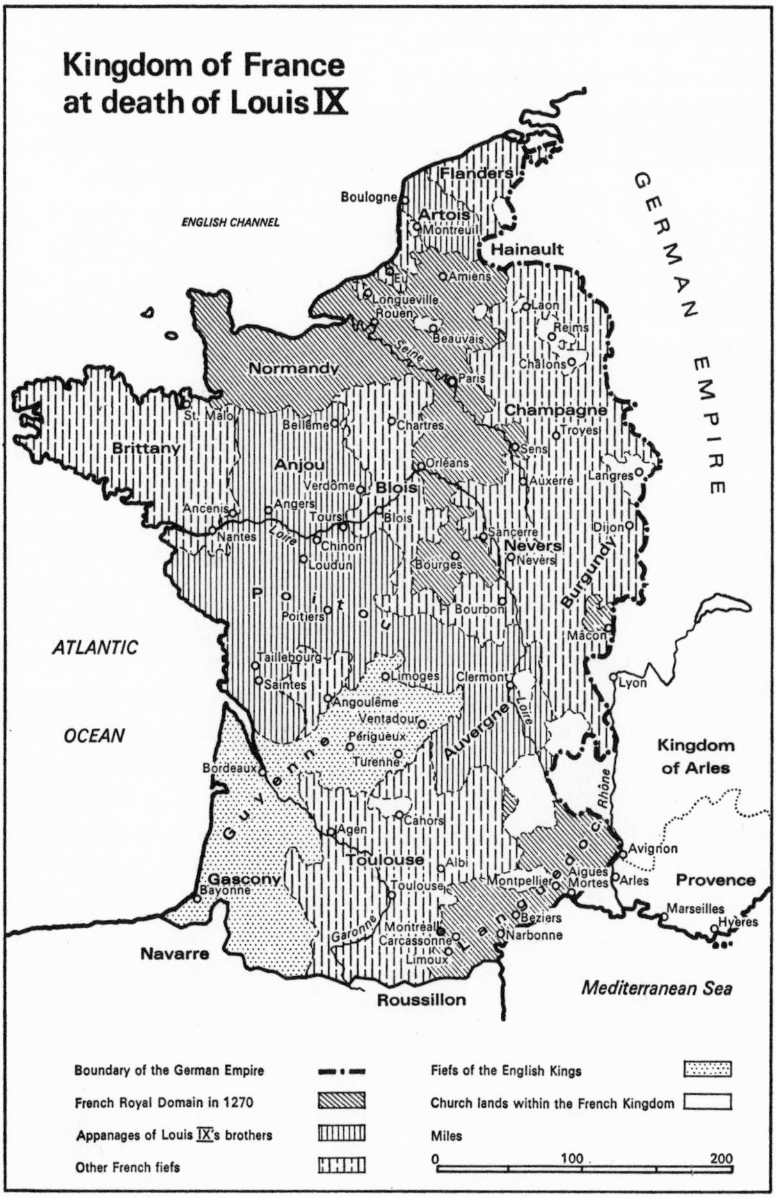
Kingdom of France
at death of Louis IX
ENGLISH CHANNEL
GERMAN EMPIRE
ATLANTIC
OCEAN
Mediterranean Sea
Kingdom
of Arles
Provence
Navarre
Roussillon
Flanders
Artois
Hainault
Normandy
Brittany
Champagne
Anjou
Blois
Nevers
Burgundy
Poitou
Auvergne
Guyenne
Gascony
Toulouse
Languedoc
Boulogne
Montreuil
Amiens
Eu
Longueville
Rouen
Beauvais
Laon
Reims
Châlons
Paris
Seine
St. Malo
Bellême
Chartres
Troyes
Sens
Orléans
Auxerre
Langres
Verdôme
Angers
Tours
Blois
Ancenis
Nantes
Loire
Chinon
Loudun
Sancerre
Nevers
Dijon
Bourges
Bourbon
Poitiers
Mâcon
Taillebourg
Saintes
Limoges
Clermont
Lyon
Angoulême
Ventadour
Périgueux
Turenne
Rhône
Bordeaux
Cahors
Agen
Avignon
Albi
Montpellier
Aigues Mortes
Arles
Bayonne
Toulouse
Marseilles
Béziers
Hyères
Garonne
Montréal
Carcassonne
Narbonne
Limoux
Boundary of the German Empire
French Royal Domain in 1270
Appanages of Louis IX's brothers
Other French fiefs
Fiefs of the English Kings
Church lands within the French Kingdom
Miles
0
100
200

IV

Campaign in Poitou 1242

The unruly barons of Languedoc and Poitou were obviously not willing to settle peacefully under the overlordship of the king of France. For centuries the area had been a cockpit of controversy where ambitious lords battled for every small advantage. Now the long arm of royal power and ambitious officials dealt more effectively with the turbulent barons and they bitterly resented their loss of independence. They hated the strength even more than the oppression of the officials. Queen Blanche and Louis had already suppressed several minor revolts in both Poitou and Languedoc, but a more vigorous attempt was more than likely and only awaited an opportunity. The investment of Alphonse of Poitiers with his appanage of Poitou and his marriage to Jeanne, daughter and heir of the count of Toulouse, provided the pretext for an uprising.

By the terms of the Treaty of Paris, Jeanne was not only to marry Alphonse, she was to inherit the city and diocese of Toulouse, and also the rest of her father's lands if he died without a male heir. As well, all her lands were to escheat to the French king if she and Alphonse died childless. When his daughter married in 1237 Count Raymond had explored a number of possible marriages for himself but without success. The count bitterly deplored the likelihood of the loss of all Toulouse to the French influence and resented the royal success in putting down the revolt of 1240. The barons of Poitou were equally intransigent. They were headed by Hugh, count of La Marche, whose ambition and resentment of the royal power were spurred on by the intrigues of his wife, Isabel. She was the widow of King John of England and an extraordinarily fiery character even in that age rich in colourful and dominating characters.

This background clouded the feast held at Saumur on June 24, 1241 to celebrate Alphonse's knighting. The festivities were of much the same type and splendour as those held four years before for Robert of Artois, but on this occasion we have not only the testimony of the accounts, with their lists of expensive horses and rich and valuable robes, but also the eye-witness description of Joinville. He was then sixteen, serving as squire to his overlord Theobald, count of Champagne and king of Navarre. On this great occasion he carved Theobald's meat and so was splendidly placed to observe the glamour of the feast with the king and his barons and their ladies dressed in their glittering finery. Joinville reports one little detail which helps to give Queen Blanche a touch of humanity she often seemed to lack. One of the young lords waiting on the queen was eighteen-year-old Herman, son of St Elizabeth of Hungary, who had been canonized only six years before. Blanche devoutly kissed the boy's forehead, because she thought his mother must have kissed him there so often.[1] The festivities over, the king and Alphonse went on to Poitiers where Alphonse received the oaths of homage from his vassals in Poitou. Despite hints by the chroniclers of trouble between the king and Count Hugh, the count of La Marche did homage to Alphonse, and reached a settlement with the king.[2]

Little stock could be put in Hugh's fidelity, especially since his wife worked steadily to encourage his rebellion. Isabel was furious that the king and his brothers had been received in the castle of Lusignan and was galled by the conviction that the king and queen at Poitiers had not paid her the respect that was due to the widow of a king. Influenced by her, Hugh set to work to devise an alliance of rebellious barons. He called a conference of the important lords of Poitou at Parthenai, a few miles west of Poitiers, which was held by his cousin. The tone of the discussions, is reported in a letter by a bourgeois of La Rochelle, a secret agent of Queen Blanche, and suggests the basic reason for their revolt.

> Above all, as one of them said, as the French have always hated us Poitevins, they wish to seize from us all our goods, in order to array us by right of conquest in their domain, and they would treat us worse than the Normans and the men of the Albigeois,

> because today the king's least groom does on his own whatever pleases him, in Champagne, in Burgundy, and in all his land, because none of the barons, like servants, dare to do anything without his order. The bourgeois also fear their domination because of the pride of their servants, who bring on their ruin, because they are far from the court and cannot go there.[3]

After the conference at Parthenai the Poitevin barons sought allies in Gascony where the seneschal of the English king, who was overlord of Gascony, and the Gascon lords and bourgeois greeted them with considerable enthusiasm. They all feared the spread of French dominance, and the bourgeois of Bordeaux and Bayonne were particularly anxious for an excuse to attack La Rochelle, their perpetual competitor and enemy. The personal influence of Isabel assured the intervention of Henry III even before Hugh Le Brun precipitated the revolt by his insolent behaviour during the Christmas festivities of 1241. When the count of La Marche was called to Alphonse's court for the great feast, he refused to do homage and, on the advice of the choleric Isabel, turned on Alphonse with a defiance, burnt the house where he had been staying, and hastily fled. The young count of Poitiers at once wrote to his brother for help. Louis declared the lands of the count of La Marche forfeit and began to organize his army for a spring campaign. Meanwhile Henry III had announced his intention of mounting another overseas expedition although the barons of England at the Candlemas Parliament of 1242 deplored his decision.[4]

The other great lords of the south had also taken advantage of the unrest to forward their own concerns. The king of Aragon, who continually meddled in the affairs of Languedoc, met with the counts of Provence and Toulouse to cement an alliance and strengthen their positions. When Louis's army was ready to march in the spring of 1242 the king was faced by a coalition of rebellious Poitevin barons, the forces of Henry III, and those of the count of Toulouse, who had token support from Aragon and Castile.

The campaign can be divided into three main segments, as Louis dealt in turn with each of his three main opponents.[5] The French king had set April 28 at Chinon as the rendezvous for his army. We do not know the exact size of his force, although he raised contingents from twenty-three bishops, two abbots, and two hundred and fourteen counts and knights.[6] Matthew Paris, with his customary inflation of numbers, talks elaborately of the presence of 4,000 knights 'who flowed into the army like rivers into the sea', and estimates the number of sergeants and bowmen at 20,000, an impossible figure.[7] It seems that even the appearance of a French army was sufficient to discourage some of the less bellicose Poitevins: the viscount of Thouars and his brother submitted at once. By May 4 the king and his brothers had arrived at Poitiers and for the next two and a half months they besieged and captured several castles belonging to the count of La Marche and his Poitevin allies. During the attack on the strong fortress of Frontenai, held by one of Hugh Le Brun's sons, Alphonse of Poitiers was seriously injured in the foot by a crossbowman. This mishap encouraged Louis and the French army to even greater struggles. Frontenai and Vouvent were taken in May and June.[8]

Henry III arrived at Royan, on the mouth of the estuary of the Gironde, on May 13 after a quick and easy passage from Portsmouth. He led a relatively small force, since the messages of Isabel and Hugh had convinced him that he was assured of plentiful Poitevin support. Soon after Henry landed, messengers were sent to Louis bearing the English claim that the French king had broken the truce: such infractions were usually easy to discover and served as a formal excuse for the resumption of hostilities. By the middle of June these legal preliminaries had been completed and both sides expected battle.

As the French army moved south Henry III's moved north, with the river Charente flowing between them. Henry and his forces camped in the fields near Tonnaye, some ten miles from Taillebourg, on which the French king was advancing. Taillebourg, which was of strategic value because of its excellent stone bridge over the Charente, was in the hands of Geoffrey of Rancon who was so at odds with Hugh of La Marche that he gladly surrendered the town to Louis. After a minor skirmish there Richard of Cornwall arranged a truce so that the English could retreat to Saintes, about ten miles away. On Tuesday, July 22, Louis and his army crossed the Charente into lower Poitou, using both the stone bridge at Taillebourg and a wooden one constructed by his engineers, and marched towards the English army at Saintes. The French foragers skirmished with the men of the count of La Marche, but the main battle began just outside the town, 'between the vines, in the narrow alleyways'.[9] Several English barons, including Simon de Montfort, son of the Albigensian conqueror, who had sought his fortune in England, distinguished themselves in the fighting, but the victory was to the French. Fearing capture, Henry and the count of La Marche evacuated the town and fled to Blaye, while Saintes surrendered to Louis who garrisoned it and prepared to pursue the fleeing English.

The victorious French army moved onward and the Poitevin nobles crept in, one by one, to make peace on whatever terms they might, surrendering their castles and strongholds. Their leader, Hugh of La Marche, had lost confidence in the efficacy of English support after Henry's defeat at Saintes and the siege and capture of many of his fortresses. Hugh withdrew from the rebellion and sent messengers to the French king to see what terms could be arranged. Louis's settlement with Hugh, although harsh, was not vindictive in view of Hugh's conduct. Count Hugh kept the great body of his lands although he recognized the king's possession of the places Louis had already conquered, but he lost his favoured position. The king was quit of the yearly rent which had been paid to Hugh under the terms of the Treaty of Vendôme (1227), and also of the provision that Louis could not make peace with the king of England without the consent of Hugh and his wife. The count of La Marche and Isabel had to do homage to Louis for their lands in Angoulême, Cognac, Jarnac, and Merpins, as well as some other lesser lordships, and to Alphonse for Lusignan and the county of La Marche.[10] Isabel's character did not allow her to submit gracefully. The chroniclers tell of her attempted revenge, for she sent two of her servants to poison the king and his brothers. The servants were caught in the act and Louis had them summarily executed. When Isabel heard this, she attempted suicide, and when that was frustrated by her servants, she fell ill from rage. It does not seem surprising that Matthew Paris said that the French and Poitevins described her as 'rather Jezebel than Isabel'.[11]

The French army was not totally victorious, for the heat of the southern midsummer brought Louis and his men fever and dysentery, always the deadliest foe of the medieval army. The primitive ideas of sanitation were further weakened by the general habit of polluting the supplies of pure water in the van of an approaching army. The debilitated French could not continue to harass the demoralized English so Louis and his men withdrew and were back at Tours before the end of August. King Henry returned to Bordeaux where his queen had recently given birth to a daughter. There he made a somewhat qualified treaty of alliance with the other main conspirator, the count of Toulouse, but Count Raymond was to be no more successful against French power than Hugh of La Marche had been. Enough of the French army had been left in the south under the command of Humbert of Beaujeu to rebuff easily Raymond's attempt to besiege the castle of Penne-l'Agenais, in the disputed land of the Agenais, and even to menace the borders of Quercy. The count of Toulouse was further weakened by the defection of the count of Foix, usually one of his strongest supporters. By October 20 Raymond too had to beg for peace, and humbly requested Queen Blanche to intercede with the king for him. Raymond had gained little by his attempted rebellion. Not only did he have to swear once more faithfully to carry out all the provisions of the Treaty of Paris, he also had to surrender further strongholds in the Agenais for five years. The Treaty of Lorris in January 1243 confirmed the definitive political eclipse of the count of Toulouse.[12]

Once the Poitevin nobles and the count of Toulouse had been subdued and firm settlements made with them, there remained only the question of the smouldering hostilities with England. The English attempted a blockade of La Rochelle during October and November 1242. King Henry himself remained at Bordeaux, sending for further supplies from England, but to no military purpose. Matthew Paris felt that he achieved nothing more than to make himself a laughing stock among the French.[13] Matthew also reports that Louis recognized Henry as a devout and charitable Christian and rebuked his own men when they passed on tales of the Gascons' dislike for their English overlords. Although Louis was quite ready to oppose the English king when he trespassed on French interests, he always respected him personally and was sure that his charities and masses would free him from all shame.[14] It took until April 1243 to arrange another truce between England and France, which was to run for a period of five years from Michaelmas. By its terms, the French king was to retain all his conquests and even some towns captured with the help of the Gascons after Louis himself had withdrawn to the north. As well, the English king was bound to a payment of 1,000 pounds a year for the term of the truce.[15] Henry had lost heavily by his ill-advised interference in the affairs of Poitou.

The truce of 1243 marked no particular change in English policy. The relations between the two countries in the half century between 1204 and 1259 were punctuated by a series of truces. They were broken and renewed, time and again, with little concern for more than the immediate issues. The basic question had not been resolved: the English king was not willing to give up his legalistic claims to the lands on the continent which King John had lost, and the French king was not yet strong enough, and perhaps not even sufficiently convinced of the total justice of his case, to force a total surrender of these chimerical claims. The truce of 1243 is noteworthy because it signals the end of open warfare between Henry and Louis. No further English expeditions were sent to France.

The campaign of 1242 had several important consequences. Louis had been successful in taming his own rebellious baronage; he had gained wealth and prestige by the pacification of his own domain and the steady enforcement of his legal claims to control and suzerainty. This campaign also marked his appearance as a soldier king, one who, as was then required, personally led his own troops and gave a good account of himself as a warrior and tactician. In many ways, 1242 marked the emergence of Louis the king from the shadow of his mother's influence. From that time on Louis was free to put into effect his ideas of good administration, of justice and peace without hindrance from leagues of insurgent nobles. France was to have internal peace for the remainder of his reign, even during his years in Outremer, and the glow of this achievement illuminated his personal qualities and his efforts for Christian government.

This campaign also marked the beginning of the end for the

organized resistance of the Albigensian heretics in the lands of Languedoc. After the Treaty of Lorris, the count of Toulouse, previously lukewarm, genuinely tried to strengthen the image of his own orthodoxy, while the loss of such other strong supporters as the old count of Foix left the Albigensians shorn of their secular protectors. In 1244 the great Catharist stronghold of Montsegur, the mountaintop castle which for a generation had been the impregnable tabernacle of the Perfect, fell at last to the royal troops led by Raymond of Toulouse. Two hundred of the Perfect among its defenders were burnt without trial, and the rest were imprisoned. Before the capture of the castle four of the Cathars had escaped with the holy books and some of their greatest treasures, which they took to mountain communities of the faithful hidden away in the Pyrenees. Although some Albigensians persisted throughout the thirteenth century, despite the zeal of the inquisitors and the frequency of the burnings, the Catharist Church in Languedoc had perished. Albigensianism had been important because of its close relationship to the secular powers in Languedoc. It had provided them with an excuse to plunder the riches of the established church and to uphold their own regionalism against the pressing claims of outside monarchs and foreign prelates. When this secular support vanished, with conquest and the victory of different values, the creed perished too.[16]

In 1242 the land of Languedoc submitted to the control of Alphonse of Poitiers whose rule aided the gradual absorption of the south into the French nation. Alphonse had many reasons to be grateful to his brother: Louis had not only given him his promised appanage and made sure that he would enjoy his wife's lands, he had also fought bravely and successfully to uphold Alphonse's power and rights. For the next thirty years Alphonse repaid his debt with the enforcement of peace and good government in his lands, and the employment of methods and officials who shared much of the king's own philosophy of ruling. The cataclysms of revolt and heresy receded into the distance as law and order were stringently enforced.

V

The King, the Pope and the Emperor

1235–1247

A constant problem of all thirteenth-century rulers was their correct relationship with the pope who played a dual role as temporal and spiritual lord. The forceful Innocent III had greatly extended the range of papal claims in temporal matters and during much of the thirteenth century there were frequent conflicts between the popes and the secular rulers. The most obvious example of this was the long-drawn-out and desperate warfare between Frederic II, the great Hohenstaufen emperor, and a series of competent, combative popes bent equally on preserving the spiritual freedom of the church and the temporal sovereignty of the papal territories.

Frederic II was one of the most glamorous and controversial figures of the century. He was accused by some of his contemporaries of atheism, scepticism, and ruthlessness – a sweeping indictment which owes rather more to the violent propaganda of the papal party than to verifiable facts – while he was praised by others in terms equally extravagant. Frederic was a brilliant and capable monarch, bent on reviving the greatness of the empire and welding his kingdom of Sicily (which included both the island of Sicily and the mainland territories of Naples and Apulia) and the imperial lands in northern Italy into a cohesive whole. Such a policy inevitably aroused papal opposition since the papal states lay across central Italy as a barrier to Frederic's ambitions. Further strain was added to their relations by the fact that the pope claimed to be overlord of the kingdom of Sicily and thus, according to feudal law, had certain rights there. Frederic loved Sicily, where he had been brought up and where he felt most at home: its multi-racial and multi-lingual nature as well as the diverse religious background of the men of his court gave some colour to the accusations of heresy made against him. Frederic was unusual for his time in being a man of primarily scientific interests: he was learned in geometry and mathematics while in his treatise on falconry, *On the Art of Hunting with Birds*, he made a notable contribution to natural history. His pragmatic and rationalist cast of mind and his relentless exploitation of every possible means of establishing a strong unified society met opposition from both the popes and the powerful nobles. Nevertheless this merely heralded the growing secularization and centralization of medieval society. Most of Frederic's actions were essentially orthodox but his struggle against the temporal power of the papacy and his insistence on a more precise delimitation of papal powers in the temporal sphere were some decades ahead of his time.[1] In cast of mind, he was the counterpart of Philip the Fair, not of St Louis.

Although Louis IX did not share the temperament or the outlook of Frederic II, the saintly king did not believe in or allow the interference of the pope or any other ecclesiastic in what he felt were temporal matters rightly under his own jurisdiction. Normally he proceeded in a diplomatic and tactful way but he was undeterred by papal complaints, the grievances of provincial synods, or sentences of excommunication. The case of Beauvais, which was handled primarily by Queen Blanche, is only one example. Soon after Louis himself took full power there was a similar incident with the archbishop of Rheims.[2]

Archbishop Henry of Braine (still another brother of the redoubtable Peter Mauclerc) had quarrelled with the bourgeois of Rheims over financial matters at the beginning of 1235. Neither side would give ground so the archbishop excommunicated the townspeople and asked the king to give effect to the sentence. The king refused to do so unless the secular court was allowed to review the grounds for the sentence, which the archbishop refused as infringing on the competence of the spiritual power. The matter was appealed by the archbishop to the pope and became involved with the still smouldering dispute at Beauvais. In a provincial council at St Quentin in July 1235 which included both the bishop of Beauvais and the archbishop of Rheims, the ecclesiastics made a series of complaints against the king, some in general terms about his power and others about its specific applications. The king did not answer them at once, but in September he assembled the barons of the realm at St Denis to join him in complaint to the pope. They wrote to Gregory IX about the abuses of the clerics, and especially the refusal of the bishops of Rheims and Beauvais to appear in the king's court on temporal matters. They emphasized the need for maintaining the royal rights and insisted that these ecclesiastics were trying to impose new customs which were detrimental to the king and the nobles.[3] Before the pope could reply the provincial council decided to reimpose the interdict throughout the ecclesiastical province.

The king finally sentenced against the bourgeois of Rheims in January 1236 and they had to make reparation to the archbishop but the matter was still clouded by the decision of the pope to call the bourgeois to his papal court – which neither the church nor the commune of Rheims wanted.

In February 1236 the pope wrote to Louis in answer to the complaint of the previous autumn and a decree which seems to have sprung from it. The French gathering declared that lords were not bound to answer in an ecclesiastical court on secular matters, and ecclesiastics were obliged, in all civil cases, to answer to the courts of their lords and the king. If the ecclesiastical judge excommunicated the lords on this matter, he was to be forced to lift the excommunication by the seizure of his temporalities. The pope claimed to be astounded at this extraordinary innovation which curtailed the liberties of the church and upset ancient custom, and reminded Louis and the barons of the statute of Honorius III which decreed excommunication for all those who made statutes against the church.[4] Despite the veiled threat, the king did not withdraw and the pope did not press the matter further since he needed the king's help against Frederic.* The issue of royal competence over ecclesiastics in civil cases was settled almost inadvertently. After Rheims it was not really questioned, and

*Matters at Beauvais, where Bishop Godfrey had reimposed the interdict, were also at an impasse. When Godfrey died soon after, Louis seized the see by regalian right, and refused to allow the election of a new bishop until the interdict was fully raised. A conciliatory bishop was finally chosen in June, 1238 but the last echoes of the controversy did not die away till ten years later when the king and the bishop finally agreed on the amount and terms of the *gîte*.

after Louis's return from Outremer it was even actively sought. The same issue had helped to cause the explosive quarrel between Becket and Henry II in England and the martyrdom of the archbishop of Canterbury had sealed his claim with blood. Louis, aided by a firm tactfulness and the growing laicization of society, won his point without fireworks.

The troubles at Beauvais and Rheims exemplify the fact that his piety in no way interfered with his interpretation of royal power. Nor did his opinion change: Joinville has preserved a later and less formal complaint of the bishops against this royal policy:

> 'Sir, the archbishops and bishops here present have charged me to tell you that under your rule Christendom is falling into decay and dissolution; and it will fare still worse, since nowadays no man has any respect for excommunication. We call on you then, sir, to order your judges and officers to force those who have been under sentence for a year and a day to give satisfaction to the Church.' The king answered, without taking any advice, that he would willingly order his judges and officers to do as they asked provided he received sufficient evidence to judge whether the sentence was justified or not. The bishops consulted among themselves and replied to the king that they would not submit to his judgment a matter that concerned the ecclesiastical courts. The king in turn answered that he would not submit to their judgment a matter that was only his own concern, and refused to order his officers to force the excommunicate, right or wrong, to obtain absolution. 'Were I to do so, I should be acting against God and justice.'[5]

The king also went on to remind the bishops that the count of Brittany had been excommunicated by the bishops of Brittany for seven years, but the sentence had been finally quashed by the pope, so the king would have been at fault if he had compelled the count earlier.

Louis showed a more conciliatory tact towards the pope, but this was not allowed to compromise his position of independence. His relations with Gregory IX and Innocent IV in their quarrel with Frederic II illustrate this. Gregory IX had been elected to the chair of Peter in 1227, when he was possibly already in his eighties. He had been made a cardinal by Innocent III at the beginning of his pontificate and had been a respected adviser at the Roman curia ever since. Pope Gregory was an impulsive and passionate man and absolutely certain that the rule of the Hohenstaufen would be fatal for the church: the fourteen years of his pontificate were marked by unremitting hostility on both sides, despite a temporary truce arrived at in 1230. From 1235 on the contest between Frederic and the papacy rushed to a climax. The emperor's military successes in Lombardy and the territories of the papal states had infuriated the pope, whose position in Rome was already perilous, and had also roused the antagonism of the great trading cities of Lombardy. Milan, Genoa and Venice had no wish to surrender their profitable independence to the heavy hand of imperial rule. In this essentially secular struggle against the emperor Gregory IX constantly turned to spiritual weapons because of the weakness of his temporal power. He desperately sought aid from other European monarchs and tried to facilitate the raising of money and arms for his struggle against Frederic by dignifying the war with the name of a crusade. In March 1239 the pope invoked the full thunder of excommunication against Frederic.

Louis had remained very correctly neutral during the early stages of this struggle. He did not break off relations with Frederic II nor did he aid the pope, but he made clear to both parties the independence of the French king. When Frederic had ordered Louis to come to Vaucouleurs in 1238 for a conference, Louis arranged to have a sizeable army at Compiègne to accompany him. This was not what Frederick had expected, and the conference was called off.[6] The only authority for a papal effort to make Louis agree to the deposition of the emperor and his replacement by Robert of Artois is Matthew Paris; according to him, the king, with the joint baronage of France, replied that they considered the pope's plan unwise since he was rash in judging such a great prince. The tone of the answer, as given by Matthew Paris, echoes more of Paris's unshakable anti-papal prejudice than the likely wording of the tactful king and his careful clerks, but the offer may well have been made and refused. The report is particularly interesting for its emphasis, so often to be found in Matthew Paris, on the innate superiority of the French king.

Ambition does not strike us; for we believe that our lord the king of France, whom the line of royal blood had brought to the sceptre of France to rule, is more excellent than any emperor who is only promoted by voluntary election. It is sufficient for Count Robert to be the brother of such a king.[7]

Relations between Frederic and Louis deteriorated when, in an attempt to counter the emperor's successes in the field, Gregory called a general church council at Rome for Easter of 1241. Frederic swore that he would capture any prelates going to Rome by land or sea, and this threat so disheartened some that they turned back at once. Other more stalwart clerics tried to reach Rome in ships offered by the Genoese, since Frederic controlled all the land routes through northern Italy. Many of the prelates, including French bishops and abbots, were captured by a Pisan fleet under the command of Frederic's son Enzio. Most of the captives were elderly and in poor health and they were thrown into prison by the triumphant Frederic and harshly treated. This naked tyranny was more than Louis could bear: he would not fight against the rightful emperor, but he would insist that the emperor recognize Louis's own royal rights and not maltreat his subjects, particularly clerics who deserved special respect. After two progressively stronger letters from the angry French king Frederic let the French bishops go. The emperor's position was too awkward to permit him to offend Louis irretrievably.[8] Before a truce could be arrived at, Pope Gregory died. Frederic was only ten miles from Rome and the outlook for the papacy was black indeed.

After a prolonged interregnum Sinibaldo Fieschi, an active, vigorous Genoese in his fifties, was elected pope in June 1243 and took the name of Innocent IV. Innocent was a great canon lawyer, but he carried to the furthest extremes the canonist's insistence on the universal and absolute nature of the papal power in all matters, both spiritual and temporal. This uncompromising attitude was bound to force a direct and immediate confrontation with Frederic's theory of unbridled imperial supremacy. The contest was not long in developing, and Frederick's armies seemed to hold the balance of power. By the summer of 1244 Innocent had to flee from Rome, in a Genoese fleet. Safely arrived in

Genoa, the pope looked for a secure place to settle and immediately thought of France. The general chapter of the Cistercians met at Cîteaux at Michaelmas 1244 and its deliberations were attended by Louis and Queen Blanche, as well as Robert of Artois and Alphonse of Poitiers. The papal letter asking for the French king's help and for refuge in France was delivered to the king by the assembled abbots. The king agreed that 'so much as honesty would permit' he would aid the pope against the emperor, and he would receive him in his realm if that was the advice of his barons.[9] Louis had chosen a polite escape from a difficult situation, since he knew that his barons were notoriously anti-papal. Innocent then decided on the city of Lyons as his refuge. Lyons, at the juncture of the Rhône and the Saône, was nominally a city of the empire, but it had maintained practical independence under the control of its archbishop. As well, it was comfortably close to the lands of France in case of an imperial attack. After a long and difficult journey over the Alps the pope finally arrived at Lyons in the beginning of December 1244.

Louis himself fell gravely ill at Pontoise in December. The king had never fully recovered from the fever and infection he had contracted during the campaign in Poitou and now the fever and a 'flux of the stomach' returned with greater virulence. For several days Louis was so ill that, at one time, those watching him thought that he had died and wanted to draw the sheet over his face. Prayers and processions were offered by the people of Paris and the agitated barons and clergy, who dreaded the death of the king when his heir was less than a year old. A few days before Christmas Louis began to recover, but he had decided that, if he was spared, he would go on crusade, and immediately after his recovery he took the cross.[10] The king's policy was now primarily directed towards the crusade and towards creating the conditions within and without the realm which would make the crusade possible.

Within a month after his arrival at Lyons Pope Innocent called a general council for the coming June. The summons mentioned the danger to Christendom from the tide of the onrushing Mongols, and from the successes of the Saracens in Outremer, but the pope's real reason in convening it was to force the struggle with Frederic to a final decision. When the Council of Lyons opened its deliberations on June 24, 1245, it was attended primarily by the French and Spanish bishops: there were few from Germany, because of the trouble with the emperor; none from Hungary, which was suffering the devastations of the Mongols; or from the Holy Land, although the bishop of Beirut arrived during the council with news from Outremer. Frederic had been summoned by the pope to appear in person or by proxy to clear himself. The emperor sent as his representative Thaddeus of Suessa, a distinguished knight and judge of the imperial court. On Frederic's behalf, Thaddeus renewed the promises made – and broken – so often before, and skilfully defended his master against the charges hurled by the pope. His eloquence convinced the bishops that it was not just to convict a man for heresy without his personal appearance, and the council was adjourned, though only for nine days, to allow Frederic to appear in person. Frederic did not, probably could not, appear in that time, for he had to come from Verona. On July 17, with Thaddeus prevented from making any further rebuttal, the council proceeded to the prearranged sentence of excommunication and deposition.

The council had only added fuel to the fire in the contest between emperor and pope. Not surprisingly, Frederic defied the authority of the council and wrote innumerable letters justifying his position and insisting on his peaceful intentions. At the end of September, for example, the emperor declared that he was willing to submit the quarrels between himself and the pope to Louis's arbitration. Frederic argued that the pope had acted against God and justice, since he truly wanted peace with the church. Knowing how dear the project of the crusade was to Louis, Frederic wrote that he was ready to go overseas with him if only peace could be achieved, or at least he would send his son. In any case, even if the dissension continued, he was ready to help Louis and the crusaders with ships and provisions.[11] Louis never took up the task of formal arbitration: he must have realized the impossibility of reconciling such opposites. The deposition was not recognized by any of the other monarchs of Europe, but Innocent acted on it, continuing to fight the emperor doggedly and to treat those who battled against Frederic as crusaders. Invective and insult mark the literature of both sides to an extraordinary degree. Frederic won some victories, but none decisive enough, and with his sudden death in 1250 the Hohenstaufen power rapidly crumbled. Innocent too was dead by 1254 and the troubled question of the kingdom of Sicily entered a new phase.

Although Louis had refused the suggested arbitration he was most anxious to see the conflict settled. In the face of the Moslem and Mongol menace he felt that the relationship between all the Christian rulers should be one of peace and mutual support. Prompted by Frederic's letter, Louis gathered his army in the autumn and went to visit the pope. He met Innocent IV at Cluny, the great abbey in Burgundy which for centuries had been the centre of so much Christian inspiration and which was still rich and magnificent. The appearance of his company seems to have been designed to warn Frederic that Louis would not tolerate any interference with the pope while he was on or near French soil. As the chroniclers describe it, his retinue looked like a battle array – there was a company of mounted sergeants with crossbows, as well as the usual detachment of armed sergeants, and a great body of knights surrounding the king. Louis was accompanied by his mother and his brothers.[12] They were all entertained at the abbey for a week, but the discussions between the pope, the king, and Queen Blanche were kept secret, though they may have discussed how peace between the church and the empire could be honourably achieved, and here Louis would have tried to restrain the belligerency of the pope. Louis not only wanted peace in Christendom; he was also anxious for the crusaders to be able to pass through the imperial territories. Probably the rulers also dealt with the question of a peace treaty between England and France, or at least the extension of the truce which was to expire in 1248. Louis was anxious not to leave his enemies an opportunity for mischief-making in his realm during his absence in Outremer.[13]

When this conference ended Louis returned to his domain, stopping at Mâcon to take possession of the county he had bought from the Countess Alix in 1239. The king had earlier divided his company and sent a strong force of armed men to Provence. The troubled state of that county may well have been the primary reason for his large retinue at Cluny. At this moment Provence was a rich and tempting prize. When Count Raymond Berenger of Provence and Count Raymond of Toulouse had met at the Council of Lyons they had discussed the possibility of a marriage between Count Raymond and Beatrice of Provence, Raymond Berenger's youngest daughter. No final decision had been made when the counts parted, and Raymond Berenger died soon after his return to Provence. His wife was in England, where she had taken their third daughter, Sanchia, to marry Richard of Cornwall, and young Beatrice was left alone. With her father's death she had become an even more tempting matrimonial prize for, by the terms of his will, she inherited the counties of Provence and Forcalquier. Her father had hoped in this way to ensure Provençal independence, and his other daughters had been less generously treated. Marguerite, married to Louis, and Eleanor, married to Henry III, received only 100 marks in addition to the 10,000 marks given them as dowries – and these had not yet been fully paid. Sanchia received 5,000 marks, as did the count's widow.[14]

The government of Provence was in the hands of Romée de Villeneuve, the chief counsellor of the dead count and a capable man who realized that the only hope for the independence of Provence was to refrain from giving open offence to the French king. He understood that Beatrice's marriage to the count of Toulouse would be regarded as provocative and against Louis's interests. Count Raymond was not told bluntly of the unacceptability of his suit, but one delay and difficulty followed another. James of Aragon was also interested in Beatrice's marriage. Since he was lord of Montpellier he hoped to increase his penetration and influence on the southern borders of the French kingdom by marrying his son to Beatrice. James brought an army as far as Aix to reinforce his suggestion, but Louis's armed men soon dissipated that threat. The problem of Beatrice and her county remained unsolved for the moment. The French king did not feel entitled in strict justice to seize the county because of his wife's claims, nor did he wish to see it divided among the sisters, as this would put the English king and his brother, Richard of Cornwall, in still another strategic position on the French frontiers. However, there was one solution which would safeguard the French interest while not destroying the apparent independence of the high-spirited Provençals. Louis's youngest brother, Charles, was still unmarried, and the decision to marry Charles to the young heiress soothed both the royal interests and the royal conscience.

The marriage took place in Provence on January 31, 1246 in the presence of the bride's mother and her three uncles, the count of Savoy, Thomas now count of Flanders after his marriage to the widowed Countess Jeanne, and the archbishop of Lyons. After the wedding Charles and Beatrice travelled back to France and on Pentecost (May 27) Louis knighted his brother and gave him his appanage of Anjou and Maine. Matthew Paris tells a story which suggests that Charles had already begun to display the arrogance for which he was to be so famous. He is reputed to have complained to his mother that the celebrations at his marriage were not as elaborate as at those of Louis. This was not proper, because Louis, although king, was the son of merely a prince – having been born before his father ascended the throne – while Charles was the son of a king and queen.*[15]

The presence of the pope so close to the borders of France encouraged the prevailing undercurrent of anti-clericalism to rise once more to the surface. During the thirteenth century as the government and administration of the church became more centralized and uniform, as canon law became codified and was generally applied throughout church jurisdiction, and as the growing bureaucracy and expensive wars of the papacy encouraged a more efficient system of taxation, there was an inevitable friction between the secular and the spiritual powers. The old, shadowy no-man's land between secular and spiritual claims was disappearing and the lay power too had begun to define and defend its frontiers and to resent vigorously any incursion on what

*This sequence of events seems to reinforce the belief that Charles's birth, of which the exact date is unknown, must be placed in the autumn of 1226, before his father's death rather than in the early months of 1227. It seems difficult to believe that Blanche could have had a posthumous child during the hectic months which followed Louis IX's accession without some chronicler commenting on the fact. Equally, it seems unlikely that Charles would have been knighted and invested with his appanage before his twenty-first year, since such had not been the practice with the king's other brothers.

it felt was its own privileged territory. The barons, as well as the king, often attempted to dispute the ecclesiastical claims. For example, in November 1246 a league of French barons banded together to defend their rights against the clergy. The leaders included Count Peter of Brittany, the duke of Burgundy, Hugh le Brun, son of the count of La Marche and himself count of Angoulême, and the count of St Pol. They felt strongly enough to agree to pay one hundredth of their revenues to the association, and, in a manifesto issued at the time of the forming of the league, they complained about the invasion by the ecclesiastical courts of what was properly under secular jurisdiction.[16] The ecclesiastical initiative in the courts meant, of course, not only a loss in the barons' prestige, but also a distinct loss in income, as the profits of justice were among the most valuable elements of a lordship. The pope quickly responded to the challenge. On January 4, 1247 Innocent ordered the papal legate, Eudes of Châteauroux, who was in France to aid in the preparations for the crusade, to proceed against all the members of the league and their supporters. The pope demanded the excommunication of all even remotely connected with the confederation and its manifesto, and insisted that the clergy of these barons were to leave their service and council as soon as the sentence had been made public, or forfeit all their benefices and privileges.[17]

The king had already called a great council in mid-Lent to discuss the major business of the realm, including the crusade on which Louis was determined to embark and for which he had already set the date of departure as June 24, 1248.[18] The grievances of the league of barons were also thoroughly debated, and the king was willing to send a personal complaint to the pope on these issues. At the beginning of May, a French embassy arrived at Lyons to present to Innocent the charges made against the church in France. The embassy did not only represent the barons: more seriously it represented a wide spectrum of French thought and power. Ferry Pâté, the marshal of France, represented the king, and he was joined by the bishops of Soissons and Troyes, on behalf of the prelates, and by the archdeacon of Tours and the provost of Normandy on the behalf of the chapters and the university clerks. They complained about the usurpation of jurisdiction by the ecclesiastical courts – the crucial and central issue; of the disposition of French benefices and pensions to Italians; of the indiscriminate use of excommunication; and of the intolerable weight of financial demands made by the pope and his nuncios, and of the insistence of his collectors. The following day the pope replied. He promised to revoke any usurpation by the church on temporal jurisdiction, but only if this usurpation was new – there was to be no change in powers of which the church was already in possession. The pope would not revoke benefices held by Italians, but he would stop the practice of papal provisions.[19] The messengers withdrew, but their report led to another embassy.

The first embassy was clearly described by Archbishop Boniface of Canterbury in a letter written from the papal court to his brother Peter of Savoy in England. The account of the second is less certain. Matthew Paris gives what seems to be the report of a speech, but was probably a memorandum prepared for the use of the embassy. Though substantially authentic it is not an official royal complaint, but was placed before the pope in the king's name. It is unfinished, confused, less carefully divided, and some of the points sound most unlike the devout and tactful king of France, and must have been drawn up by the unknown envoy. In a very sharp tone the document detailed two major complaints brought forward again by the French in late May or early June 1247. The document argued particularly against the money exaction by the pope and complained at the papal appointments to ecclesiastical benefices. It claimed that the temporalities of the church in France belonged to the king for his own needs and those of the realm, and even suggested that the king had the power to use church property as his own in time of necessity.[20] The most extreme claim, the royal right to church property, seems to have been supplied by the envoy himself and does not fairly represent Louis's views. Even in his moments of greatest need, the king did not seize the goods of the church but asked for grants.[21]

These protests of 1247 are worth noting because they strikingly underline Louis's independence of papal control or any subservience to ecclesiastical pressures. Beauvais and Rheims were later echoed in a similar insistence on his bishops obeying the civil statutes. The year Louis died he threatened the seizure of the temporalities of the bishop of Clermont who had altered the money he had the right to coin and then had excommunicated all those who would not accept it at the episcopal valuation. The bishop was to lift the excommunication at once or suffer the seizure of his goods.[22] Yet Louis never denied the papal leadership of the whole church, or tried to make the French church an almost separate unit under his own influence. The Pragmatic Sanction of 1269, which is attributed to Louis in the *Ordonnances*, is a fifteenth-century forgery.[23] It covers much of the same ground as the memorandum of 1247 but is markedly different. The document of 1247 was a request for the reformation of papal abuses in France, while the Pragmatic Sanction was meant to be an ordinance of the king legislating for the church in his own right.[24]

Louis always showed honour and respect to the pope and did not allow the emperor to attack him. But despite the papal sentence of excommunication and deposition, Louis had correct, if none too cordial, relations with the emperor. In his own realm Louis would not abdicate his position of supremacy. He made sure that his bishops, and ultimately the pope, recognized and bowed to his power in the purely temporal affairs of the church. Louis was a very good Christian; he was far from being a clerical puppet.

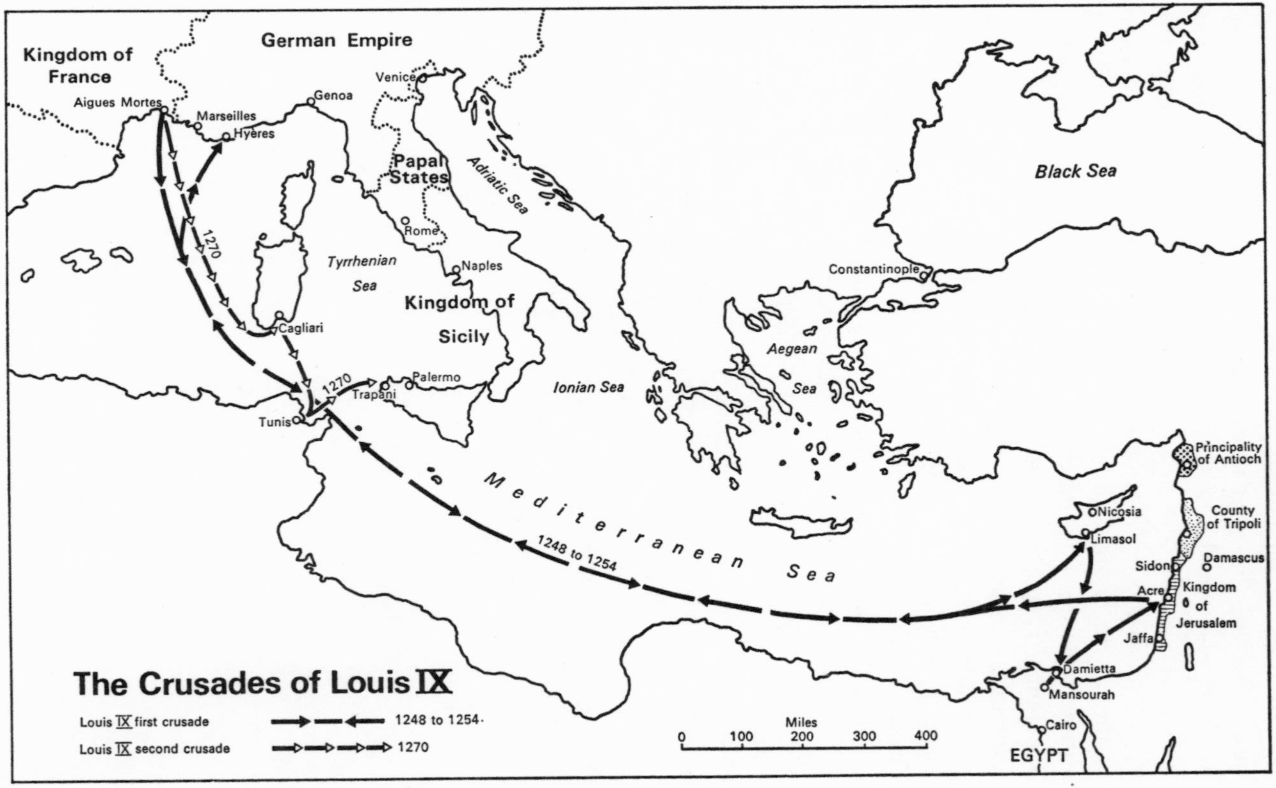
The Crusades of Louis IX
Louis IX first crusade
1248 to 1254
Louis IX second crusade
1270
Kingdom of France
German Empire
Aigues Mortes
Marseilles
Hyères
Genoa
Venice
Papal States
Rome
Naples
Adriatic Sea
Tyrrhenian Sea
Kingdom of Sicily
Cagliari
Palermo
Trapani
Tunis
1270
1270
Ionian Sea
Aegean Sea
Constantinople
Black Sea
Mediterranean Sea
1248 to 1254
Principality of Antioch
County of Tripoli
Damascus
Nicosia
Limasol
Sidon
Acre
Kingdom of Jerusalem
Jaffa
Damietta
Mansourah
Cairo
EGYPT
Miles
0
100
200
300
400

VI

Preparations for the Crusade 1245–1248

Louis IX had taken the cross during his serious illness in December 1244. Unlike many of his contemporaries who cheerfully vowed to go on crusade in moments of danger and then bought release from their crusading vows as soon as the emergency had passed, the French king was truly convinced of his duty to lead the Christians of the west against the Moslems, and to strive once again for the reconquest of the Holy Land.

Crusading had been a constant element in Christian policy ever since the emotional launching of the First Crusade by Pope Urban at Clermont in 1095. In the first wave of fervour the kings and princes of the west had mounted several serious military expeditions to free the Holy Land and there had also been such ill-fated mass movements of the poor and weak as the Children's Crusade and that led by Peter the Hermit. By the thirteenth century, the idealistic concept of the crusade had declined from its first emotional height and the overseas expeditions, although still called crusades, became more practical and more limited in their aims. Christians had settled in Outremer,* many of them the descendants of the landless knights who, in the early crusades, had seen scope for their territorial ambitions as well as their religious fervour. Gradually these adventurers had consolidated their position in small principalities along the coast of present-day Syria and Lebanon, in southern Greece and on the island of Cyprus. Some of this acquisition of territory had been at the expense of the Greek Christian Byzantine empire, toppled by the

*In western Europe at this time the term Outremer referred to all those lands which lay beyond the seas, either under Moslem control or open to Moslem attack. Outremer included the Moslem territories of North Africa, Egypt and Asia Minor as well as the Christian principalities of the near east. The term serves as a convenient geographical abbreviation.

joint attack of the Venetians and the men of the Fourth Crusade. Constantinople and its territories were now ruled by the weak Latin Emperor Baldwin. The Fourth Crusade's scandalous pitting of Christian against Christian, and the papal insistence on describing as crusades its primarily political wars in Europe combined to bring the original militant ideal of a Holy War against the infidel into disrepute. Yet most European feudal lords, and many of their lesser men, still felt bound to make at least one crusading expedition during their lifetime. Their motives were undoubtedly mixed. The excitement of campaigning in strange lands, of which they had heard tales from returned crusaders; the obligation to lend useful support to their friends or relations in Outremer, who desperately needed it; the legal and spiritual benefits extended to crusaders, such as freedom from prosecution and massive indulgences; all these must often have helped to weigh the balance of genuine religious belief in the spiritual benefits of the crusade. Then too, in a civilization where the law court was gradually replacing recourse to private war, where the military class was finding the king's peace firmly enforced by his officials, the crusades offered church-sanctioned adventure and violence, heroism and excitement, all extremely tempting.

The Christian hold in Outremer was always perilous. Despite their original success the crusading forces had never been able to push their territorial gains beyond the coastal plains and the control of some of the mountain passes: they never captured Damascus, key to the inland route, which allowed the Moslems to transfer their forces at will from Egypt to the north. On the other hand, the Christians were upheld by the unquestioned Italian naval superiority and control of the Mediterranean, and by the constant infusion of new fighting strength from the west, sporadic and disorganized though it might be. When King Louis decided to go on crusade the outlook was at once darker, and yet more promising, than it had been for many years.

The politics of Outremer were a constant source of frustration to men from the west who thought the world was merely divided into good Christians and bad Moslems. Those knights who had spent some time in Outremer knew that the alliances and alignments of the Moslem world were infinitely changeable, so that the

5. Louis and Marguerite kneeling at the feet of Christ, from the tympanum of the Porte Rouge at Notre Dame, Paris

6a. Louis receives the Crown of Thorns (from the *Chroniques de St Denis c.* 1275 begun at the end of Louis's reign and inspired by him, they give the history of France until the death of Philip Augustus. In the 14th century a life of St Louis was added)

6b. The Sainte Chapelle and royal palace – although an early 15th century representation the impression is essentially that of Louis's reign

enemy of one day was the ally of the next, and they had learned from costly experience to balance in this confused and shifting sea. Two recent events had conspired to change the old patterns beyond recognition. The Khwarismians, swept out of their lands in Persia by the onrush of the Mongols, had combined with the Egyptians to attack the Frankish states. They captured Jerusalem in the summer of 1244 and defeated the Christians decisively in a major battle at La Forbie, near Gaza. The immediate future of the Christian states in the near east looked perilous, and the frequent agitated letters from the prelates and lords of Outremer to those in Europe make clear how desperate was the concern for the future of the Christian principalities.

The most important shift of power in the first half of the thirteenth century, however, was the great westward sweep of the Mongols, or Tartars, as the medieval men called them, from their centre north of Lake Baikal, in Mongolia. They flooded into India, onward to Persia and Armenia, and, in Europe, into Russia, Hungary, up to the Danube, and even to the shores of the Adriatic. Only the death of the Great Khan Ogodai at Karakorum in December 1241, and the subsequent return of Batu, the Mongol chief in charge of the forces invading Europe, to join in the choice of the new khan saved Europe from being overrun by the Mongol horde. The Tartar invasion was terrifying, for the Mongol warriors killed all those who resisted them, and devastated the territory they conquered. Whole cities were wiped out and all their inhabitants killed, and those whom the armies had overlooked were felled by famine, hunger so fierce that 'living men ate the bodies of the dead, dogs, cats, and whatever they could find'.[1]

The Mongols nevertheless presented the rulers of western Europe with a ray of hope. As the invaders came closer to the borders of the known world, where it was possible to get credible and regular reports, it became obvious that perhaps in this wild and terrible new race lay the counterpoise to the Moslems. The Mongols had not yet espoused any religion, and if they could be converted to Christianity they might unite with the Christians to end Moslem rule. A great new Christian world might stretch right across Asia. This optimistic dream was not without some foundation. The Mongol khans had accepted Christians within their lands: Nestorian Christians held positions of power and influence at court, and Christian practice was respected. The unparalleled success of the Mongol conquests in the thirteenth century reopened the overland route between Asia, Europe, and India – the old 'Silk Road'. For almost a hundred years missionary friars and adventurous merchants travelled back and forth unmolested across the great stretches of inland Russia and Mongolia from Europe to China. In the end the noble dream of one great world perished with the Christianized Mongols. The Mongols became Moslems, the great land route was again closed, and the noble vision faded. But in the thirteenth century optimism was still possible. In 1244, although Louis was most impressed by the immediate danger of the Mongols to Europe and to the crusader states, he was not unaware that he might find in them a common ally against the Moslems.[2]

The king was determined that his crusade would be a large and well equipped expedition, since recent efforts, such as those of Theobald of Champagne, had suffered from a lack of men and provisions. Louis's first need was to encourage men to take the cross. The method of recruiting had changed since the first crusade, but it was still based on preaching. By the thirteenth century manuals had been written to instruct those preachers, and one of the most famous was that written by Humbert of the Romans, the Master General of the Dominicans who died in 1277 after fifty years as a friar. Humbert had been one of Louis's counsellors and a godfather to one of his sons, so his treatise *On Preaching the Cross* mirrors the accepted practice of Louis's reign.

Preaching and recruiting were carried on in public assemblies as well as churches, but the formal taking of the cross usually occurred at a special ceremony in church which was marked by hymns, prayers, an insistent sermon, the presentation of crosses, and the taking up of a collection. The whole tone appears to have been markedly revivalist, with strong emotional appeal. The atmosphere must have been that of an evangelical camp-meeting, calling sinners to repent and to make a decision for Christ. More interesting to us than the frenzied tone of the appeals are the homely illustrations used by the preachers. Those who feared shipwreck – a universal bugaboo – or the difficult climate and terrain of Outremer were compared to fat palfreys, which spent their time in being groomed or parading ostentatiously, instead of working or fighting. Those who were afraid to leave their native land were contemptuously compared to hens, or the placid cows of Flanders tethered to their houses. The preachers emphasized how the crusade was the quick, sure way to Paradise.[3] The famous Stephen of Bourbon gives the most startling simile, comparing the crusade to a pole vault:

> In Flanders there are many canals. When men cannot cross them unless they find a bridge with great expenditure of time and labour, agile men take great staffs or perches or lances, and with their aid with one leap they cross the water. Thus with the staff of the cross in the crossing of death the crusaders, avoiding even the long pain of purgatory, cross to heaven as if with one leap.[4]

The sermons were full, too, of vivid stories about the discomfiture crusading vows caused the devil. One particularly popular tale, which turns up in several guises in the collections of *exempla* (the illustrative tales included in medieval sermons and circulated among preachers) and even in a supposed chronicle of Louis's reign, tells of the knight who was passing through a great wood in early October on his way to Paris. He heard horrible wailings of devils bemoaning the loss of men they felt they had possessed and naming eminent barons and knights. The knight and his squires recognized the names and were terrified for their own future. They immediately promised to take the cross and go overseas with the king, making themselves a cross of leafy branches as a token of their vow. When they got to Paris and told their story they discovered that those whom the demons had named had taken the cross at that very hour in the great assembly called by Louis and the papal legate.[5]

But it was not only the preachers who tried to rouse public opinion for the crusade, the poets were also propagandists. The poems of Rutebeuf, the most famous among them, apply to Louis's second crusade, but other poets, especially in the south of France, joined the crusading chorus earlier. Their *sirventes*, as they were called, were composed for a large audience and often dealt with some question of public life. Since the Provençal poets hated the papacy because of the Albigensian Crusade their songs were often bitterly anti-papal. Nevertheless they found it much more subtle, and less likely to provoke retaliation, to encourage crusading and to blame the papacy because it was insufficiently devoted to the Holy Sepulchre.

Such popular exhortations and songs were meant to influence especially the less affluent knights and the lower classes. The great barons and prelates were approached with more dignity. The king requested a legate from Innocent IV charged with the special responsibility for the crusade. After the Council of Lyons in 1245 the pope sent Eudes of Châteauroux, the bishop of Tusculanum and one time chancellor of Paris to France with a commission to preach the crusade throughout the realm. Louis called a great parlement at Paris in October, before leaving to visit the pope at Cluny, and both the king and the legate exhorted those attending to take the cross. Many of the prelates and a fair number of the great lords, including the king's brothers, yielded to Louis's plea.[6] The king was not completely satisfied with the response. Matthew Paris tells of Louis arranging for the robes which he was required to distribute to the knights of his household at Christmas to be of specially fine material this year, but also to have a cross worked on the shoulder. The mantles were distributed in the dark and the knights in their new robes were called to join the king at early mass on Christmas Day before the sun had risen. In daylight they saw the pious trick the king had played on them, but felt constrained to accept the cross calling the king 'a hunter of pilgrims and a new fisher of men'.[7]

The French members of Louis's crusade were in the majority. The Germans and the Italians were totally absorbed in the great contest between the pope and the Emperor Frederic. The lords of eastern Europe were hard pressed to hold their own borders against the Mongol encroachments, while Henry III of England was not anxious to see many of his barons enrolled in an expedition led by a king with whom he was formally at war. The crusading army was primarily composed of men from the royal domain and the lands of the king's brothers, although it included forces from Burgundy, Champagne, and Flanders and a small English contingent headed by William Longsword, earl of Salisbury.

Money was the first prerequisite for building up a large crusading army with its necessary supplies and reinforcements. Louis's first crusade was extremely well financed. The Council of Lyons had ordered a grant of one-twentieth of ecclesiastical revenues for this purpose, and the French clergy, under pressure from both the pope and the king, increased their contribution to one-tenth for five years. By the middle of the thirteenth century the papal system of taxation had been developed and elaborated and its efficiency helped to fill Louis's crusading coffers. Not much accrued to the king from the twentieth outside of France, except in the dioceses in Lorraine and Burgundy which were coming more and more under French influence. In France itself, however, the returns from the church provided valuable sums. It has been estimated that the total cost of the crusade was something over 1,500,000 pounds, and that the French clergy, in the five years during which the tenth was collected, paid some 950,000 pounds, or nearly two-thirds. The king's normal revenue at this time was about 240,000 to 250,000 pounds a year and much of this came from fixed payments which could not easily be augmented. However, the towns could be required to give the king financial aid, and this source was vigorously exploited. Not only did the towns provide at least 66,000 pounds before the king's departure, but they continued to contribute to his expenses after he had gone overseas. Years later they were still complaining of the debts thus incurred.[8] The great barons also collected as much capital for themselves as they could. Some profited from various grants made them by their vassals but others must have been like Joinville, who had to pledge a great part of his estate to equip and sustain himself and the nine knights under him.[9] Even this was not sufficient for a long campaign, and ultimately the payment of much of the army devolved upon the king. Louis's credit remained good throughout his time in the east and his bills of credit and loans were speedily honoured by the Italian bankers and merchants.

Once the financing of the crusades was settled Louis had next to decide on the main port of embarkation and arrange for the necessary transport. The king's choice of a port was easy: it had to be Aigues-Mortes, since no other port on the Mediterranean was in the royal domain. Narbonne, although temporarily in Louis's hands, was too close to Spain and would have seriously lengthened the overland journey; Montpellier was in the hands of King James of Aragon; while Marseilles, the most convenient port and best harbour, divided its allegiance between the counts of Provence and Toulouse. The king had previously purchased the port of Aigues-Mortes from the abbey of Psalmody and had decided on a town there which would provide a royal foothold on the Mediterranean.

The town of Aigues-Mortes[10] is now a remote backwater approached over the flat, watery land of the Camargue, where the Rhône finds its way to the Mediterranean. Girdled by the great encircling wall built by Louis's son Philip and dominated by the Tower of Constance which Louis had built for his own headquarters in 1248, the town reflects in almost suspended animation its brief period of importance and prosperity. The harbour at Aigues-Mortes illustrates the conditions typical of this stretch of the coast. The town had a good outer harbour which had been in use long before the place was inhabited permanently, but the town itself was built on an inland *étang*, a large shallow lake of brackish water, which was separated from the sea by narrow strips of land, cut by *graux* or channels. These channels needed constant dredging and supervision to keep them from silting up and all the loading and unloading had to be done by lighters, since no big ships could come into the inner harbour. Even in the time of Louis, Aigues-Mortes was not directly on the Mediterranean and only vessels of shallow draught could come directly to its walls. The outer port, or bay, which has now become only another *étang*, opened directly to the Mediterranean, and the wide shallow opening into the inner port was a continuation of the Little Rhône. Aigues-Mortes had other deficiencies as a harbour. It was plagued by violent winds which whipped up sand storms: its fresh-water supply was inadequate for large numbers: and it probably suffered as well from the plague of malaria-bearing mosquitoes. The king had done all he could to make the place attractive and habitable. The charter of liberties given to Aigues-Mortes in May 1246 was the only one issued in Beaucaire during his reign, and offered special inducements to encourage settlement in the town. There were valuable financial concessions and the inhabitants of the town were allowed wide powers of self-government, although Louis retained control of all criminal justice and many of the civil cases.*[11] However, despite all the king's efforts and some commercial prosperity during the second half of the thirteenth century, Aigues-Mortes remained primarily a military port, to be abandoned when better harbours, more easily maintained, became available.

The provision of ships for the crusading army was a major concern of the king and required protracted negotiation with both Genoa and Marseilles, which were then the great ship-building and ship-renting centres. Although the king had made tentative efforts to deal with the Venetians, he found their prices too high and their assurances of delivery uncertain. Fortunately some of the contracts made in the king's name with both Genoa and Marseilles have survived and provide a factual check on the size and nature of the ships used in the profitable transport of soldiers and pilgrims to the Levant. These early contracts are particularly interesting for the proof they give of the large size of ships at this time. The largest Genoese ship, the *Paradise*, seems to have been a little over eighty-three feet. It was equipped to carry a hundred horses below decks, as well as crusaders and their attendants. The exact number of passengers cannot be estimated exactly, since the wealthy and important crusaders with several horses took up more space than the average humble pilgrims, who were allowed very little space for themselves and their necessary provisions. The poor pilgrims are probably described with reason as 'the medieval steerage',[13] and it appears that on an ordinary voyage these ships accommodated at least a thousand passengers. The king's party and the magnates occupied the chambers built on

*The extraordinary detail of medieval charters is often startling. Aigues-Mortes' first charter, when dealing with judicial procedure, ordered that adulterers should be fined or driven naked through the streets. When the charter was confirmed in 1279 some experienced clerk added to this provision that adulteresses had to be at least *slightly* clad when driven through the streets.[12]

deck, both fore and aft, known as the 'castles', which were the luxury cabins of the day. Men of substance were on deck while the poorest lived below decks at a considerably reduced price.

Royal officials, including representatives of the great crusading orders of the Templars and Hospitallers, who were expected to know what kind of transportation was required, were named to supervise the renting and purchasing of the ships. After the negotiations with Genoa had opened, the king appointed two admirals (the first time the title had been used in France) to represent him in making contracts with the individual ship-owners and builders. They were two eminent Genoese, Hugo Lercari and Jacopo d'Levanto, recommended by the Genoese Innocent IV because they had commanded the fleet which had brought him safely from Rome to Savona. Lercari had also been in charge of many convoys to the western Mediterranean. The Genoese admirals also bought naval stores and necessary arms, both in Genoa and elsewhere.[14] The ships had originally been ordered for the summer of 1247, but departure was postponed until 1248. In the summer of that year about thirty-eight large ships awaited the king and his forces at Aigues-Mortes. Other great lords made their own arrangements for transportation. Joinville joined the lord of Apremont in hiring a ship, and they sailed from Marseilles; the count of St Pol had one of his ships built at Inverness; while Raymond of Toulouse ordered his ships from Brittany for the crusade he had vowed, but never embarked on.[15]

As well as providing the major part of the transport, the king saw to it that large quantities of supplies were sent ahead to Cyprus, the final rallying point for the crusaders before their attack on the Moslem lands. Louis spent some 11,000 pounds in Burgundy in 1248 for cloth, wine, and supplies and also purchased six shiploads of food, wine and other stores from the Venetians which they delivered to Cyprus in their own ships before the king's arrival.[16] Statistics come to life in Joinville's vivid description.

> There was such a supply of wine that in the middle of the fields by the seashore his men had built great piles of barrels of wine which they had been buying for two years before his arrival;

> they had put them one on top of the other, so that when you looked at them from the front you would have thought that they were great wooden barns. The wheat and barley were also heaped out in the fields. At first sight you thought they were hills; the rain had been beating on the grain for a long time and had made it sprout on the outside, so that all you could see was the green grass. But when they were ready to ship it to Egypt they tore off the outside crust of grass, and inside the wheat and barley were as fresh as if they had been newly threshed.[17]

The care with which the king oversaw these preparations is adequate proof of his essentially practical outlook. Louis was more than a careful organizer; he was above all a king with a highly developed conscience about the Christian responsibilities of his exalted position. His primary duties as king were the provision of justice and peace for his realm and he made strenuous efforts to put the affairs of his kingdom in order before his departure.

The exercise of justice was the keystone of the royal power. The king's court was theoretically the final court of appeal, and the king the ultimate judge in secular cases. As both the royal domain and the royal power expanded, more of the king's exercise of justice was being delegated to his lesser officials, to the baillis and seneschals who represented him even in the remote corners of the kingdom. Such delegation could give rise to many abuses and exactions and of this Louis was well aware. In order to keep the abuses in check Louis decided to send out enquêteurs* before his departure. The terms of the commission given to the first enquêteurs in January 1247 underlines their essentially reforming nature. Their prime function was:

> To hear and to write and to inquire simply and openly concerning the injuries and exactions, services unjustly received and other burdens, if they were made by others or caused by our bailiffs, provosts, foresters, sergeants, or families of the same, in the time of our rule, and to enjoin the aforesaid or their

*It seems best to use the term *enquêteur* for these officials, as open to the least misinterpretation. Its proper translation, 'inquisitor', now implies an official whose only function was to pursue heretics. In fact, the Latin term, which was accurately applied to both kinds of officials, only means that these men decided their cases by the means of an inquest.

heirs that they restore those things to the restitution of which through their confessions or through proofs the aforesaid friars shall see them to be held following God.[18]

This office was not abolished after the crusade; the enquêteurs served throughout the king's reign, although their most extensive journeys were in 1247–48 but their value and the effects of their work can best be discussed against the background of the whole system of local government. Undoubtedly the main inspiration for their creation was Louis's own conscientiousness in all matters of justice, which was reinforced by the vow of all crusaders to settle their temporal affairs and right any injuries before their departure. This same spirit is obvious in other crusaders who accompanied Louis. Alphonse of Poitiers, in a document given at Aigues-Mortes just before his embarkation empowered his executors to amend his wrongs and those of his officials.[19] Joinville, in the middle of the celebrations of the birth of his son, called all his people and his vassals together and arranged to settle with any who felt they had a claim on him.[20] Louis having promised rightful restitution through the enquêteurs could depart feeling that he had done what he could to maintain justice in his realm.

The problem of ensuring peace was more difficult, as it did not rest wholly in the king's hands. Since 1245 Louis had been trying to bring the pope and the emperor together. That contest had become too bitter and too deeply rooted to allow any compromise; neither contestant could be satisfied except by the death or total surrender of the other. Still another source of concern was the simmering quarrel with England. The settlement arrived at after Louis's successful campaign in Poitou was due to expire in 1248 and the French king naturally wanted to be sure that, during his absence, no unfair advantage was taken by Henry III. Louis persuaded the pope to forbid Henry to attack the French kingdom during the period of the crusade, and this papal prohibition, combined with Henry's own difficulties in Gascony, prompted the English to renew the truce.[21] Louis had previously attempted by arbitration to regulate the troubled affairs of Flanders,[22] but, despite a temporary calm, further unrest developed during the king's absence.

Once matters within and without the realm were as well regulated as Louis could arrange he was ready to go. The regency presented no problem: Queen Blanche, still an important voice in the councils of state, was the obvious choice. Alphonse of Poitiers did not go overseas with his brothers but stayed a year with Blanche to aid in the care of the realm, while both Alphonse and Charles returned to France in 1250. Despite the presence of his brothers the parting of Blanche and Louis must have been sad. Blanche of Castile was sixty, and so could wonder if she would ever see her best loved son again. She accompanied the great procession of the king and the young queen, the legate, the king's brothers and their wives, and the lesser barons and knights as they went to St Denis for the king to receive the staff and scrip of the crusader. Blanche then stayed with them for three days of the journey until the king ordered her to return, saying that he had left her his three children to guard and his kingdom to govern and he had full confidence in her. According to a contemporary chronicler, the queen replied in tears: 'How can my heart suffer the parting of you and me? Certainly it would be harder than stone if it did not break in half, because you have been the best son that ever a mother had'. With these words, the king and his brothers Robert and Charles took their leave.[23]

The great cavalcade rode down through a countryside bright with the full bloom of early summer. It passed through Sens, where the king turned aside to visit the provincial chapter of the Franciscans. Salimbene, the itinerant and gossipy Italian friar, was fortunately present and sketched the appearance of the thirty-four year old king, who 'was slight, spare and slender, somewhat lean, and of a proper height, having the face of an angel, and a countenance full of grace'.[24] The friar had a lively curiosity and interest in all that went on. He commented on the fact that French women in the city were poorly dressed, and then remembered that they were only bourgeois, the French nobles lived in the country. He managed to get next to the king when Louis emerged from the Franciscan church and was able to see with his own eyes the great living pike which had been presented to the king by the treasurer of the cathedral of Sens and which was still swimming in a huge wooden tub 'such as was used for bathing babies'. The king sought the prayers of the Franciscans, and then entertained them all to a special dinner with good wine and unusual luxuries, a feast which the friar describes in detail with considerable gusto.[25] But Salimbene's testimony, besides its valuable firsthand description of the king's appearance, is still another witness to the seriousness with which the king embarked on this crusade – a seriousness shared by others in his retinue, who saw themselves as pilgrim soldiers supported by the strength of God. The friar followed the king's cavalcade after it had left the Franciscans and, as he says, it was easy for him to catch up with the king because Louis turned off the high road so frequently to visit the convents and monasteries that lay near his path. Once when Louis had already left the church after finishing his own prayers, he waited patiently outside for Charles who still prayed fervently within.[26]

Louis's journey to Aigues-Mortes was not merely a pious pilgrimage. He stopped at Lyons for a last meeting with Pope Innocent IV, requesting the pope's intervention in the truce with England. From Lyons the great expedition moved down along the bank of the Rhône, probably as described by Joinville, loading their bulky goods into boats for easier carriage and walking the heavy warhorses along the river path. The king paused to besiege and capture the castle of La Roche-Glun, north of Valence, whose lord had used his fortress as a shelter from which to rob and terrorize unprotected pilgrims and merchants.[27]

The king had left Paris on June 12, he did not arrive at Aigues-Mortes till the middle of August, and the heat during the last part of his journey must have been particularly oppressive. A few matters remained to be settled before the great expedition could set sail, but much of the work of embarking the less important crusaders and their belongings filled the last days. During his remaining time at Aigues-Mortes the count of Toulouse came to see Louis. Raymond had not yet fulfilled the vow to go on crusade which he had taken in 1229, so he had ordered ships and supplies to depart on Louis's expedition. But before he left Raymond was most anxious to secure papal permission to bury his father in consecrated ground, a request which had been denied because of Raymond VI's sympathy with the Albigensians. Louis interceded with the pope but was unable to gain any concession. After the meeting Raymond went to Marseilles to set sail, but instead wintered there, perhaps he thought he would wait and depart with Alphonse and Jeanne, his son-in-law and daughter, the following summer.[28]

Finally all was ready for the royal embarkation. Louis and Marguerite took ship on Tuesday, August 25, but then the great fleet had to wait another two days for a wind. At last on Friday the ships set sail for Cyprus, with the horses safely secured below, and the priests asking the aid of the Holy Spirit as they moved away from land. Joinville's own apprehension as the coastline of France faded from sight expresses the general medieval terror of shipwreck.

> Soon the wind filled the sails and had taken us out of sight of land, so that we could see nothing but sky and water; and every day the wind took us further from the homes in which we were born. How foolhardy then is the man who dares to run so grave a risk when he has in his possession what belongs to another, or is in mortal sin. For when you go to sleep at night you do not know whether you may find yourself in the morning at the bottom of the sea.[29]

This dread of the sea was not restricted to Christians. A Moslem emir talking with Louis after his capture asked the king why so intelligent and sensible a man had trusted himself to the sea in a fragile boat. One of the Moslem doctors had thought that anyone who exposed his person and his goods twice to the sea ought to be regarded as a madman, and his testimony unacceptable in court. Louis smiled quietly and agreed.[30]

Despite all such forebodings the whole convoy reached Limasol, on the south side of Cyprus, after three weeks.[31] Charles of Anjou arrived in the late afternoon of September 17, and landed immediately with his wife and men. The king's ship dropped anchor that same evening, but Louis waited till the following day to disembark, when Robert of Artois and his company also appeared. The reunion of the king and his brothers was happy, for everyone was delighted to have survived the perils of the sea and to be with each other again. The king was ready to press on immediately to

Egypt and encounter the Moslems, but his own men and the barons of Cyprus advised him to remain on the island, since his army was not yet complete. Louis agreed, but as a result the whole French army wintered in Cyprus. The delay seriously damaged the morale as well as the painfully gathered supplies of the crusaders. Many fell ill, including Charles of Anjou who had a serious quartan fever. The army lost the counts of Montfort, Vendôme, and Dreux, as well as Erembald of Bourbon and William des Barres, and the bishop of Beauvais. Many of the crusaders began to run short of funds. Again Joinville puts into personal terms the evidence contained in the long list of loans to knights for which the king made himself surety. Joinville says that when he had arrived in Cyprus and paid for his ships all he had left was two hundred and forty pounds *tournois*, and some of the knights of his company threatened to leave him unless he could raise more money. Joinville's finances were restored by the king who engaged him and gave the seneschal the money to pay his men.[32]

Louis had other problems in Cyprus. The situation in the island kingdom was far from peaceful, with continuous dissension between the rival archbishops of the Greek and Latin rites, and also between the Latin archbishop and the knights of Cyprus. The papal legate spent much of his time arbitrating these disputes and managed to settle them. The Christian princes of the near east were also unable to work together in amity. Louis received messages from the king of Armenia who was quarrelling with the prince of Antioch. The French king sent messengers to both, persuaded them to a two year truce, and also detached some 600 bowmen to aid the prince of Antioch who suffered from the continual harassment of his borders by the Turcomans, who had been driven westward by the relentless onward rush of the Mongols.

The Moslem princes, always unable to maintain a united front for more than a short period, had been thrown into considerable disarray by the news of the imminent invasion of their lands by the large and well-supplied French army. The sultan of Aleppo and the sultan of Egypt, after a futile attempt at settlement, fought bitterly over the city of Homs. As well, the Egyptian sultan was supposed to have sent spies to try and kill the French king and other leaders of the army. Some negotiations were attempted at this time through the Master of the Templars at Acre, in which the Egyptian sultan claimed that he really wanted peace with the French king. Louis was very angry with the Master, he felt that any suggestion of bargaining before a battle had even been fought would imply that the French did not have adequate confidence in their fighting strength.

The winter in Cyprus also brought Louis into closer relations with the Mongols. The first embassy to the Mongols from the west had been sent by Pope Innocent IV at the time of the Council of Lyons. The Franciscan John of Piano Carpini, the leader of the main expedition, had returned to Europe from Karakorum by 1248 and Louis had heard his story directly from him, as Innocent had sent John to Louis after his first report to him. According to Salimbene, who also met him, John was enjoying the prestige of his extraordinary journey for 'he was freely and frequently invited to dinner and supper'.[33] Around Christmas messengers came to Nicosia from Aljighidai, the Mongol leader in Persia, and were presented to the king and his court. Louis was fortunate to have with him Brother Andrew of Longjumeau, a learned and much-travelled Dominican. Not only had Brother Andrew been one of the original messengers who had brought back the Crown of Thorns from Constantinople to France, he also had been sent by the pope to the Tartar army in western Asia at the same time as John's mission. Andrew had thus met one of the present Mongol messengers and he had learned enough Persian and Arabic to be able to translate the letters of the envoys into Latin.

The letters were full of exciting news. They claimed that not only had Aljighidai become a Christian, but so had the Great Khan himself and much of the army, and that the Mongols proposed to fight against the enemies of the Christians. Naturally Louis was overjoyed at this news, which unfortunately was not true, and greeted the messengers with enthusiasm. The envoys appeared to the crusaders to act like Christians, going to mass on Christmas Day with the king and sharing the feast-day dinner in court. They also went to mass on Epiphany. Louis decided to send his own envoys back to the Mongol khan, bearing letters and jewels and also a scarlet tent-chapel, magnificently embroidered with scenes from the life of Christ. In the middle of February 1249 Brother Andrew and two other Dominicans set off on their mission. They went to Aljighidai's camp in the heart of Persia, but the leader had died and they could only speak to his widow who simply regarded their gifts as signs of tribute and a recognition of the Great Khan's sovereignty. Brother Andrew and his companions returned to report to Louis before he left Outremer, but their mission had no immediate or visible result.

Spring approached and the king faced serious problems in reorganizing the expedition. The forces had already been plagued by squabbles which naturally arose among large groups of men who were insufficiently occupied. The perennial rivalry between the Genoese and the Pisans was smouldering beneath the surface, ready to flare at the slightest provocation. The king's most pressing need was for more ships, as not all the ships he had rented so carefully had remained with the expedition during the winter. In February the king sent Humbert of Beaujeu and two leading prelates to Acre. They were to bring back enough ships and sailors, and settle a quarrel which had arisen between the bailiff of Cyprus and the Venetians. They also had to put an end to a major dispute between the Pisans and the Genoese. While these messengers negotiated for enough boats for the force, the men in Cyprus put their time to good use making small landing craft to aid the disembarkation from the great galleys.

By the middle of May all was ready. Many of the knights who had wintered in other islands returned to Nicosia, and there were other new additions to the army. The duke of Burgundy, who had wintered in Rome, and knights from the Morea, the southern part of Greece, arrived. The long preliminaries were at last over. According to John of Beaumont, the chamberlain of France, the fleet consisted of more than 120 great ships and eighty lesser ones. Joinville put it in more colourful terms when he said that the whole sea, as far as the eye could reach, seemed to be covered by the canvas of the ships' sails.[34] One of the more conservative chroniclers estimates that there were about 2,500 knights in the force, of which 700 were from various parts of Outremer, and 5,000 bowmen.[35] It is, of course, impossible to check medieval figures, which were always inflated. One of the present-day

7a. Louis sets out for his first Crusade 1248 (from the *Chroniques de St Denis*)

7b. Setting out for the Crusade (from William of St-Pathus, *Life and Miracles of Saint Louis* written before 1350 by the confessor of Queen Marguerite at the request of her daughter Blanche)

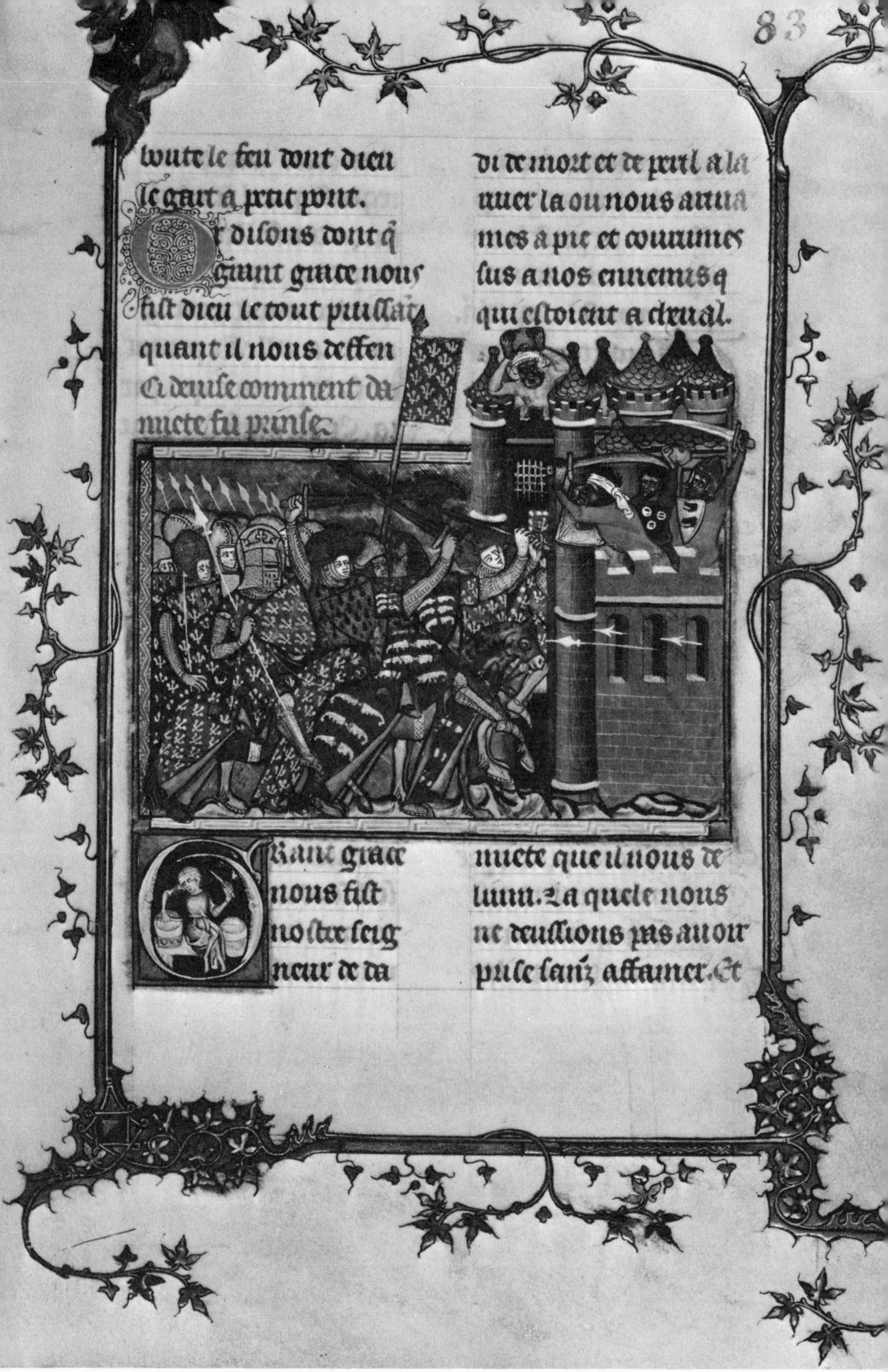

8. Capture of Damietta (from the oldest existing MS of Joinville's *Life of St Louis c.* 1360)

authorities on the crusade feels that the largest army Louis could have had, counting mounted sergeants and foot-soldiers as well as the knights and bowmen was 15,000 men.[36] This was undoubtedly large for a medieval army but any major losses would reduce it to a level dangerously low for the conquest of Egypt. Full of enthusiasm and optimism, the army sailed in the middle of May to attack Egypt.

VII

The Crusade: Victory and Defeat 1249–1250

Optimism did not last long. On leaving Cyprus the royal fleet was attacked by a storm which not only delayed but weakened it.[1] Many ships were blown away and took a long time to rejoin the expedition. Despite the setback when the king's ships left Limasol at the end of May they headed directly for Damietta. Louis and the other leaders of the crusade seem to have chosen Damietta as their first point of attack soon after they arrived in Cyprus.

It was always difficult for the western leaders to obtain enough local information to make satisfactory military decisions. Although the crusaders were gradually gaining practical knowledge of the terrain of the near east, from the failures of their predecessors and the detailed information of returning crusaders and widely travelled merchants, there were dangerous gaps. They had grasped the fact that the Frankish kingdom of Jerusalem was an impossibility so long as there was a strong Egyptian army. In these circumstances, it was eminently reasonable to plan an invasion of Egypt. They hoped to reach Cairo, the capital, and destroy the power and military forces of Ayub the sultan of Egypt. Nevertheless, Damietta was a poor choice for attack. It was favoured over Alexandria because it was felt to be less strongly defended and to have a much better port – an important advantage for the crusaders who had to rely on their ships for reinforcements and supplies. But the line of march from Damietta to Cairo was almost impossible, as it was criss-crossed by a net-work of canals and lesser branches of the Nile.

Unfortunately, the geography of the Nile delta was not sufficiently well known to King Louis or his advisers, and this put him at a disadvantage from the very beginning, even though he had assimilated the importance of the Nile Flood. The extraordinary phenomenon of the yearly rising of the waters had been known in Europe for centuries, but the earlier interest shown by such diverse authorities as the Venerable Bede and Peter Abelard was primarily theological, for these scholars enjoyed deducing all kinds of religious symbols from their limited geographical data. More factually, William of Tyre, at the beginning of the thirteenth century, had described in vivid detail the flood which covered the delta between June and September and emphasized its importance for the fertility of the land it watered.[2] Louis's interest was primarily military. He had heard the accounts of the disasters of the army of the Fifth Crusade; their long siege of Damietta and then their catastrophic defeat in the delta. He fully realized that extensive marching was impossible during the flood and tried to time the movements of his forces accordingly. Nevertheless, the difficulties of the terrain and the delays caused by this and by flood conditions made a coherent campaign impossible.

The French forces arrived off Damietta on Friday, June 4 and anchored some leagues off shore. The sultan of Egypt, who had spent most of the winter besieging the castle of Homs, had heard in good time of the French departure from Cyprus and the plan to attack Damietta. Although Ayub was seriously ill, he had himself transported to the stronghold of Ashmun-Tannah, a little distance up river. He made arrangements for Damietta to be provisioned and armed, and ordered the emir Fakr ad-Din, with his Egyptian troops, to the aid of the threatened city. The beauty of Damietta and its massive fortifications were well known by reputation to the leaders of the French army. A German chronicler, who had taken a leading part in the Fifth Crusade, included in his work a careful description of the city the crusaders had besieged so long and desperately. Damietta was not only protected by triple walls and many towers but was also made more difficult of access by the Nile and by a large navigable ditch which surrounded it on its landward sides. The Moslems seemed to have the natural advantage in any attack on the city launched directly from the ships.

The crusaders were optimistic and in a council of war on board the king's flagship, the *Montjoie*, they agreed to attempt the landing early the following morning. The rest of Friday was spent in great activity: the galleys and small landing craft were made ready, and the crusaders prepared themselves for battle by confession and making their wills. Early Saturday morning, after mass, Louis armed himself and ordered his followers into the boats. John of Beaumont and Geoffrey of Sergines, a valiant knight from Languedoc, had the honour of manning the leading barge which bore the great oriflamme* of St Denis, while the king shared a cog with some of his household and the papal legate who displayed the relic of the True Cross. The beach chosen for the assault was situated on the west bank of the Nile, across the river from the town. The French knights urged their little boats towards the shore where they saw the Saracen troops drawn up to face them. The boats were driven as far up on the sand as possible while the impatient knights jumped into water up to their waists, wading ashore with their shields and lances. Many of them did not even wait to wrestle their horses free, but turned immediately to attack the enemy. Louis, when he saw his companions battling so valiantly on the shore, could not be restrained and, undaunted by his full mail, leaped into the water up to his armpits and struggled to the beach to urge on his men.

The colourful scene was very confused, since it consisted of innumerable individual combats with no overall coherence. The French won the day with relative ease, aided by their numbers and their determination, as well as the relative weakness of the opposing forces and the death, early in the battle, of the emir in charge of the Saracen troops. By Saturday noon the Moslems had retreated into the city, and the Christian forces had gained a firm foothold on the beach. The rest of the day was occupied in extending their hold along the shore, and in bringing up their horses and supplies from the ships lying offshore.

This success of the French army discouraged the troops assigned to the protection of Damietta. According to Joinville, they sent

*The oriflamme was originally the banner of the abbey of St Denis which came to the French kings after their acquisition of the French Vexin. It became the banner of the whole kingdom, and was preserved over the altar of St Denis except in times of war. In appearance, the oriflamme resembled religious processional banners – almost square, the base cut in points and ornamented with fringe. The oriflamme was made of red samite and attached to a cross of gold. The shape, the colour, and the effect of the wind on the pointed tails probably gave it its name of oriflamme, i.e., gold flame.[3]

several messages by carrier pigeon to the sultan at Ashmun-Tannah, but had no responce. The Moslem defenders were afraid that the sultan had died, or that no further help was forthcoming, so they withdrew quietly from the city during Saturday night. On Sunday morning a Saracen renegade came to the French camp and informed the king that the city had been abandoned. Louis prudently sent one of his knights to check the report, but not only was it true, but the Moslems had also decamped with such speed that they had neglected to destroy the bridge of boats connecting the city itself to their battlefield on the shore. Access to the city was made so easy that many Christians had entered Damietta by Sunday afternoon, June 6, and the king's banner was placed triumphantly on a high tower.

The king made his formal entrance into the captured city on June 12 at the head of a great procession. The Great Mosque, which had been a Christian church during the occupation of Damietta by the earlier crusaders, was again converted to Christian use and the legate led the assembly in the Te Deum, which the Christians had good reasons to sing. The army of Louis IX had succeeded in winning, almost without effort or loss of men, the second strongest place on the Egyptian coast, which the Moslems had reasonably regarded as the cornerstone of their defence. By great and unmerited luck the Christains had gained immediate access to valuable Damietta which had not been destroyed, although the retreating troops had set fire to the market and some of the provision stores.

The French were not willing or able to exploit this initial success by pressing on relentlessly. The king was afraid that his army would be cut off from its supply base if it marched immediately towards Cairo. Then too, Alphonse of Poitiers was expected in the autumn with reinforcements, and Louis was anxious to have his brothers' assistance and counsel. Therefore it seemed best to settle the army as adequately as possible at Damietta and await an autumn campaign. The queen and part of the royal household were installed in the palace of the sultan. The legate had the house of the emir who had been killed in the fighting, and each of the barons received a handsome house within the city. Louis, the legate and the greater part of the army, did not lodge within the city but remained in camp on the island where the first landing had been made. The army had to contend with regular harassment from Bedouin raiders, who infiltrated the Christian lines and beheaded those who did not keep careful watch. The sultan had taken strong measures to restore the morale of his army, even hanging a number of emirs who had not shown sufficient firmness, and encouraged these raids by the offer of a bezant* for each Christian head. Louis countered attacks by ordering protective ditches dug around the camp. In an effort to maintain his army's full strength he forbade the rash and bellicose barons to sally out in private combat against the elusive Moslem attackers, but often in vain, all bold deeds, even at the cost of death, attracted the undisciplined knights. The inactivity was galling and there was much suffering in the camp, both from the appalling heat so unfamiliar to the northerners and 'the great plenty of flies and the great large fleas'.[4] The barons sought distraction in frequent entertaining and extravagant feasting, while the common men found diversion with the women who flocked around the camp. The morale of the army was seriously affected, and the long idleness in Damietta, added to the stay in Cyprus, created further problems of provisioning and maintenance.

Surprised gratitude at their easy success and considerable boredom at their lack of activity, encouraged the writing of a large number of letters to friends and relations in Europe which described the taking of Damietta in careful detail. Even Robert of Artois wrote for his mother, Queen Blanche, a good summary, which she quickly passed on to Henry III. She had family news for him as well: she was sure that the English queen would be glad to hear that her younger sister Beatrice, wife of Charles of Anjou, had had a healthy son during the winter at Cyprus.[5] However, truth was not the only passenger to Europe on the returning ships; Louis was credited with the conquest not only of Damietta, but also of Alexandria and Cairo, and some even said that all Egypt was in his power.[6]

At the beginning of October, when the Nile flood had begun to

*The bezant was a gold coin originally struck by the Byzantine emperors. Although gold coins were rare at this time, the bezant enjoyed a wide circulation in both Europe and the middle east and was universally accepted.

subside, Louis awaited anxiously the arrival of his brother. Alphonse had not only stayed in France to assist Blanche, he was particularly anxious to have in hand the 6,000 pounds promised him by the pope, but this had not yet been received in April 1250. Instead his mother lent him two-thirds,[7] and at the end of August 1249 Alphonse, his wife Jeanne, and his sister-in-law, the countess of Artois, set sail from Aigues-Mortes. They had a good passage, stopped briefly in Cyprus, and arrived at Damietta on October 24, barely avoiding a dreadful storm which battered the harbour at Damietta so badly that many ships foundered and their companies were drowned. The safe arrival of Alphonse and the welcome reinforcements he brought cheered the French camp. There was no time for rejoicing, since final decisions had to be made quickly about the subsequent campaign, because the ideal weather for military operations was beginning.

There were really only two possible choices open to the French leaders: they could aim for Alexandria or Cairo.* Joinville echoes the prejudices of most of the other chroniclers in describing Alexandria as the most sensible point of attack – primarily because its harbour was so useful for their seaborne provisions and reinforcements. According to Joinville, the weight of opinion among the barons favoured Alexandria, while only the count of Artois was outspoken in favour of Cairo, but the king insisted on listening to his brother.[8] In fact, the plan put forward by the count of Artois was based on some reasonable arguments. Even if Alexandria were conquered the crusaders still faced the necessity of destroying the Egyptian army if they wished to hold the Holy Land: there was no adequate substitute for an ultimate attack on the Egyptian capital.

Once the decision had been made, Louis began to arrange the necessary support for the army. The king clearly recognized,

*The chroniclers frequently confuse modern readers by referring to the capital of Egypt as Babylon. Babylon was the ancient city, probably built by some Babylonians from Chaldea, and made into an impressive fortress by the Romans, who used it as the centre for one of their legions. It was later superseded by a succession of Moslem settlements, the last of which was Cairo, built a couple of miles away. Thirteenth-century Cairo owed its plan to Saladin and had been much improved by the Ayubite sultans. Although Cairo was now the actual seat of the sultan the western chroniclers usually preferred to refer to the original fortress – Babylon.

although the point was not sufficiently understood by the western chroniclers, that the movement of his army from Damietta towards Cairo was not just a military manœuvre. It was, in modern terms, a 'combined operation', and required the support of ships operating on the Nile. When the expedition was at last ready to set out at the end of November so many ships, large and small, had been stocked with provisions, siege machines, extra armour, and other necessities that they covered the river at the harbour of Damietta. As the great force started upstream, heading for Mansourah, some forty-five miles south-west of Damietta, the army marched on land, accompanied and strengthened by the ships on the river. The crusaders' last stroke of luck was the death of the ailing sultan only a few days after their departure from Damietta. Turanshah, the son and heir, was still far away and the Christian exploitation of the possible confusion in the Moslem camp could have done much to win their objective. But the sultan's wife, who was resolute and far-seeing, prevented it. With the aid of certain key officials, she managed to conceal from the Moslem army the fact of the sultan's death and she reinforced the authority of Fakr ad-Din, whom she placed in charge.

The French march towards Mansourah was slow and difficult. Minor canals had to be dammed to allow the army to pass, contrary winds hindered the upstream passage of the ships. During the march various skirmishes were fought with the Moslems, but there was no major confrontation. Finally, on December 21, after a month, the army came close to Mansourah. They were separated from their Saracen opponents by the canal of Bahr as-Saghir, which here divides from the Nile. The crusaders decided to camp in the triangle of land between the two arms of the river, and attempt various methods of crossing the canal and facing their opponents.

The French first tried to build a causeway, but the canal was deep and the situation unpromising. King Louis had great cat-castles made – fortified movable towers which protected the men working – and set the barons to protect them. Despite these cumbersome defences, the causeway made little progress. As the French workmen proceeded with the dam, the Saracens dug away the bank on their own side, leaving as great a gap to be filled in as ever. The Moslems also attacked the cat-castles vigorously, hurling stones and the dreaded Greek fire.* Joinville describes vividly the terror that Greek fire aroused among the crusaders.

> This is what Greek fire was like: it came straight at you as big as a vinegar barrel, with a tail of fire behind it as long as a long spear. It made such a noise as it came that it seemed like the thunder of heaven; it looked like a dragon flying through the air. It gave so intense a light that in the camp you could see as clearly as by daylight in the great mass of flame which illuminated everything.[9]

More than a month was spent in these futile efforts at direct assault across the river, until it became clear to the king that it was imperative to find a ford and attempt to outflank the Moslems' position. At the beginning of February a renegade Moslem came to the king, informing him of a possible ford a little further downstream, and Louis decided that they should try to cross. On February 8, before dawn, the king and his brothers and the greater part of the knights mounted and rode towards the ford. The king left a strong rearguard in the camp under the command of the duke of Burgundy and arranged for the building of a pontoon bridge so that the bowmen might be able to give their support as soon as the knights had succeeded in crossing the river. Once more Louis repeated his constant orders: each should maintain his proper place in the host, the sections of the army should stay close to each other, and those who were first across should wait for the king and the rest of the force. Louis knew only too well, and thoroughly distrusted, the fighting barons' incurable rashness and desire for lone exploits. Throughout the campaign Louis tried everything to make these individualistic heroes recognize the overwhelming importance of the common good.

The crossing took longer than the king had hoped. The water was deep and swift and in many places the horses had to swim, encumbered by their riders in heavy armour. The banks of the river, too, were steep and difficult to climb. As soon as the first

*Greek fire was a highly inflammable mixture, which included sulphur, pitch, tow, and naptha or petroleum. The formula was developed to the highest degree at Constantinople, where they even employed a wet fire, utilizing quicklime, which was sprayed at attackers. The Moslems had learned the secret from the Greeks.

contingents had crossed, under the command of Count Robert of Artois, the king's oldest and best loved brother, the very thing happened against which Louis had tried to guard. The rash Count Robert ignored his brother's orders and immediately went in pursuit of the Saracens without waiting for the rest of the army. Robert and his men hastened along the river bank to the spot opposite the French camp, where the Moslems had their machines, and were fortunate enough to catch the defenders asleep. They fell on the unsuspecting men and surprise gave them a great advantage. Even Fakr ad-Din heard of the attack only while he was in his bath. He rushed to mount his horse without waiting to arm himself fully, and was soon killed. There was great slaughter among the Saracens and an important immediate advantage had been gained.

Unfortunately, Robert of Artois was intoxicated with his success, and he refused to heed either the king's commands or the warnings of the Master of the Temple who shared with him the lead of the vanguard. He insisted on pursuing the fleeing Moslems into the centre of the town of Mansourah, some two miles away. The Saracens, now led by the Mameluk Baibars, were quick to see the advantage that the impulsive count had given them. In the narrow streets of a medieval town the crusaders' use of the cavalry charge, their great offensive weapon, was impossible. Heartened by this unexpected turn of events, the Moslems sounded their horns and trumpets to rally their men: they let the Frenchmen sweep through the gates, and then turned to fight them. The French horses were tired and were easily cut down in the narrow streets, and once unhorsed and facing hand-to-hand combat, the French were bound to be overcome by the sheer weight of Moslem numbers. The count of Artois was killed, as were most of the Templars, William Longsword, and many other knights. What had promised to be a substantial crusading victory had turned instead into a Christian rout. The remaining Christian cavalry finally managed to re-form and fight its way out of town to the riverbank, pursued by the emboldened Moslems. A further struggle took place there since the main body of the French army had now arrived, led by the king himself. Joinville always remembered affectionately the king's appearance: 'Never have I seen so fine a man in arms; he towered head and shoulders over his people, a gilded helmet on his head, and in his hand a sword of German steel'.[10] The French fought doggedly but they were harassed by the Saracen bowmen on their light, swift horses and needed the support of their own footsoldiers. The crusaders suffered heavily from the loss of their horses due to the heavy fire of the arrows, but the king and those surrounding him fought valiantly. The French crossbowmen had not been able to cross the ford but when they realized the ferocity of the battle they hurriedly constructed a makeshift bridge and crossed over to help. Enough of the French footsoldiers and bowmen eventually got across to turn the tide of battle. As evening came on the Moslems once more withdrew to Mansourah.

The crusading army were now encamped in the spot occupied the previous night by their enemies, but they had paid a heavy toll for this success. The count of Artois, many important barons, and all but a handful of the highly trained Templars had been killed. The strength of the army had been so reduced that there was little hope of regrouping and making a further attack on Mansourah when there would be adequate communication between the two sides of the river. The king strengthened the bridge connecting the two shores of the canal and fortified his camp as best he could to await the attack he was sure would come. On Friday, February 11, the Egyptian troops attacked in great force, and a bitter battle raged. The Moslem bowmen advanced under a cloud of arrows, to the cost of the crusaders' horses, which were not sufficiently protected. The army fought bravely and, this time, obeyed the orders of King Louis, who held the knights back until they could countercharge effectively. He himself charged to the rescue of the weaker French barons in the centre, giving them new courage. At last the Moslems wearied: finding themselves unable to dislodge the crusaders, they retreated in good order to Mansourah. Once more there was stalemate, but this time geography and climate were on the side of the Egyptians. Immediate retreat to the fortified walls of Damietta would have been wise, but it would also have been an acceptance of failure, a heartbreaking decision that Louis's crusading zeal would not let him make.

All during Lent the crusaders remained in their camp on the banks of the canal, while the situation deteriorated. Turanshah arrived from the east and revived the Egyptian army. He was particularly clever in exploiting the possibilities offered him by the geography of the Nile. Turanshah had a number of light boats built and transported in sections by camel-back to the borders of the Nile between Damietta and Mansourah where they were reassembled. They were then launched to prey successfully on the shipping which brought provisions and reinforcements from Damietta to the Christian camp. This blockade, though not totally effective, still caused great hardship and famine. The lack of fresh food, as well as the unaccustomed heat and poor sanitation, brought on those diseases which were the plague of every crusade, scurvy and dysentery. Many died and the rest of the army were weakened. By the end of March it was bitterly obvious to Louis that the army had to be evacuated from its unhealthy and dangerous camp, that it had to retreat to the relative safety of Damietta. His decision to withdraw was reinforced by heavy Moslem attacks upon the Christian camp between Holy Thursday and Easter which the crusaders found difficult to repel.

By the time the Christians were ready to abandon camp on April 5 they faced appalling difficulties. There were so many sick or wounded that the king arranged for them to be loaded into the galleys to be taken down to Damietta by river. The debilitated army was to march along the bank, close by the ships, so that one might protect the other. Louis himself insisted on sharing the army's march, although his dysentery was so bad that he could not stand without support and he had constantly to descend from his horse. The household knights with him tried to persuade him to go in one of the ships, but Louis refused to abandon his people. His brother Charles added his pleas, suggesting that Louis's painfully slow movement by land retarded the whole army and might be the cause of their downfall. Charles was a young and impatient man of twenty-three and he grasped at any argument in his anxiety for the king's safety. Louis's reply summed up his obstinate insistence on his personal responsibility: 'Count of Anjou, if I am a drag on you, get rid of me, but I will never rid myself of my people'.[11] Such determination and self-abnegation were noble but they were no substitute for strength. The Moslems had observed the loading of the sick and wounded into galleys and set out in pursuit. Unfortunately the French engineers in their desperate flight had made the same mistake as the Moslem defenders of Damietta – they had left their bridge over the canal unbroken. The Moslems swarmed across and were soon in full pursuit of the weak and outnumbered Christian army, which fought with heroism and obstinacy, but these virtues were not enough. Louis in his weakness may well have remembered the prophetic lines in the Song of Roland, and echoed their only hope:

> Barons of France, for me you go to death,
> Nought can I give you of safeguard or defence;
> Now aid you God, who ne'er failed any yet![12]

Philip de Montfort, one of the most highly regarded Frankish barons in Outremer, took control of the impossible situation and went to the Egyptians to try and negotiate a truce. During this meeting and in the middle of all the clamorous confusion Marcel, a French sergeant, who may have been bribed by the Moslems, rode through the Christian army telling them all to surrender at once, that it was the king's own order and would save Louis from being slain. At this the bewildered Christians dropped their weapons and Philip de Montfort, who had almost succeeded in negotiating a truce on the basis of surrendering Damietta in return for their free passage, discovered the uselessness of his work. The Saracens did not need a truce – they had already taken the whole army captive. Meanwhile the Moslem galleys on the river had attacked and surrounded the Christian ships. There was turmoil as many of the sick and wounded were massacred, ships were burned and sunk, and only the rich and wealthy were saved since they might provide profitable ransoms. A few fortunate individuals, including the legate and the eighty-year-old patriarch of Jerusalem, managed to outride the attacking Moslems. They found an abandoned barge and made Damietta safely without knowing that the whole army behind them had been captured. Louis himself had been forced to take refuge in a village just north of Sharimshah, and there he was taken into captivity by the victorious Moslems.

When none of the army followed the legate to Damietta, and there was no news, the queen and the prelate, with the agreement of the magnates, sent ten galleys upstream to the king's aid. The ships got as far as Sharimshah, but could find no signs of the army. Then, scouting the surrounding countryside, their crews discovered in a field near the village the first confirmation of the disaster they had feared – a great number of beheaded naked men, grisly evidence of the massacre by the Moslems after they captured the army. The scouting party returned to Damietta with their terrifying news and by Sunday, April 10 further credible reports of the disastrous battle and the capture of the king and the army had reached the garrison there.

Queen Marguerite's situation was particularly hard as her baby was due when the news came of Louis's capture. Joinville vividly pictures her terror when he writes that whenever the queen slept she dreamt the room was full of Saracens and cried 'Help, help!'. An old knight, some eighty years of age, slept by her bed and held her hand to comfort her. Just before her child's birth the queen, on her knees, asked this knight to behead her rather than let the Saracens take her alive, a decision which the old man had already made himself.[13] But the queen bore a healthy son, though he was always known as John Tristan from the days of sorrow in which he was born. Queen Marguerite now had a chance to show her courage and force. The very day of her son's birth she was told that the Italian merchants had decided to leave Damietta, and she knew that without them the city could not be held. She had the merchants called to her bedchamber and reproached them with their decision which, she argued, might well cost the lives of the king and all the army, as well as her poor newborn child. They pleaded famine as an excuse but she brushed this pretext aside, bought up all the provisions in town herself at a cost of 360,000 pounds, and engaged the merchants at the king's charge. Rather shamefacedly they agreed to stay,[14] and Damietta was preserved as a bargaining counter for the crusaders.

King Louis had been removed by his captors to a private house in Mansourah, and, according to the Moslem chronicler, Maqrisi, was taken there loaded with chains.[15] Only one French sergeant, Isambert the Cook, remained with the king because everyone else was sick. Isambert cooked for his king whatever he could get from the sultan's court but Louis was still so ill from his dysentery that his teeth chattered and the bones of his back showed through his skin. The king was so weak that Isambert had to carry him to the privy. Despite all these indignities Louis's good temper and patience never deserted him.[16] It does not appear that the king was badly treated by his captors. William of Nangis emphasizes the fact that the sultan sent his own doctors to take care of the king and praises the greater skill of the Arab doctors.[17] Louis's clothes had been lost in the retreat and he had only a rough green surcoat handed to him by a poor man. The sultan fitted him out in black satin, lined with ermine and grey squirrel, fastened with many solid gold buttons.[18]

As soon as the king had begun to recover slightly, he began to negotiate freedom for the remaining French prisoners. There was only a remnant of his army, for the Moslems had rid themselves of the poor and sick by massacres. Joinville's excited narrative shows plainly how essential it was to be identified as rich or important if your life was to be spared.[19] Charles of Anjou warned his brother, when he saw Louis after their capture, that the richer barons had already begun to try and make individual terms with their captors. The king was totally opposed to this piecemeal approach. His anxiety and responsibility was for all the crusaders, rich and poor, and he also wanted to negotiate from a stronger position by keeping the great lords with the rest of the army. Louis gave orders that he himself would negotiate the general deliverance of the prisoners and would pay the ransome of all.[20]

After some bargaining on terms a truce was arranged to last for ten years. Louis was to return Damietta to the Moslems and to pay a ransom of a million bezants.* In return, Louis and all the Christians taken in the present campaign, as well as those captured since the last truce had been arranged with Frederic II in 1229, should be freed to go wherever they wished. Those lands which the Christians had held at the time of Louis's coming were

*There is some question as to the actual value of a bezant in French money. 400,000 bezants, the half of the ransom finally paid at Damietta, was thought by Joinville to equal 200,000 pounds *tournois*, but the royal accounts made up later give the amount as 167,000 pounds *tournois*. It was, in any case, less than a year's income for the king.[21]

to remain Christian. Louis was to free any Saracen prisoners, but the French king's goods in Damietta and those of the Christian merchants were to be kept under the sultan's protection until they could be sent to Christian territories. The Christian sick in Damietta were also to be protected. The terms were harsh, but considering the scope of the Christian defeat, not unreasonable. Louis owed a great deal to Queen Marguerite whose treatment of the Italian merchants had preserved the French hold on Damietta, the fortress which was the essential factor in the negotiations.

The surrender of Damietta and the payment of the ransom money were to take place at the end of April. The sultan and his army loaded the French king and the remaining crusaders into galleys and took them downstream to Fariskur, some ten miles from Damietta, where they were to await the settlement of the final details of the truce. On May 1 the patriarch of Jerusalem came to the king from Damietta for a last conference on methods of liberating the prisoners. The following day the sultan's bodyguard, the Mameluks,* rose against Turanshah and murdered him. Turanshah had only ruled for two months, but once he had achieved success against the French he tried to replace the trusted officials of his father with his own favourites from the Jezireh. The Mameluks had been consistently gaining in power and influence: their leader Baibars was an able soldier and general, and they resented the changes and feared for their own safety when the sultan should have regained valuable Damietta. The bodyguard fell upon the unprotected sultan as he rose from dinner: when he tried to escape their swords they pursued him into the Nile and killed him there.

Louis, his brothers, and their immediate retinue were lodged in a pavilion on the river bank not far from the sultan. Into their tent burst the men who had murdered Turanshah, brandishing their bloody weapons and with their white clothes covered with

*The Mameluks have a long history in Moslem territories. They were slaves, always white, and originally Turks from Central Asia. A privileged caste, they were carefully trained from childhood as soldiers for the Moslem dynasties. After successfully completing their service they could be freed and rise to almost any position of military or political eminence. Ayub, the father of Turanshah, had developed to its highest pitch the system of employing Mameluks for his bodyguard and army.

blood. The French feared immediate massacre, but the Mameluks, though threatening, were not anxious to lose the enormous ransom. They were full of excuses for the murder of the sultan, even claiming that they could not stand Turanshah's faithlessness towards the king and the Christians, for, they claimed, he had resolved to kill them whether they gave up Damietta or not.[22] Meanwhile, the murderers of the sultan had also boarded the galley where the other French barons were confined, and the Frenchmen too fell at once to their prayers expecting to be massacred. But the Mameluks were again more interested in terrifying their prisoners than in breaking the advantageous terms of the truce. The following day, May 3, the truce terms were again discussed with the emirs now in charge, and the king's ransom was reduced to 800,000 bezants, half to be paid before the king was released, and the remainder after he had reached Acre and the conditions concerning the release of the prisoners had been met. Only one obstacle to the settlement now remained. The Moslems had sworn to their acceptance of the truce with oaths which suggested that they would renounce their religion if they broke their word, and they wanted King Louis to swear in the same form. The king adamantly refused, although he was told it might mean his death, and even resisted the pleas of the aged patriarch who was tortured by the Moslems to encourage the king's acquiescence. Finally the Moslems renounced their insistence on this guarantee. Louis had impressed his adversaries. Joinville tells of a current story that the emirs had been anxious to make Louis sultan of Egypt, and the plan was only not carried out because the king was so steadfast a Christian.[23]

The truce was sworn and the last arrangements made to surrender Damietta and pay the agreed half of the ransom on Friday, May 6. Then another argument arose about the choice of sureties: the Moslems suggested either the king himself, or all the other prisoners. Louis immediately chose himself, but his brothers and his household knights disputed this vigorously, fearing treachery. In the end the Saracens agreed to accept one of the king's brothers, so Louis chose Charles of Anjou. The Moslems, thinking that Alphonse of Poitiers was better loved by the king, then insisted on him. Agreement was finally reached: the king was to be released as soon as Damietta was surrendered and Alphonse of Poitiers as soon as the agreed half of the ransom had been paid.[24]

On Friday at sunrise Geoffrey of Sergines went into Damietta and arranged for the ransom to be handed over to the Saracens, though the queen and all the Christians well enough to travel had been evacuated to the ships and dispatched to Acre before the surrender. Despite some threats and delays, the king was duly released on Friday and embarked on one of his Genoese galleys. Saturday morning the payment of the ransom money was begun, a tedious proceeding that was to last till Sunday evening since the counting of such a vast sum was done by weight. Late Sunday it became obvious to the king's men in charge of the business that they were some 30,000 pounds short. At Joinville's suggestion the money was seized from those moneys which the Templars had on deposit:[25] it was merely a *pro forma* seizure, since the Templars were not supposed to release their deposits to any but their rightful owners but knew they could compensate themselves with the royal moneys they held at Acre. The king's credit was still good. With this involuntary assistance, the whole sum of the ransom was paid over within two days.

Even in dealing with the Saracens, the king would not countenance any dishonesty. When Louis asked his knights if the ransom was all paid Sir Philip of Nemours announced proudly that they had completed the tally and cheated the Moslems by some 10,000 pounds in the weighing of the silver. The king was furious, for he had pledged his word to the payment in full of the promised amount. Joinville, knowing his master's tender conscience, stepped heavily on Philip's foot and winked at him while assuring the king that there was no question of believing the story for the knight was a joker. Thus warned, Philip quickly agreed that he had been joking but Louis took the matter very seriously and endeavoured to be quite sure that his enemies had received the proper payment.[26]

At last the king ordered his galley from the river, where he had remained for the long hours of counting, and commanded the crew to make for the ship offshore, although there was still no word of the release of the count of Poitiers. Worried over the fate of Alphonse, they had already travelled some distance in silence when Philip de Montfort came up in a barge and joyfully informed the king that he had the count of Poitiers with him. At last the king and the remnants of his once proud crusading army could escape from Damietta and the Nile, the scene of their discomfiture, and the crusading fleet raised anchor at once and sailed for Acre.

Thus ended in tragedy the campaign begun with such enthusiasm and high hopes. The French king had spent prodigally, but all that had been achieved was the death of many important French barons and the loss of thousands of fighting men. Louis, so pious, so wholeheartedly committed to the crusading ideal, must have wondered why God allowed these reverses. In earlier crusades the evil and weakness of their leaders had been the excuse for failure. Such an allegation could not be made against Louis and yet his crusade was as great, or an even greater failure than the others. An Arab poet put the king's dilemma in its most sardonic form.

> May God reward you for having brought to death the adorers of Jesus, the Messiah.
> You came to Egypt with the plan of conquering this kingdom; you believed you would meet there only hautboys and tambours . . .
> You have led your companions by your noble counsels to the gates of the tomb.
> There are fifty thousand never to be seen again, dead wounded, or prisoners.
> God be merciful to you for such an enterprise![27]

The insoluble dilemma of this unsuccessful crusade was to haunt Louis for the rest of his life.

VIII

The Years in Outremer 1250–1254

As the crusaders' ships sailed for Acre those on board gave thanks for their deliverance and exchanged stories of their capture and imprisonment. Louis remained weak but his spirit was undaunted. One day he asked for Charles of Anjou, who had not come to see him and heard that he was playing backgammon with another knight. The king was furious – he did not approve of games of chance under any circumstances and certainly not at a time when the crusaders should have been doing penance. Louis made his way to the deck, seized the dice and the board, and threw them overboard. Charles's opponent got the best of the affair for, while Louis reproached his brother, the quickwitted knight scooped the large pile of money on the board into his lap and went off with it.[1] The voyage to Acre took six days, and the arrival of the ships was a signal for great rejoicing by the people of the town who came out in procession to the seashore to greet the king and his companions. At Acre the king was reunited with Queen Marguerite and first saw his son.

The joys of reunion and safe arrival did not dispel the many problems which faced the king. Louis had to decide almost immediately whether he should return at once to France or remain in Outremer in hopes of salvaging some advantage for the Christians there. Many of the barons of the crusading army had now been away from their homes for over two years and their funds were running low. They had entirely lost their first enthusiasm, and hoped for a swift ending to this ill-fated expedition which would allow them to return to their own affairs. Their basically selfish interest was camouflaged under a mask of concern for the welfare of the realm of France and, especially in the case of the king's brothers, their desire to assist Queen Blanche. On the other hand, the barons of Outremer fully realized that their only security lay in Louis's prestige and resources, and in the strength he could exert: despite his defeat, the French king was still the only hope of the Christian cause in the near east. Louis himself recognized the force of their argument, and was influenced by their claim that only he could make the Egyptians carry out the terms of the truce and release the prisoners; for these men, victims of his failure, he felt a personal responsibility. After several sessions with his council, Louis announced his decision at the end of June. He himself would stay in the kingdom of Acre, and would also engage at his own expense those knights who were willing to remain with him. To ensure the safety of the realm and to console his mother he would send both of his brothers back to France. By their first-hand description of what had happened to the army, and of the desperate state of the Christian cause, they could raise more money and men to come to the aid of the crusaders. Once again it is Joinville who brings to life the violent discussions between the barons, and their mixed motives. The seneschal was a leader of the small group that advised the king to stay on in Outremer and for this he was so much reviled by his companions that he slipped away from the council afraid that he had angered the king. Louis himself came to reassure him with the playful affection that marked his relations with Joinville. Thus strengthened, the seneschal reacted vigorously to the taunts of his opponents who nicknamed him a *poulain*, or colt, as the half-Syrian half-French natives were called. Joinville retorted that at least it was better to be a colt than a broken-down horse like his tormentors.[2]

At the beginning of August Charles of Anjou, Alphonse of Poitiers, and many of the French barons returned home. They carried with them a letter from King Louis to his realm describing the crusade and underlining the needs of the Christians at Acre. In factual, unemotional terms Louis described the calamities which had befallen them and explained the reasons he felt required his presence in Outremer. He begged all those who could, to come themselves, or to be ready to send help by the first passage in the following spring, and assured them that, like the gospel parable, even the latest worker in the vineyard would receive an everlasting reward.[3]

One ray of hope had brightened the deliberations of the crusaders during the summer. The sultan of Aleppo, the chief city of Syria, was a member of the Ayubite family, and he bitterly resented the murder of Turanshah, the last of the Ayubite rulers of Egypt. The sultan of Aleppo seized Damascus and then proposed to move against the Mameluk ruler who had replaced Turanshah, so that the Egyptians now found themselves faced with the dangerous possibility of invasion from Syria. Although the Frankish forces were pitifully small, they could now make a decisive difference and both sides sent envoys to Louis, seeking Christian support. The sultan of Aleppo's messengers offered to surrender the kingdom of Jerusalem to the Franks if the sultan received Louis's help against the Egyptians. Louis preferred to temporize on this offer, to use it as a bargaining counter against the Egyptians, who still held so many French prisoners, and sent his own envoys to Damascus to see the sultan. One of his ambassadors was a friar, the Dominican Yves the Breton. As we have seen, friars, especially the Dominicans, frequently appear in embassies because of their knowledge of languages needed for missionary activities. In Spain many studied Arabic among the Saracens there, and in the east some learned the various dialects as well as Persian and Mongol.[4] The friars could also travel without the splendour and protocol required by more important men and were useful sources of information to the king.

Meanwhile, Louis had been in almost constant touch with the rulers of Egypt. Soon after his arrival in Acre Louis had sent one of his knights, John of Valenciennes, a favoured negotiator (he later appears in England on Louis's business) to the court of the sultan of Egypt. John's mission was to complain of the Egyptian disregard of the terms of the truce. The Egyptians had destroyed the king's goods and war materials in Damietta, burned the supplies of salt pork, and massacred the sick Christians. As well, they were very reluctant to release any of the Christian prisoners they held. The Egyptians now declared that they would be glad to carry out their commitments if only Louis would aid them against the sultan of Aleppo, but John warned them that his master was more likely to be responsive to their plea if they returned the imprisoned knights. By the middle of October twenty-five Hospitallers, fifteen Templars, ten Teutonic Knights, and a hundred secular knights, as well as some six hundred other prisoners were returned. However, there were still more prisoners and the king lost no opportunity to push his claims whenever circumstances seemed favourable.[5]

Other envoys also visited the king's court at Acre. Soon after the king's brothers and their company had sailed, messengers came from the Emperor Frederic II in Europe. He had heard of the king's capture but not yet of the sultan's death or of Louis's release. His messengers claimed that the emperor wished to assist in bringing about the king's freedom. Despite the French suspicion of Frederic's real motives, the claim was probably true, since Frederic prized Louis's neutrality in his struggle with the pope and wanted the good will of a powerful prince of unimpeachable orthodoxy. Frederic, of course, was interested in the existence of the crusader states, since his son Conrad was legally king of Jerusalem, though he had never exercised his rule in person, and Frederic himself had great prestige among the Moslems.

The most colourful envoys who waited on King Louis at Acre were those sent by the Old Man of the Mountain, the name given by the Christians to the Assassins, a sect formed in Persia almost two centuries before. They were Shiite* rather than Sunnite Moslems and their constant struggles for political power were less remarkable than their well-known habit of murdering swiftly, secretly, and successfully those who oppose them. Essentially a religious secret society at the total disposal of their leader, their unwavering obedience to even the most impossible commands seems to have been achieved by the use of hashish. The Assassins were known and feared throughout Europe, as well as in the middle east, and gave their name to the practice of political murder or assassination. Baldwin of Avesnes, the Flemish chronicler,

*The Shiites were a fanatic sect of Moslems who believed that they must be ruled by an *imam*, a prophetic and infallible teacher, who could be chosen only from the descendants of Ali, the cousin and son-in-law of Mohammed. The Shiites were marked by an extreme intransigeance towards their fellow Moslems as well as Christians and Jews. The Sunnites, who were much the larger group, were less aggressive and intolerant. They were ruled by a caliph, who was in essence an executive charged with the defence of the faith and the faithful, not necessarily a quasi-divine prophet.

even claimed that Assassins had been sent to kill King Louis some years before but that the leader had soon regretted his command and warned the king by other messengers to guard himself.[6]

By the thirteenth century the Syrian branch of the Assassins, headed by the Old Man of the Mountain, had a stronghold at Masyaf, north of Krak des Chevaliers, and their relations with the Christians varied. For example, they had agreed to pay a tribute to the Templars and the Hospitallers, for against such orders, with their numerous knights, the threat of assassination was not a decisive weapon. In their embassy to King Louis, the Assassins demanded the king's recognition of them and also requested the removal of the tribute which they now paid to the religious orders. The king convinced the messengers of his closeness to the Templars and the Hospitallers, and their Masters, who were present at the interview, reprimanded the Assassin messengers for their temerity and warned them to try and pacify the king with presents and promises of friendship. Since the Assassins were trapped in a position of troubled neutrality between the opposing Syrians and Egyptians, they decided to conciliate the French king. They returned with protestations of the Old Man's friendship and magnificent presents, including a chess set carved in crystal and gold and scented with ambergris, and other finely carved objects in crystal, among them an elephant and a giraffe. The king sent gifts in return with his own envoys, the less exotic fine woollen cloths and jewels of Europe. Brother Yves the Breton, who knew Arabic, went on this embassy too, and it was he who was able to explain how the Assassins' religious beliefs differed from those of the ordinary Mohammedans.[7]

Meanwhile the contest between Aleppo and Egypt had broken into open warfare. The sultan of Aleppo invaded Egypt and a battle was fought at Abbasa, in the Nile delta, at the beginning of February 1251. The Egyptians won and the sultan of Aleppo withdrew, but made further advances to the French, offering to return if they would only help. Louis again sent John of Valenciennes to the Egyptian court to warn the sultan that unless the Egyptians released all prisoners, and made other concessions, including the cancellation of the remaining ransom money, Louis would make an alliance with the sultan of Aleppo. It took another year but the king, by his skilled diplomacy, had restored his prestige and heartened the barons of Outremer.

Louis also turned his forces and finances to the rebuilding of the fortifications of the main Christian strongholds along the coast. He first prepared to march his men to Caesarea, some twenty-five miles south of Acre, to repair the defences there which the Moslems had destroyed. Since the sultans of Aleppo and Egypt were at war, there was no one to hinder him, and the reconstruction encouraged the inhabitants who had felt forgotten and helpless before their dangerous foe.

Before Louis departed for Caesarea he had satisfied the claims of devotion by making a pilgrimage to Nazareth, some fifteen miles east of Acre. On March 24 Louis came to Cana and Mount Thabor and then went on to Nazareth where, as a mark of piety he entered the town on foot. The next morning, the feast of the Annunciation, mass was said at the altar of the Annunciation and the king received communion. The legate celebrated high mass at the main altar and preached a sermon in honour of the king's visit.[8] This was the only pilgrimage Louis was to make during his years in Outremer. The sultan of Damascus later offered to allow him to go to Jerusalem under a safe-conduct and Joinville suggests that the king was tempted by the offer. The council persuaded him to decline the invitation, reminding him of Richard the Lionhearted who refused to look on Jerusalem since he was not able to deliver it from its enemies.[9]

The king remained in Caesarea about a year. He received messengers, settled breaches of the peace or of the regulations of the army, and led a reasonably peaceful life. Louis summed up his activities admirably when he wrote to Alphonse in the middle of August. He described the state of constant alert and the frequent skirmishes between the Egyptians and the forces of the sultan of Aleppo, but he reported with pleasure that the Christians had not been bothered by the Saracens, not even by the Bedouin raiders. The army was well supplied and victualled and the king had seen to the safety of the sea lanes by posting armed ships at sea to intercept and terrify pirates. Nevertheless Louis impressed on those at home the need for further help to enable him to make 'good truces, and useful for Christendom'.[10]

By March 1252 Louis had achieved his purpose. He arranged a fifteen year truce and alliance with the Egyptians, offering French aid against the forces of the sultan of Aleppo in return for the release of all remaining survivors, the cancellation of the second half of the ransom, and the cession of Jerusalem and the lands west of the Jordan when – and if – the Egyptian campaign succeeded. Louis's most urgent preoccupation had always been the return of the prisoners, since he felt a dual responsibility for them both as military leader in a disastrous expedition and as Christian ruler responsible for the safeguarding of the Christian faith of his subjects. All the Christian captives were finally returned, even those who had been captured as children and had abjured their faith. As a further token of goodwill the sultan sent Louis an elephant and a zebra. The elephant was sent back to France and was later given to Henry III, who kept it in his menagerie at the Tower of London.

After the conclusion of the alliance Louis had planned to move on to Gaza and there meet the Egyptian troops but the sultan of Aleppo, who had heard of the new alliance, sent a strong force of his own to prevent the meeting. Louis then changed direction and went on to Jaffa, some forty miles north of Gaza, and still in Christian hands. His coming was greeted with tremendous enthusiasm by the count of Jaffa, delighted by the prospect of French reinforcement of his outlying position. The count decorated his battlements with some five hundred shields, 'a noble sight to see', according to Joinville.[11]

The king remained in Jaffa for nearly a year while there were occasional skirmishes with the forces of the sultan of Aleppo and further discussions with the Egyptian emirs. Louis put his time to good use by rebuilding the walls of the town, clearing the ditches, and generally improving the fortifications so that they included the town as well as the castle. This was his general practice while in Outremer, since he wished to make the Christian community more able to withstand the Moslem attacks which he felt sure were inevitable. The king's stay in Jaffa ended when the caliph of Bagdad, much disturbed by the internal struggles of the various Moslem states, succeeded in mediating the dispute between Aleppo and Egypt. Peace was made between them in April 1253 and the forces of the sultan of Aleppo then withdrew from Gaza. They passed close by the Christian troops at Jaffa on their way north, and there were some minor skirmishes. The Moslem troops had heard that the king had not yet been to Sidon, where he also proposed to strengthen the fortifications, so they decided to attack it. The Christian fighting men withdrew to the safety of the castle but they were not able to shelter many of the townspeople and there was a dreadful massacre. The Moslems killed more than two thousand Christians and looted the town.[12] They then returned to Damascus with only this dubious victory and some plunder to show for their year on the frontier of Egypt.

When the news of the successful Saracen assault reached Jaffa it reinforced the arguments of those barons of Outremer who wanted Louis to rebuild the fortifications of Sidon, rather than one of the inland castles between Jaffa and Jerusalem. The barons had already realized that they no longer had sufficient strength to hold a castle which was even a few miles inland – they had to remain on the coast where they could count on the support of their ships.[13] At the end of June 1253 King Louis and his army set out for Sidon. They marched northwards towards Acre, but they did not enter the city, camping instead on the sands. At this same time a great troop of pilgrims from Greater Armenia were making a pilgrimage to Jerusalem, under Moslem escort and at considerable expense. They felt that merely a sight of the holy French king, whose name was already widely known in the middle east, would add greatly to their journey, and they begged Joinville, by an interpreter, to see if this was possible. Joinville duly went to find the king and deliver the message, but the seneschal was quite sure that, no matter what such pilgrims thought, he did not want to treat his king as a saintly relic, which much amused Louis.[14]

The king continued his march to Sidon, although some of the barons, including Philip of Montfort, the Masters of the Temple and the Hospital, and Joinville went to attack the Moslems in the city of Baniyas, the ancient Caesarea Philippi. As is usual in

Joinville's description of a battle, the minor skirmish in which he takes part is described in loving detail. The town was captured from the Moslems, although Joinville and his detachment were for a time in considerable danger and were saved by the quick-wittedness of Oliver of Termes, one of the bravest and most capable of the Provençal knights.[15] When the king arrived at Sidon he first saw to the burial of the dead. Their corpses had been unceremoniously pitched into cisterns or had been left, in the hot summer weather, to rot where they lay. Louis wanted to give these martyrs – as he felt they were – Christian burial, but he was also interested in safeguarding the health of the city he wished to rebuild. The king had great ditches dug in a newly blessed cemetery and supervised the collection and removal of the remains. So many of his men complained or tried to avoid this grisly occupation that Louis set the example by carrying the stinking corpses with his own hands. As a special mark of the king's charity, William of St Pathus comments approvingly, while the bishops saying the service for the dead at the side of the ditches plugged their nostrils with their vestments, the king joined in the prayers and did not even hold his nose.[16]

At Sidon the news came from France of the death of Queen Blanche. She had died in November 1252, but the news only arrived in Outremer in the summer of 1253. Louis was overcome with sorrow, because his love and devotion to his mother had dominated his life. He himself said when the legate broke the news that 'he loved his mother above all mortal creatures',[17] and, for a time, the king altogether withdrew from the life of the camp. Queen Marguerite, who had just rejoined the king after sailing from Jaffa where she had borne a daughter, Blanche, the third child she had had during this crusade, was overcome with grief. Her mourning was beyond Joinville's understanding, for he knew how cruel Blanche had been to her, but Marguerite wept for her husband's sorrow and the thought of her daughter Isabel, alone in France and so far away.[18]

The shock of Blanche's death and his concern for the situation at home turned Louis's mind once more to France and his duties there, especially as he had successfully completed the walls and fortifications of Sidon. The king tried to discover his duty by prayers and processions and his natural inclination to return to France was reinforced by the advice of the leading men of Outremer. They felt that Louis had achieved all that he could for the Christian states. He had fortified the main cities; he had succeeded in freeing all the Christian captives; he had restored the prestige of the French by his conduct, and had even helped to improve the situation of the beleaguered principality of Antioch. Now it was more important that the men of Outremer should have a powerful ruler in Europe who could continue to send them support and who had himself experienced their problems and needs. The king finally decided to return to Acre at the beginning of Lent, 1254 and he prepared to sail soon after Easter.

On April 24, the king and queen and their remaining company weighed anchor at Acre. Only nine ships and nine galleys remained of the great fleet which had sailed so proudly from Aigues-Mortes nearly six years before. The day after the departure, Louis confided to Joinville, was his fortieth birthday. The loyal and practical seneschal said, with considerable relief, that the king might add that he was born again on that day, 'for his escape from that dangerous country was certainly a second birth'.[19] But ahead of them lay the long voyage to France, with all its attendant dangers of high wind and shipwreck. Louis sought spiritual help against these perils. He obtained permission to have the Blessed Sacrament kept on the ship in a special tabernacle on a decorated altar. Every day the king heard mass, which was normally said on shipboard in a shortened form, the sick were able to receive the sacraments, and the dead were buried with the proper rites. Louis liked sermons and three were given every week during the long and tedious voyage, and there was a special sermon for the sailors when the sea was calm and their work was light. He arranged too for the sailors to go to the sacraments, which many of them had not been able to do for years.[20]

On the third night at sea, when the fleet was approaching Cyprus, the king's ship ran onto a submerged sandbank. The whole ship's company began lamenting and exclaiming. The king prostrated himself before the altar on the ship's bridge, barefoot and in his tunic, expecting to die. But the ship floated free of the sandbar and on the following morning Louis ordered the master of the ship to send down divers to discover the extent of the damage. They reported that some twenty feet of the keel had been torn away and they feared for the safety of the ship: the timbers might have shifted from the shock and be unable to withstand the pounding of the waves when they got to sea. Their unanimous advice was for the king to abandon this ship and to embark in another. The king thought over the problem and then called the most important men on board for their counsel; they agreed that he should trust the technical knowledge of the sailors. When Louis asked the sailors what they themselves would do in such a case, they admitted that they would remain with the ship because of their investment in it, but they hurriedly added that gold and silver alone could not be equated with the safety of the king and queen and their children. Finally the king decided to continue: characteristically, he feared that if he abandoned this ship the other eight hundred passengers would do likewise. Since it would be very difficult for the average person to obtain another passage from Cyprus, they might never be able to return home. This was proved by Joinville's example of Oliver of Termes, who had distinguished himself by his bravery in the Holy Land but who was so afraid of drowning that he left the ship at Cyprus. It was another year and a half before he could get back to France, and he was wealthy and important: poorer crusaders would have been even worse off.[21]

The fleet was later buffeted by such heavy winds that Queen Marguerite wanted to promise a pilgrimage if they escaped from danger, but could not find the king to gain his permission. Joinville suggested that instead she promised St Nicholas, the patron saint of travellers, a silver ship, and he would take it to the shrine, as he had already promised to go there barefoot if only they were spared.*[22] They were threatened by fire as well. One night a careless serving-woman in the queen's cabin left a kerchief where it could catch fire from the queen's night-light. Marguerite awoke to a cabin full of flames, and with considerable presence of mind

*Marguerite kept her promise and had a silver ship made in Paris with the king, queen, and the three children on deck all in silver. The sails too were sewn with silver thread. Joinville took this votive offering to St Nicholas-de-Port, near Lunéville, on the river Meurthe, where similar *ex-votos* of miniature ships were made until late in the eighteenth century.

she threw the kerchief overboard and hastily beat out the flames in the sheets. After this the king ordered the extinction of all the fires on board at night, except for the main galley fire, and insisted that he should be notified when this was done.[23]

Louis's strictness when he felt the general good was threatened was again illustrated by his treatment of the unfortunate youths who had been sent to the island of Pantelleria to get fruit for the royal children. There was danger of Moslem attack and the king had warned the small boats to be ready to come alongside as soon as the royal ship passed the island, in order not to delay the convoy. At the appointed moment there was no sign of the small boats and the king's ship had to come about, since Louis refused to obey the sailors' suggestion and abandon the men, whom they thought had been caught by the Saracens. Just then the galleys appeared and it was discovered that some young Parisians were the cause of the delay, for they had been greedily eating fruit in the gardens and would not answer the command to embark. Louis ordered the culprits to be kept in the ship's boat until they reached land. Since the boat was towed behind the ship, it was an uncomfortable as well as a dangerous place, and one of great disgrace. The young men, and even the queen, pleaded with the king for a mitigation of the punishment, but he refused to relent.[24]

The voyage was very slow, for it was only after some ten weeks at sea that the royal convoy arrived at a port near Hyères. Louis was not anxious to land there, since Hyères was in the county of Provence, and would have preferred to go on to Aigues-Mortes. For once he was overruled by the combined objections of his council and the queen, who advised him that stubborn insistence on reaching Aigues-Mortes was rash and unwise. The king and queen and their children disembarked and stayed for a time at Hyères while they were awaiting horses for the long journey north. They travelled by way of Aix, where the king and Joinville turned aside to see the cave in the Ste-Baume where Mary Magdalen was reputed to have lived. At the boundaries of royal territory at Beaucaire, Louis had at last returned safely to France.

Louis's first crusade was over, its achievements and failures could be summed up. His military defeat and the catastrophic retreat from Mansourah had undermined the hopes of crusaders, both in Europe and Outremer. If a most respected and devout king, with almost unlimited resources and careful planning, was unable to win a decisive victory, and indeed was ignominiously captured, then any hopes for real military success were unfounded. The Latin kingdoms of the east were more and more circumscribed by the strong Moslems and their own inability to make a firm alliance. King Louis's new fortifications and paid knights had given them some temporary security and a few more years of existence, but had not solved their basic problem. The only thing that might have saved them would have been an alliance between the Christians and the Mongols, but this grew more and more unlikely. Once the Moslems were no longer preoccupied with the onward rush of Mongol power they could easily turn and sweep the Christian fortresses into the sea. The end did not come for another forty years, but it was already foreseeable.

But the most lasting effect of the crusade was on Louis himself. The king had always been a devout and pious Christian, but he became something more than that in the hardships of the Egyptian campaign and the long years in Outremer. Louis was still attuned to the ideal of the Christian monarch which he had absorbed from Queen Blanche, but his interpretation from now on would be slightly different. He never seemed to lose the sense of personal responsibility for the failure of the French expedition and the death of so many courageous knights, including his own much loved brother. Matthew Paris's description of the king's grief is highly coloured, but coincides with the other evidence.

> The king of the French with a mind and countenance distraught, did not wish to admit any consolation; cheerful or consoling tales and musical instruments would not make him smile or rejoice. Not the visit of his own native land or his proper realm, not the salutation of venerable visitors, not the recognition of lords with due gifts pleased him; but with his eyes fixed on the ground, with the greatest sorrow and growing sighs he thought of his capture, and the general confusion of Christianity because of it.

A bishop tried to console him, but the king replied:

> If only I could suffer alone the opprobrium and the adversity, and my sins should not recoil on the universal church, then I could bear it with equanimity. But woe is me, by me all Christianity has been covered with confusion.[25]

The appalling experiences of his captivity, his sense of personal guilt for the death and imprisonment of so many of the crusaders, weighed Louis down with the conviction that the failure of the crusade was primarily his fault, to be blamed on his own sins and weaknesses. From this time on his asceticism, his shunning of luxury, display, and even comfort were much more marked. Louis did all he could during the later years of his reign to do penance himself and to make his realm a place where holiness was encouraged. The king's fondness for clerks and religious increased as he sought to guide, and if necessary coerce all his subjects into the paths of piety and godly conduct. His devotion to the Holy Land continued to manifest itself in his constant support of knights and levies for use there. In addition when he departed from Acre he left Geoffrey of Sergines at the head of a company of one hundred knights maintained at the king's expense.[26] Louis's first crusade was the watershed of his reign. From 1254 on he would look at his royal business from a slightly new angle, and his emphasis on peace and justice within his realm would make him the most sought after arbitrator in Europe. Louis never put aside his royal responsibilities but he always dreamed of another crusade, another chance to free the Holy Land and its Christians. His judgment on the value of a further crusade was based only on spiritual conviction. He could not, or would not, see the futility of another crusade as a means of political action.

IX

Return to France 1254

During Louis's six-year absence in Outremer peace in France had been seriously disturbed only once. Queen Blanche had enforced the policy of firmness and pacification which had marked her years of rule during her son's minority. Her second regency was easier than the first for, by the time Louis left, the barons had learned the futility of rebellion against the royal forces, and many of the older rebel leaders, such as Peter of Brittany and the high-tempered Le Bruns of La Marche, had joined the crusading army. Queen Blanche, with the three prelates who apparently served as her council, had dealt competently with the affairs of the kingdom.

All France, and indeed much of Europe, had been elated by the news of Damietta. Matthew Paris's description of the effect of the news of Mansourah and Louis's capture on France reflects the extremely emotional responses of medieval people.

> The appearance of women was changed; garlands of flowers were thrown away; songs were broken off; musical instruments were prohibited; every song of joy was turned into mourning and lament. And, what is worse, accusing God of injustice, they broke into blasphemy. . . . And many began to vacillate in their faith.[1]

The city of Albi threatened to revolt after the disaster and Philip Berruier, the bishop of Bourges and one of the queen's trusted counsellors, had to go and pacify the city.[2]

Alphonse of Poitiers and Charles of Anjou set sail from Acre in August 1250. They were willing to aid their mother and maintain the peace of the realm but both were primarily concerned with developments in their own important territories. During his absence, Alphonse had become heir to the extensive lands of the count of Toulouse, his father-in-law, who had died soon after his departure. Although Queen Blanche had helped Alphonse's own officials and Sicard Alaman, the leading official of Count Raymond, in achieving the peaceful recognition of the new overlord, Alphonse was understandably eager to oversee personally his new inheritance. When he arrived at Aigues-Mortes at the beginning of October, he remained in the south until November 1251, only travelling to Lyons to see the pope at the end of 1250. He inspected his appanage of Poitou as well as the new lands that had come to him by right of his wife.[3]

Charles of Anjou was also anxious to see the pope because he wanted his help in dealing with the upheavals among his Provençal vassals and in his quarrels over jurisdiction. It is obvious that the two brothers' visit to Lyons was prompted by selfish motives, as well as by their dutiful support of Louis's request to enlist new help from Pope Innocent.

At this time the pope was still most concerned with his war with the Emperor Frederic. It was only early in January 1251 that Innocent heard that Frederic had died on December 13 in southern Italy and the pope's exultation on his hated rival's death passed all bounds of reason or charity. Frederic's death did not end the papal crusade against the Hohenstaufen: the papal enmity continued to pursue Conrad, Frederic's son and heir. Innocent was thus far too concerned to give much assistance or encouragement to Louis's crusade, and he was also planning his own return to Rome. Queen Blanche, disgusted with the pope's lukewarm support, sent messengers to him, suggesting that she came to see him in Lyons before his departure. She felt the force of her personality might push Innocent to more helpful measures. The pope, although he sang her praises in a long and diplomatic letter, firmly discouraged her. He reminded her that she had been ill and should not run the risk of a relapse. But the pope did send one of his chaplains to promote Charles of Anjou's interests and encourage the pacification of Provence, Marseilles, and Avignon where communal insurrections and divided jurisdictions were creating much unrest.[4] Blanche summoned the French barons to attempt to find reinforcements for Louis, and in her exasperation with the pope's emphasis on the war against the empire she seized all the lands and possessions of those who joined the crusade against Conrad. 'Those who fight for the pope,' Paris reports her saying, 'can be supported by papal officials, and may go not to return'.[5]

The despair and anger of the people of France over the defeat and capture of their kind boiled to the surface in the spring of 1251 in one of those recurrent popular movements inspired by the public preaching of crusades. The poor and ignorant could not reckon in terms of military strategy, financial aid, or limited objectives; for them, a crusade was a straightforward matter of going to fight the hated Moslems. A spellbinding leader could easily whip the masses into an emotional frenzy, rousing them to fever pitch over the danger to the Holy Land. Around Easter a wild-eyed fanatic, known as the Master of Hungary, claimed that he had a special revelation from the Blessed Virgin ordering him to bring together all the shepherds, who would then go overseas and rescue the Holy Land. The movement started in the north of France in Picardy, and the Master rapidly gathered an unruly mob of armed followers. They came to Paris and were received by Queen Blanche, who seems to have hoped, in her frustration and despair, that perhaps they really might rescue the Holy Land and aid her son. The movement soon proved to be more anti-clerical than truly crusading. The *Pastoureaux*, as they were known, attacked all clerks, denounced the monks and friars, and caused riots and bloodshed. After wild scenes in Paris, the throng moved on to Orléans where their behaviour was denounced by the bishop. The clamour and complaint reached Blanche who was finally disillusioned and ordered their excommunication, capture, and destruction. The Master of Hungary was slain in one of the encounters and the leaderless mob wandered southwards to be gradually dispersed, or caught and hung.[6]

The general uproar caused by the *Pastoureaux* again exacerbated the relations between the queen and the university. Blanche had always regarded with suspicion the university's constant effort to gain exemption from the authority of any outsider, and the pope himself had had to complain to the queen about the unjustified imposition of customs duties and tolls on students coming to the schools in Paris. After the invasion of the *Pastoureaux*, the queen succeeded in getting sworn promises from both the bourgeois and the members of the university to do everything possible to preserve order.*[7]

The last year of Blanche's life was saddened by the serious illness of Alphonse of Poitiers, who was attacked both by paralysis and eye trouble. Alphonse's chaplain wrote to Louis in Outremer before Queen Blanche's death announcing Alphonse's grave illness, but said that he was getting better, was anxious to see Louis, and did not even discount the possibility of again taking the cross.[8] Alphonse also tried to cure his eye trouble, writing to one of his vassals who knew of a Jewish doctor particularly brilliant in treating diseases of the eyes. The Jew was convinced that Alphonse could be cured if he could distinguish one thing from another at short range and could tell green from blue.[9] Although Alphonse did not go overseas before his brother returned, his health improved noticeably, and he lived an active and vigorous life until his death in 1271, after Louis's second crusade.†

But neither age, nor worry over her sons, or even illness were sufficient to change the imperious Blanche or her insistence on the maintenance of the royal rights. The most celebrated example during her second regency was her intervention in the affairs of the serfs of Orly, which is colourfully but rather inaccurately described in the *Grandes Chroniques*.[11] The chapter of Notre Dame decided to raise a *taille*, or tallage, upon their serfs at Orly. The peasants refused the payment and questioned its legitimacy, which naturally provoked a case in the chapter's court. The court condemned the non-payment and threw a certain number of the serfs in prison until the tax was paid. The peasants appealed to the

*It is interesting to note the particular cases in which the masters of the faculties of the universities agreed not to insist on the release of a scholar, merely because he was a scholar, but to follow an agreed-upon procedure for investigation. These special offences were 'frequent rioting, rape, housebreaking, night-wandering, theft, public robbery, and murder'. A formidable list for supposedly studious clerks.

†Roger Bacon, the scientifically-minded Franciscan, seems to be referring to Alphonse when he praised a magnificent medicine, known as the 'treasure of the sages', which transformed a French prince from a covetous, mean-spirited, depressed and feeble man to a generous, cheerful and healthy individual. From the nature of its ingredients this medicine would probably have cured constipation, colic, and flatulence – important factors in improving any patient's disposition.[10]

queen to bring the case before the royal court. Blanche tried to get the canons to agree to the holding of an inquest on the validity of their right, and also to liberate the serfs until a decision was reached. The chapter reacted quickly and vehemently. They insisted that the queen had no right to intervene in a strictly domestic affair between them and their serfs over whom they had absolute power, and as a lesson to the serfs, they threw their wives and children into prison where it was so hot that some of them died. Queen Blanche finally decided on action. Accompanied by the castellan of the Louvre, the provost of Paris and a troop of men-at-arms, she entered the cloister of the canons, on the north side of the cathedral, from which the canons had withdrawn, closing the doors but not barring them against the queen's entry. Even this unopposed entry was a breach of the recognized immunity of the canons' cloister from royal judgment. Blanche, knowing that her legal position was questionable, did not want to exercise force, and her men tried to find the keys for the cellar and for the gaol in the cellar where the serfs were imprisoned. Without her express command, and apparently without her knowledge, the doors to the cellar and the gaol were broken open and the serfs were rescued.

The controversy did not end there, for three bishops then supervised an arbitration on the legality of the queen's action. The matter dragged on for some time. The queen had intervened between the end of August 1251 and the beginning of March 1252, and the arbitral sentence was not finally given until December 1, 1252, a few days after her death. It decided that the chapter had the right to tallage its serfs and had been legally correct in its treatment of them. The queen had overstepped her rights in trying to exercise royal justice. Although the *Grandes Chroniques* attributes to Blanche the enfranchisement of the serfs at Orly, this was not actually achieved until later, and by the serfs' own payments. The vivid picture the chronicler draws of a determined Blanche striking the first blow on the prison door is more colourful than correct.[12]

The tragedies and worries of the last years had all taken their toll of Queen Blanche. She was, after all, a woman in her sixties, who had borne twelve children and carried much of the burden of the rule of France since 1226. In November 1252 when she realized she would soon die, she went to her dearly-loved Cistercian abbey of Maubuisson, near Pontoise, which she had founded in 1236. Blanche then devoted her last days to spiritual exercises, having had the bishop of Paris clothe her in the habit of a Cistercian nun. Charles of Anjou gives the most vivid picture of Blanche's death.

> Having received the sacraments and death approaching, she had lost her speech. The priests and clerks there hesitated, not knowing what to do. All at once she herself began to intone the prayer for the dying *Subvenite Sancti Dei*, and gave up her soul little by little, muttering between her teeth the rest of the prayer.[13]

Blanche's burial took place at Maubuisson on November 29,[14] two or three days after her death. Her two regencies had well earned her the eulogies of the chroniclers. One anonymous scribe described her as 'the wise, the valiant, the good queen . . . who so well and so wisely governed the country and the kingdom'. Even William of Nangis's pedestrian style seems brightened by an unaccustomed touch of emotion when he writes of her as 'the wisest of all women of her time, and all good things came to the realm of France while she was alive'.[15] After their mother's death Alphonse of Poitiers and Charles of Anjou held joint custody of the realm, since Louis's oldest son was only nine. They immediately sent messengers to Louis in Outremer with the sad news and urgently requested him to return.

Before Louis could return a serious problem erupted on the frontiers of the realm, which intimately concerned Charles of Anjou. The affairs of the county of Flanders were particularly tangled, aggravated by the complications of inheritance and by the fact that the county divided its homage, Flanders proper being a fief of France and Hainault a fief of the Empire. Countess Jeanne, who had been countess of Flanders and Hainault in her own right when Louis IX came to the throne, had had two husbands, but no children. When she died in 1244, she was succeeded by her sister Marguerite whose difficulties arose from a typically medieval dispute over the legitimacy of her marriages. Marguerite had first married Bouchard of Avesnes, a clerk, and had two sons by him, John and Baldwin. Since Bouchard was a clerk, the marriage was dissolved and the children declared illegitimate, although they were later legitimized by both the pope and the emperor. In 1218 Marguerite married William of Dampierre, a younger brother of Archambaud of Bourbon, and had three sons by him, William, Guy, and John. Her husband was dead before she inherited Flanders from her sister. The quarrel between the Avesnes and the Dampierres had already caused difficulties and had been submitted to Louis for arbitration before he left for the crusade. In July 1246 the king and the papal legate had given a sentence dividing Marguerite's lands. They adjudged the county of Hainault to John of Avesnes, and the county of Flanders to William of Dampierre.[16] This sentence shows once again how Louis often combined the exercise of justice with the exploitation of an advantage for France, since William of Dampierre, as the nephew of one of the most loyal of all French vassals, was much preferred by the royal interest as count of Flanders. In October 1246 the king accepted William's homage for the county,[17] and from that time on William was given the title of count of Flanders.

William joined Louis on the crusade where he distinguished himself. He returned home in 1250 with the king's brothers and the following summer was killed in Hainault while participating in a tournament, his favourite sport. There was considerable talk that his death was not an accident, but had been brought about by the supporters of his half-brother. Certainly John of Avesnes was angry because he had not received the title of count of Hainault although his stepbrother had been invested as count of Flanders. In 1252 John encouraged William of Holland, king of the Romans* and his brother-in-law, to seize from Countess Marguerite all her lands which paid homage to the empire. Marguerite attempted to assert her rights by force, and the inhabitants of Hainault rose in revolt against their countess and her Flemish supporters. The dispute led to open warfare and in

*This was the title given to the man elected as Holy Roman Emperor, but not yet crowned by the pope. Both William and his successor, Richard of Cornwall, never were crowned, and, in fact, never gained the support of all the imperial electors.

July 1253 Marguerite and her Dampierre sons were defeated by the Avesnes in the battle of Walcheren. Guy and John Dampierre were taken prisoner but even this setback did not discourage the truculent Marguerite,* who refused to treat for her sons' freedom.

The countess turned instead to Charles of Anjou for help. Although she had applied to Queen Blanche before, she had offered no reward for assistance, now she appealed to Charles's cupidity and desire for power by ceding him the county of Hainault in return for his help. Since his mother was dead and Louis far away, there was no one to restrain his ambition and Charles moved eagerly into the breach. He sent a strong garrison to Valenciennes, seized the town, and then with a large army, entered Hainault and besieged Mons. John of Avesnes was again supported by William of Holland. Though both armies were in the field no major battle was fought and both sides gradually withdrew. No final decision had been reached but Charles was in possession of much of Hainault. This uneasy equilibrium existed until Louis, who at Acre learnt what had happened, returned to intervene.

In the summer of 1254 as Louis rode north through the French countryside, rich and green and wooded and in sharp contrast to the heat and sand of the near east, he had time to ponder the good advice of the Franciscan, Brother Hugh of Montpellier, who had preached to him during his stay at Hyères. Brother Hugh, much esteemed for his sanctity, was one of the most famous preachers of his day. Although he was dark and short, he had a 'voice like a sounding trumpet and great thunder and the rushing of many waters' and was as successful preaching to cardinals as to poor townspeople.[19] Louis had been informed of his reputation and asked him to preach before him, but Brother Hugh did not attempt to mollify the great. He berated the religious who spent their time at the king's court for, he said, they were likely to lose their souls for being so far away from their own cloister. His advice to the king on matters of government was, if idealistic, both sound and in accord with the king's own ideal of kingship.

*Matthew Paris describes Marguerite as 'another Medea', and asserts that she wrote to John of Avesnes after her sons' capture: 'My sons, your brothers, are in your hands. I will not bend because of them. Sacrifice them, truculent meat-eater, and devour one of them cooked with a pepper sauce, and the other roasted with garlic'.[18]

> In his sermons he taught the king that he should act in accordance with the will of his people; and he finished by saying that he had read the Bible and books that correspond to the Bible, and he had never, either in Christian or infidel books, seen any kingdom lost, or transferred from one government or king to another, except through some lack of justice. 'The King, then,' he said, 'should be careful, now that he is returning to France, to do such justice to his people that he may thereby retain the love of God, so that God may not deprive him of his kingdom during his lifetime'.[20]

The problem for Louis, as for any conscientious medieval ruler, was to translate into practical forms this concern for justice within his realm and peace without. Although Queen Blanche and his brothers had managed well, Louis had some urgent decisions to make. There was the immediate and pressing problem of Flanders and Hainault There was his interest in the further change in the affairs of the Empire and Sicily, since Conrad, Frederic's heir had died in May, during Louis's journey home, and Innocent IV had tried to persuade Charles of Anjou to accept the crown of Sicily and oppose Conrad and his half-brother Manfred. The king had vetoed Charles's involvement because he felt Conrad's right was unassailable, despite the pope's hostility to him, but Conrad's death made a difference. Louis was also concerned over the relations of France with England. Although truces continued, and there were no overt hostilities, there was still no real peace.

Within his own realm there was the basic question of the best means of governing his kingdom, the difficult but necessary compromise between the strictest possible justice for his subjects and the firmest possible assertion of the royal rights. Undoubtedly Louis had thought about these matters during his years overseas, where his encounter with other methods and forms of government had provided him with useful comparisons and suggestions. By the time the king returned to Paris at the beginning of September 1254 he was ready to take up, with both firmness and compassion, the reins of government he had laid down six years before.

X

Paris: The King's Capital

Thirteenth-century Paris was the biggest and most important city in northern Europe. It had a population of between a hundred and a hundred and fifty thousand by the middle of the century and intellectually, artistically, and commercially it dominated its era. The pre-eminent position of the University of Paris in intellectual life ensured the city a cosmopolitan and constantly changing population, while the almost continuous presence of the French king and his court encouraged the development of the luxury trades and of the most advanced styles and methods of building. Louis IX was never as peripatetic as Henry III. Although he spent much time at the royal hunting lodges, and at favourite hospitals and abbeys, his travels were mainly within a day's journey of Paris. Except for the campaigns of the early years of his reign and his crusading expeditions, Louis only left the environs of Paris when on royal business. This made Paris the true capital of the realm, while Louis also pursued and reinforced his grandfather's policy of establishing permanently in Paris the most important branches of royal government. Even at this period in French history Paris was a magnetic force drawing talent and wealth from the rest of the royal domain.

The Paris of Louis IX was small in geographical extent and mainly contained within the walls built by Philip Augustus.[1] The Ile-de-la Cité was its centre, morally as well as geographically, containing on its island the palace, as symbol of lay power, and the great cathedral of Notre Dame, as symbol of the spiritual. The Ile was connected to the mainland by two bridges, the Grand Pont and the Petit Pont: even in those days the Right and Left Banks had the same distinctive character which they have maintained. The Right Bank was the town, the home of the merchants and the ordinary artisans and townspeople. To the west the original old tower of the Louvre was just outside the western rampart of the city wall, while the last traces of its eastern end can still be seen along the small rue des Jardins, leading to the Quai des Celestins. The ancient rue du Temple led outside the city wall to the rich establishment of the Temple, home of the military order of the Templars who during Louis's reign banked the royal funds

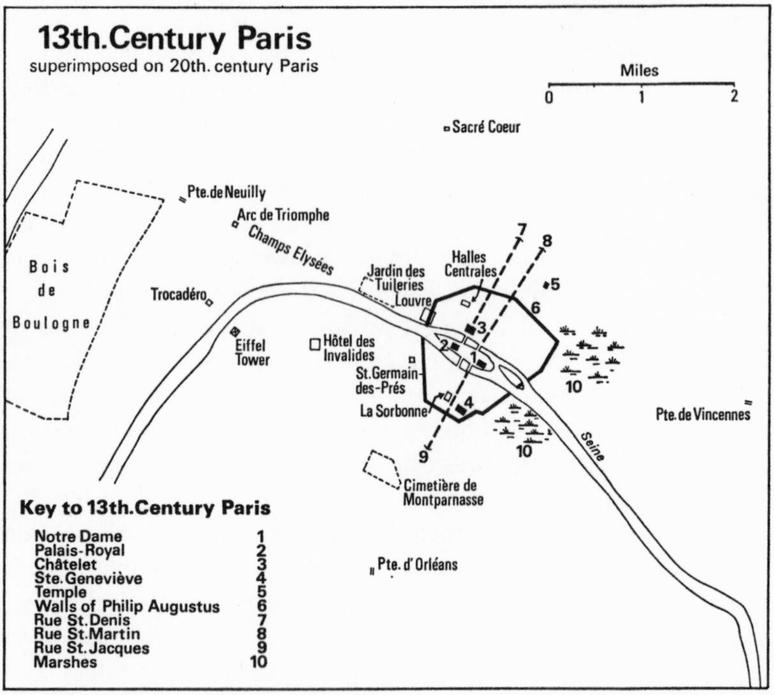

and supervised the royal treasury. A little further to the west the rue St Denis also led beyond the walls, marking the route to the royal abbey of St Denis, some seven miles to the north.

The Left Bank was even then the student quarter. On this side of the river, Philip Augustus's wall stretched from its westward anchor at the Tour de Nesle (now the corner of the rue de Nevers) eastward to the Pont de la Tournelle. The main street of the Left Bank was the rue St Jacques, the oldest street in Paris and the line of the original Roman road to Orléans and the pilgrimage road to St James of Compostela. The students swarmed around the rue St Jacques and up the Mont St. Geneviève, pushing into crowded lecture rooms and struggling for desirable lodgings. Great abbeys on this side of the river, such as St Victor and St Germain-des-Prés, were outside the walls, but the open fields near them were the popular recreation ground of the students.

Many people were building in Paris during Louis's reign. The present-day rue du Roi-de-Sicile commemorates the great town house built here by Charles of Anjou after he became king of Sicily. Various officials of Louis's household owned houses in Paris, and seem to have traded in real estate. Isambert the Cook, the squire who had stayed close to his master during his captivity in Egypt, sold his house in the rue du Sablon, worth seventy pounds, for the use of the Paris hospital.[2] A newly rich class, the booksellers, as a result of the growth of the university could invest their profits in houses and rents.[3] Throughout the thirteenth century the urban character of Paris was becoming much more pronounced and the open spaces in the district enclosed by Philip Augustus's walls were rapidly filling up. This development brought its own dangers. In any medieval city where narrow streets, lack of water, and careless methods of building intensified the danger of fire, some method of inspection was usually attempted. The chapter of Notre Dame, as enlightened landlords, provided for an annual summer inspection of their houses. They even insisted that the canons were to be accompanied by expert carpenters and masons to see what repairs had to be made to which houses.[4] Paris was advanced in its style of building. Houses were often three stories or more, with gables projecting over the street, but they were plastered on the exterior – an innovation which much impressed Henry III.[5]

Most of these houses, certainly those of the well-to-do, had their own small gardens and often their own vines, for wines of good quality were still made from grapes grown in the environs of Paris. There were no parks or public open spaces. Paris, like other medieval cities, needed protection from the countryside, not reminders of it. Just how flimsy was the barrier against the dangers of the surrounding wilderness is remarkably illustrated by the continuing payment of bounties on wolves as late as the end of the fifteenth century. Occasionally the captured wolves were even paraded live through the streets of Paris to claim the reward at the treasury. At the end of the thirteenth century, in the outlying districts of Melun, only thirty miles from Paris, thirty-two people were eaten by wolves during three winter months.[6]

As well, it was often difficult to maintain order among the turbulent population. Joinville tells of meeting a cart being taken to the king with the bodies of three men killed by a clerk. The seneschal was so curious that he sent his squire to find out what the king would do. The king was told that the dead men were minor royal officials, sergeants from the Châtelet, who used to haunt deserted streets in order to rob any passersby. They had caught this clerk and stripped him of his clothes. Furious, the clerk had hurried back to his lodgings, seized his crossbow and cutlass, and rushed off in pursuit of the offenders. He killed one man with the bow and then, with enormous vigour and skill, used his cutlass to slit the skull of one and detach the leg of another. Afterwards the clerk had come to surrender himself to justice and the royal provost was not quite sure what should be done. The king did not hesitate. The clerk had lost his clerical character by this spilling of blood, but Louis saw no need to punish him. He felt that the clerk had been justified, and besides was such a doughty fighter, that he immediately engaged him to join the royal service and to accompany him overseas.[7] So it is easy to understand why the university authorities agreed to include 'night-wandering' among their serious crimes.

The king's palace on the Ile-de-la-Cité was the seat and symbol of royal power in the realm. The overpowering impression it made on contemporary men is expressed by Guy of Bazoches who wrote a picturesque description of Paris in the last half of the twelfth century. In rather rhetorical terms he told how the royal palace towered to lofty heights and audaciously overlooked the roofs of the whole city.

> This is that house, the glory of the Franks, whose
> Praises the eternal centuries will sing.
> This is that house which holds in its power

Gaul mighty in war, Flanders magnificent in wealth.
This is that house whose sceptre the Burgundian,
Whose mandate the Norman, and whose arms the
Briton fears.[8]

The appearance of the palace at the time of St Louis is best suggested by the miniature for June in the *Très Riches Heures* of the duke of Berry, which shows a view taken across the fields from the Tour de Nesle. Although the miniaturist includes the changes made during the fourteenth century, the impression of the palace is essentially that of Louis's time – a huddle of roofs and towers dominated by the elegant Sainte Chapelle.

The palace was a residence, but it was also a centre of government and the dual nature of many of its rooms illustrate the indistinct dividing line which separated the public and private functions of the king.[9] Louis's hall was still where the *curia regis* held its deliberations, as well as being the dining hall for the household. The king's chamber, also on the ground floor, served as the king's own dining hall and had a door which opened to the garden within the palace walls. Here the king frequently listened to pleas and gave justice, and the peace treaty with England was solemnly proclaimed. Up one flight of stairs was the king's bedchamber and the meeting place of his private council, and near this was the wardrobe where his chamberlains worked and ate. Even the small building which had been constructed to serve as sacristy and treasury for the Sainte Chapelle had a third floor for the exclusive use of the king which housed the royal archives and library.

This indistinct dividing line was also evident in the king's household, although the process of development and specialization among royal officials had been progressing steadily during the twelfth and thirteenth centuries. The major offices of the king's household, such as the seneschal, the steward, the butler, had at one time been in the hands of certain great families as hereditary honours. The Capetian kings had been steadily reducing their dependence on the great lords and they left these offices unfilled or reduced them to ornamental sinecures. Instead the king gathered around himself a large group of counsellors and officials from lower levels of the feudal structure, whose hopes of future advancement lay in loyalty and devotion to the crown. The clerics could aspire to bishoprics or other important benefices in the royal gift. The lesser nobles and bourgeois were most often men from the north and centre of France – the original royal domain – where families had a tradition of royal service, and faithful service was repaid with rents and grants of lands as well as the increase in importance and social status that came from association with the king. Throughout the century, there was an extraordinary continuity of royal counsellors and officials, with frequent recurrence of the same family names and evidence of an almost hereditary caste of officials in the royal household, who often inter-married.

The establishment required to serve King Louis during the later years of his reign, both in the palace in Paris and on his travels, is given in the household ordinance for 1261. It lists the officials, some by name, their wages, their perquisites, the number of horses they were allowed, and the number of valets by whom they could be served. It is not complete, and not as carefully organized as the equivalent contemporary household documents in England, but it provides valuable hints on the extent and organization of the king's household and again illustrates the typical mingling of functions.

The highest wages went to the king's three most important chamberlains, each of whom received six shillings a day, had the right to have three valets eating at court, and received valuable perquisites of wine and candles, and smithy privileges for their horses. John Sarrasin, one of the three, was actually treasurer of the king's household, although he did not have the official title. It was his special duty to bring together his notes* and the accounts of each of the subordinate officials in charge of the other household offices and to answer every four months to the Treasurer of the Temple for the sums he had already received from him. The man in charge of each of the other main offices, such as the pantry,

*There exists a rare example of these early notes made on black wax tablets by John Sarrasin. The wax was set in wood, rather like a child's slate, and was written on with a sharp stylus. This served as a rough copy for the finished roll which was put on parchment and the wax could then be erased with the blunt end of the stylus. The tablets, with the notes on the expenses of the household in 1256–7, are preserved in the Archives Nationales at Paris.

9. Louis receives petitions from the sick (from a 16th century MS commemorating the triumphal entry into Paris of Claude of France, daughter of Louis XII – an example of the continuing royal veneration of Louis)

10a. Louis gives judgment (from William of St-Pathus, *Life and Miracles of St Louis*)

10b. Louis serves the poor (from William of St-Pathus, *Life and Miracles of St Louis*)

the butlery, and the kitchen, was paid at the same rate as the chamberlains, but the king's surgeon, Peter de Brocia, had only two shillings a day, and the barber only sixpence.

Curious items illuminating the pattern of everyday life emerge from the dry list of names, wages, and duties. One of the sumptermen of the butlery, the department primarily concerned with the purchase and service of wine, had special orders to bring the king's drinking-water every day. John the pastry cook had pleasant perquisites, the customary fragments of pastries, tarts and flawns. The domestic chaplains were remarkably poorly paid, only fourpence a day. Other clerks, such as the treasurer of Tours and the dean of St Aignan, drew wages of four or five shillings a day, but this is because they were primarily royal officials, serving as royal secretaries or dealing with special matters for the king. Two entries are typical of Louis's concern for the material welfare of those who had suffered for the faith; generous provision is made for twenty-four converted Jews and eight ransomed men.[10]

The list is not complete – there is, for example, no mention of the king's knights or armed guard – so it is impossible to draw an accurate balance of the number of people involved and the extent of their wages. But a rough estimate suggests that over one hundred people were paid wages, ate at the king's expense, and most of these were an essential part of the king's retinue when he travelled. The figures available for the year 1256–7 have been analysed to arrive at a sum of just over one hundred pounds a day for the expenses of the household offices, although this figure does not include the king's alms or his bodyguard. As might be expected Louis's alms were generous, about fifteen pounds a day, but Joinville suggests that the king kept a reasonable balance in the expenses of his household.

> Some of his household grumbled at his giving such generous alms and spending so much on them. He answered, 'I would rather my extravagance should be in almsgiving for the love of God than in the pomp and vain glory of this world.' In spite, however, of the King's great expenditure in almsgiving, his daily household expenses were none the less very high. He was liberal and generous at the Parlements and meetings of barons and knights, and entertained them at his court with greater

courtesy and prodigality than had been seen for a long time at the courts of his predecessors.[11]

At the same time as this ordinance was drawn up, regulations were also made for the strict control of the queen's household. The queen was allowed 400 pounds Paris for alms and offerings a year, although these amounts were in addition to the expenses of feeding a number of the poor every day. She had a generous number of ladies to serve her, since some twenty-six received robes at her expense. The regulation is especially interesting for the evidence it gives of the prohibitions that hedged the queen. Marguerite was not to receive any loan or present for herself or her children, except wine or other minor trifles. She was not to give any commands to any royal officials, nor to name any officials of her own authority. She was not even allowed to engage any person for her own service, or for that of the children, without the permission of the king and the consent of the council.[12] It is evident that Louis believed in strict control of all aspects of his household and those of his dependents. Although well organized and adequately staffed, the king avoided excess expenditure and was completely intolerant of any interference with his officials or his high ideals of government.

The solidity and impressiveness of the royal palace and the large household which revolved around it was counter-balanced on the Ile-de-la-Cité by the magnificent cathedral of Notre Dame, and the power of the bishop and his chapter. The task of completing and decorating the great cathedral was actively pursued all during Louis's reign, though the main plan had been achieved by 1250. Notre Dame was the church for great state occasions for all the people of Paris, but the cathedral was not yet the undisputed religious centre of French official life. The bishop of Paris and the chapter of Notre Dame had temporal as well as spiritual jurisdiction, and they frequently clashed with the royal officials over contested rights and claims. Royal and episcopal officials equally disputed the independent authority of the university over its students and the jurisdiction of the various abbeys. These points of conflict were typical of the intricate web which slowed and complicated the processes of medieval government.

Still another quarrel which racked Paris during the 1250s was the major struggle between the university and the friars, in which the king became personally involved. The secular masters of the university bitterly resented the growing importance of the friars at the university and their acquisition of so many of the important teaching chairs, especially as the friars were not willing to swear total allegiance to the university. A major crisis exploded in February 1254, before Louis returned home, and when it was appealed to the pope, Innocent IV limited the friars' privileges and upheld the Masters of the university. Twelve days later, however, Innocent died and he was followed by Pope Alexander IV. Alexander was a strong supporter of the friars, since he had been cardinal protector of the Franciscans, and he immediately repealed Innocent's judgment. The university forces then waged a pamphlet warfare. William of St Amour was the most aggressive of the secular masters. In a *Brief Tract on the Danger of the Times* he described the mendicants as the precursors of anti-Christ, full of pride and cupidity, who were destroying the universities. This vituperation did not ease the tension between the university and Louis who knew the most distinguished friars. Bonaventura, the brilliant and saintly general of the Franciscans, preached a fifth of all his sermons in Paris before the king. Thomas Aquinas, according to the often-told story, was invited to dinner with Louis and sat next to him, but his mind was so preoccupied with his refutation of the Manichean heresy that he completely forgot his surroundings, struck the table and exclaimed: 'That settles the Manichees!'[13] As well, many of Louis's closest friends and councillors belonged to the mendicant orders – Archbishop Eudes Rigaud of Rouen, Vincent of Beauvais, Humbert of the Romans.

Despite this, Louis attempted to settle the differences, and after an arbitration committee had been formed, proclaimed a reasonable compromise on March 1, 1256. The pope quashed the arbitration and William of St Amour, throwing caution to the winds in his anger, made a flagrant attack on the king in his Pentecost sermon in Paris. He described with malice a king who no longer wore elegant robes, and ridiculed him for leaping from his bed to say matins in the middle of the night. William accused the king of taking money from the towns and counties and not paying it back, but using it for a war in which many Christians were killed. Such a king was a hypocrite who should not be surrounded and counselled by self-righteous vagabonds. They should go and beg and leave the king to his own responsibilties, especially justice which was his particular duty.[14] This was too obvious an attack for Louis not to be forced to take action at once, in order to maintain the royal dignity. He complained to the pope and, after a hearing before a papal commission, William's tract was condemned and he himself was deprived of all his offices and benefices, forbidden to enter the kingdom of France or to preach or teach.[15] After the departure of William the king had no further contest with the university, but the conflict between the secular masters and the friars continued to sputter malevolently and to disturb the university quarter.

Paris was an important commercial centre and much of the real control of commercial life rested in the hands of the most important bourgeois. By the time of St Louis there had already developed a long tradition of co-operation between them and the king. When Philip Augustus went on crusade he left the government of the city in their hands. Over the years the rich families of the city prospered and kept on intimate terms with the king and his household. John Sarrasin, for example, wrote the details of the crusaders' capture of Damietta to Nicholas Arrode. The Arrodes were among the important Parisian bourgeois, as were the Barbettes, who gave their name to one of the city gates on the Right Bank. These rich and powerful men belonged to the gild of the Merchants of the Water, which owed its importance to its control of the river traffic. Situated as they were on the Seine, near the confluence of the Marne and the Oise, the merchants of Paris were able to enforce a practical monopoly on all goods carried to or through the city by water. The gild charged high duties and the goods had to be sold by the Paris merchants. This privilege caused much argument from other river towns such as Rouen, but the king usually upheld the Parisian privileges. The monopoly only applied to the river traffic, but this was the great majority, since at that time it was easiest to ship bulky cargoes by water.

In these merchants was concentrated the main strength within the city and by the middle of the thirteenth century, they had achieved their own provost, known as the provost of the merchants. The provost was aided by aldermen and other functionaries and had his own seat of power at the Parloir des Bourgeois, just opposite the Grand Châtelet, the seat of the king's provost. The provost of the merchants was, in effect, the embodiment of the city's life as a trading centre.*

The day-to-day trading was carried on at markets and fairs. The most important fair in the Paris region was that of Lendit, named from the district between Paris and St Denis where it was held for two weeks in June. Its revenues had been granted to the abbey of St Denis by Louis VI. It was not only a thriving market-place where many flocked to purchase their special needs, but was also a rendezvous for minstrels and poets who entertained the crowds with their new songs and political satires. By the time of Louis, although the Lendit fair was still popular, the Halles had already become the great market of Paris. Philip Augustus had constructed two buildings there for the protection of the merchandise and the shelter of the merchants. Near the end of his reign, Louis IX added three more buildings, including one for the sale of seafish which were imported from the northern Channel ports. The Halles were a royal market where the king's officials rented the stalls and the king received an impost on transactions. Almost everything was sold, but the Halles were only open three days a week (Wednesday, Friday, and Saturday) and they also had to close during the fortnight of the Lendit fair.[16]

The royal interest in the Halles is further evidence of mutual royal and commercial interests. The royal authority over Paris was vested in the provost, who was armed with extensive judicial and financial powers which he exercised from Grand Châtelet, the protecting fortress of the Grand Pont as it crossed from the Ile-de-la-Cité to the Right Bank. One of Louis's administrators, Stephen Boileau, who served as provost from 1261 to 1269 has been canonized by Joinville and the *Grandes Chroniques*.

It is necessary to sort out truth from legend in the stories about Boileau, and, as usual, the legend is more colourful and interesting.

*The seal of Paris still bears the fleur-de-lis and a thirteenth-century ship, symbol of the basis of its power.

It claims that until the middle of Louis's reign the provost of Paris farmed his office, that is, he bought the right to return a fixed sum to the king and to take anything above that as profit. Because of the rapacious demands of the provost, bribery flourished and the poor and weak did not dare to live in the king's land for only the rich received justice. Louis was supposed to have reformed the office – ignoring the bishop of Paris who feared loss of his profits – and, after much inquiry for a just and honest man, appointed Stephen Boileau. Boileau was so conscientious and incorruptible that no evildoer was safe from his justice: he even had his godson hung for wrongdoing. The chronicle concludes the story with this triumphant flourish.

> Because of this the king's land was freed from many services and for the good laws which the provost made, the people left the other seignories to live in the king's land. They multiplied and improved so much that the sales and seisins and purchases and other levies were worth more than four times what they were when the king took it before.[17]

The office of provost of Paris had indeed been farmed for many years, but the provosts had been drawn from men of importance and substance. Many were later used by the king in other offices – hardly a proof that they had acted unjustly during their term as provost. Boileau himself was a well-known bourgeois of Paris, who had accompanied Louis on the crusade of 1248 and shared his king's imprisonment. Louis certainly supported Boileau in his work. When the provost was involved in a struggle with the chapter of Notre Dame and was excommunicated by the canons, the king intervened to have him absolved.[18] Boileau was a good and faithful servant of the king but no such striking results flowed from his administration as the chroniclers would suggest, and any reform was part of Louis's general prescription for the whole kingdom. The accounts show that there was no particular increase in the receipts after Boileau was named provost; they remained almost the same. The exaggeration of Boileau's achievements was merely another example of the use of every possible rumour and legend by the royal clerks to inflate the reputation and sanctity of the king.[19]

Much of Stephen Boileau's fame, however, rests on the *Livre des Métiers* which bears his name. It must be realized that he was not a legislator for the Paris industries, nor the founder or organizer of the artisan communities in the city; these already existed and had their own rules. What Boileau did was to establish a register at the Châtelet which listed the regulations for the control of the artisans, the rights and tariffs claimed in the king's name, the arrangements for the entry of provisions and other merchandise, and finally the titles on which the abbots and other lords founded the privileges they enjoyed in Paris. In order to make this register complete the provost ordered the representatives of the various corporations of artisans to appear before him at the Châtelet to declare their usages and immemorial customs, and to have them registered. The clerk wrote them down under the provost's eye in a simplified form, which may perhaps have been dictated by Boileau. The *Livre des Métiers* is essentially the record of oral proceedings. It makes no effort to describe what should be done for the common good, since the rules had been elaborated for the benefit of the corporations themselves. Nor can it be considered as complete, for it does not include all of the corporations, even some of the most important. The Merchants of the Water are not included at all, and the butchers, the tanners and the glassmakers were all registered by Boileau's successors.

However, the *Livre des Métiers* is a valuable and illuminating record of the enormous scope and variety of trades practised in medieval Paris. Along with the masons, the weavers, the tailors and the shoemakers, there were the artists and those who catered for the rich and well-born. These included the workers in gold, the makers and painters of statues, the blazoners of saddles, and the makers of embroidered head-dresses. The differentiations between the various trades were minute but carefully respected. There were, for example, three separate kinds of pater-noster makers, who also made buttons; those who worked in bone or leather, those whose beads were made of coral or shells, and the most elegant of all whose beads were worked in amber and jet.[20] Equally there were five separate classifications of hat-makers using flowers, felt, fur, cotton, or peacock feathers.[21]

The bakers and brewers also listed their customs and usages, but there was no universally applied regulation comparable to the Assizes of Bread or Ale in England. The brewers acknowledged their obligation not to adulterate their beer, or to flavour it with such spices as piment or juniper.[22] The bakers were particulary closely controlled by their gild for they were restricted both in their place of residence and their place of sale. The description of the left-over bread which could be sold on Sunday at the Parvis Notre Dame suggests that they had a fair quota of failures, for they were allowed to dispose of bread that was burnt or too hard, or which had risen too high, or had been gnawed by rats or mice.[23] Among the most powerful of the lesser gilds were the criers of wine. These men 'cried', or announced, the price of wine in the street and kept the record of how much was sold. Since every tavern-keeper had to have a crier if he sold wine from an open cask, they were much in demand and had considerable power over the tavernkeepers.[24]

Paris showed many different faces, but the men of the royal household, the many artisans and artists, and even the quarrelsome clerks profited from their close association with the king and the government.

XI

The King's Justice

Louis and his contemporaries did not doubt that the primary duty of a king was justice. Louis was even more conscientious than many of his fellow monarchs in his interpretation of the accepted ideal. The growing importance and recognition of the king's justice, brought about by the steadily increasing centralization of the kingdom, was given impetus by the eager willingness of Louis to give exact justice to all, rich and poor, high and low. It was this concern which led to the acts and innovations which Louis's contemporaries found most startling. The king was not willing merely to abide by the force of custom; he borrowed and adapted from canon law, or Roman law, or from his contemporaries, whatever improvements he thought could usefully serve his kingdom.

It is difficult for us to realize that the power to legislate was not considered an essential attribute of the king during the early part of the Middle Ages. Even in the thirteenth century the concept of 'making law' was not generally accepted. Law was essentially custom, and though it was necessary for a ruler to go back and affirm the good and rightful customs, and perhaps arrange new ways for them to be carried out, these decisions were considered administrative orders rather than new laws. Actual change was often concealed under a cloak of spurious antiquity. By the middle of the reign of Louis IX, we have come to that almost indefinable area where the king is beginning to lay down new principles of law. These were not created by the king alone, but by the king in council, with the approval of his barons and his counsellors, and the making of such *établissements* was hedged by many conditions. Philip of Beaumanoir, the noted legist who had many years of experience as a royal official, described some of the factors which the king had to consider.

> Although the king can make new *établissements*, he must take special care that he makes them for reasonable cause and for the common profit and by the great council, and especially that they be not made against God or good customs.[1]

Philip's *Coutumes de Beauvaisis* were written in the 1280s and were the most famous collection of French law of the time. They illustrate the curious blending and confusion caused by the intermingling of the old feudal structure of customary law in the north with the renascent force of Roman law, and of the written law which was accepted in Languedoc.

There is no real summary of the laws of Louis's reign. The *Etablissements de Saint Louis* is a misleading title; though it is a summary of law and custom made two or three years after the king's death, it is a private work based on the custom of Orléans, Touraine and Anjou.[2] Louis's ordinances were placed at the head of the work and probably gave it its name. These ordinances, which included the banning of trial by battle, certain orders regarding the coinage, the treatment of the Jews, and most famous of all, the ordinance for the reform of the realm, were a mixture of the administrative and the legislative in proportions learnedly disputed by the constitutional historians. Their greatest importance, however, lay in the method of enforcement by the royal courts of justice, and especially the king's own court.

Early in the thirteenth century the royal palace at Paris had become the normal seat of the supreme court of royal justice, and by 1239 we find the first mention of parlement. It is tempting but illusory to insist on the equivalence of the rudimentary parliaments in England with the parlement in France. Both had the same roots, for they sprang from the old *curia regis*: they were the extension of the judicial function of the king as supreme feudal lord giving justice to his vassals while supported by the council of his barons. Unlike the comparable parliamentary development in England, the thirteenth-century parlement in Paris was never able to assert financial control over the king. It never represented the will of the concerted French barons, nor dreamed of imposing its decisions upon the king, for it was essentially the instrument and expression of the king's own will. By the time Louis returned from his crusade parlement emerges from the shadows as a visible institution with its own professional officials and its own characteristic records, the Olim.[3]*

The Olim were the registers of the parlement of Paris, a record of the decisions reached at each meeting. The first compiler was Master John of Montluçon, who was a king's clerk in 1263, serving as a notary, not a judge. His register covers the years from 1254 to 1270, but it is unofficial and incomplete. Some of the most famous of all Louis's cases are not even mentioned and there is no detailed or dated description of the royal ordinances or charters. It is merely Master John's personal summary of some of the judgments given in parlement which particularly interested him, and his notes are occasionally so brief as to be of very little use. Nevertheless, the Olim illustrate the casual and inchoate beginnings of an institution which was to grow in importance and develop into several specialized departments over the centuries.

One of Louis's contemporaries, the Dominican Humbert of the Romans, defines the make-up and function of the parlement of his day.

> The parlements which are held every year at a fixed time and where gather, with the councillors of the crown, a crowd of lords and bishops, have a triple mission: to expedite (judicial) affairs; to receive the accounts of royal officers; and to regulate the general practice of government.[4]

The primary function of parlement was judicial, and the extant lists of its varying members show the preponderant weight of royal officials, legists, and other professional men. The parlement could and did judge both civil and criminal cases and it owed its growth to one of the king's innovations – the banning of trial by battle within the royal domain.

The judicial duel had long been accepted and popular within the framework of feudal law. Trial by battle, which was used with slightly different regulations right up and down the social scale,

*These records were nicknamed the Olim from the first word of the case with which the second book began.

was employed in all kinds of disputes, even over matters of procedure. Its relation to abstract justice was tenuous and the church always opposed it, although the excuse for the procedure was that God would give strength to the man in the right. Louis was not the first secular ruler to ban it: Frederic II had already prohibited it, as had some of the cities of Italy and the Low Countries. The chronicler who comments on the king's decision gives an idea of the extraordinary variety of causes for which trial by battle was employed.

> King Louis did not want battles waged by champions or by knights in the kingdom of France, not for murder, treason, inheritance, or debt, but these were all tried by inquest of prudent and loyal men.[5]

The procedure which was to replace it was known as the inquest in thirteenth-century France. It was a mixture of public and secret procedures: the witnesses swore in the presence of both parties to speak the truth, but their evidence was not heard by both parties, although their deposition was communicated to the accused. This procedure had been suggested by the Lateran Council of 1215 which had adopted it from the Roman law, which also required that the witnesses be questioned in the presence of both parties.[6]

The barons were insulted by the new procedure; they felt it minimized the social distinction between the upper classes and the serfs and lessened their privileges. A contemporary song, probably by an aggrieved baron, echoes the exasperated fury of his class.

> Men of France, there you are, dumbfounded. I say this to all who were born on fiefs. In God's eyes you are no longer free, you have been well separated from your franchises, for you are judged solely by inquest. You have been cruelly deluded and deceived, because you have no defence able to come to your aid. Sweet France! You should no longer be called this but you should be known as a country of slaves, a land of cowards, a kingdom of wretches, exposed time and time again to violence.

The poet insists that he is really loyal to his lord; he merely wants to be sure that his king does not go to the devil for such an appalling innovation.[7]

Louis probably acted against trial by battle by 1258 or as early as 1254,[8] but the ordinance of 1260 formally forbade duels as judicial proof and substituted proof by inquest, although the king specifically limited its enforcement to the lands of the royal domain.[9] The most fruitful result of the king's action was his substitution of a legal method of appeal for the wager of battle in a suspected case of false judgment, for the case was now brought to a superior court for a new trial. The king's own court, as the highest in the realm, became the natural court of appeal from the lower royal courts and also from the principal seignorial courts.

The quantity of work of the king's court as carried out in parlement grew during the reign. Two kinds of judgments were given: *enquêtes* and *arrêts*. The enquête was not the inquest itself, but the decision given after the receiving of the report of an inquest, its examination, and the settlement of the disputed questions of procedure and fact. An arrêt was a decision given by parlement either immediately following the plea or after personal deliberation by those serving as judges. Both could deal with very minor affairs, as well as the important questions of disputed rights and privileges. An inquest could set the proper hours for the vineyard workers of Dun-le-Roi,[10] or settle the issue of the nature of the regalian rights* in Le Puy.[11] There was the judgment given against the knight who had complained of the drop in his income since he no longer received the five shillings he had been accustomed to have for each duel. The knight insisted that he should have five shillings for each inquest which replaced a duel. The court replied quickly that the five shillings had been given to him on condition of his guarding the battlefield, so that 'as he no longer renders any service, he had no right to any indemnity'.[12]

The registers of parlement during Louis's reign show a number of cases in which the king himself intervened: usually when he wished to ensure equity rather than the strict letter of the law. For example, in the case of a woman who had committed suicide by drowning, and whose goods should legally have escheated to the crown, the king intervened to allow her heirs to succeed to all her

*Regalian right was that privilege which put the king in possession of the temporalities of an episcopal see when it fell vacant through death or transfer. In Louis's time, the return of the temporalities was not made until after the new bishop had taken an oath of fidelity. In some cases Louis had a further regalian right of appointment to certain benefices normally in the bishop's gift.

goods and lands, because the woman was not sane.[13] Louis also insisted that a defendant was not to be allowed to refuse to answer to the court on the pretext that the appellant was excommunicate (and therefore incapable of pleading) until the excommunication had been proved[14] – this excuse was often used as a means to deny justice. The king would also change a custom which he felt was excessively harsh. In the province of Touraine, for example, it had been customary for any servant who stole only a loaf of bread, a drink of wine, or a chicken from his lord to be liable to the loss of a limb. Louis abolished this as undue punishment.[15] The most dramatic example of his respect for the spirit rather than the letter of the law was his judgment in the dispute over a document with a broken seal. Lord Renaud of Trie brought to the king's court a royal charter granting him the lands of the deceased countess of Boulogne, but all that remained of the seal was the lower half of the king's legs and the stool on which his feet rested. In the Middle Ages the seal was the essential authenticating element of a document and the necessary proof of its validity. The king's counsellors were unanimous that Louis did not have to carry out the terms of the charter since the seal was broken, but the king insisted on calling for another letter with a complete seal and testing the broken piece against it. It was obvious that the fragment exactly matched the unbroken seal so Louis decided that he could not in conscience withhold the grant, and Renaud received his lands.[16] Louis's characteristic eagerness to exercise the king's justice has been immortalized in Joinville's description.

> Often in the summer he went after Mass to the wood of Vincennes and sat down with his back against an oak tree, and made us sit all around him. Everyone who had an affair to settle could come and speak to him without the interference of the usher or any other official. The king would speak himself and ask, 'Is there any one here who has a case to settle?' All those who had would then stand up and he would say, 'Quiet, all of you, and your cases shall be dealt with in turn.' Then he would call my Lord Peter of Fontaines and my Lord Geoffrey of Villette and say to one of them, 'Now give me your judgment in this case.' When those who spoke for him or for the other party said anything which he saw needed correction he cor-

> rected it himself. Once in the summer I saw him as he went to the gardens in Paris to give judgment for his people. He wore a tunic of natural wool, a sleeveless surcoat of cotton, and a black satin cloak around his shoulders; he wore no cap but his hair was well combed, and on his head he wore a hat of white peacocks' feathers. He had carpets spread so that we could sit about him, and all who had business with him would stand around.[17]

When parlement dealt with great legal issues decision was normally left to the technical competence of the king's learned councillors. Parlement consistently extended the royal prerogative as far as possible, disputing the rights of bishops and abbots, confining the sovereignty of great lords, consolidating and re-emphasizing the king's supremacy.

It is odd that the most famous of all the cases of justice in Louis's reign is known to us only through the chroniclers: there is no mention of the condemnation of Enguerrand of Coucy in the registers of parlement. The case is of particular interest because it demonstrates so clearly the inflexible determination of the king to have his justice apply to the great as well as to the small. The lord of Coucy was related to most of the important barons of the realm through his connection with the farflung and violent family of Dreux and had already often quarrelled with his neighbours, especially those abbots with lands contiguous to his with whom he disputed justice and administration. On this occasion three well-born Flemish boys who had been sent to the abbey of St Nicholas-des-Bois, near Laon, to learn French, had taken their bows and arrows to hunt rabbits in the woods of the abbey. Unwittingly they trespassed on to the woods of the lord of Coucy and were promptly caught by his foresters who put them in gaol for infringing the lord's hunting rights. Enguerrand, without even a formal trial, had all three summarily hanged. The abbot of St Nicholas and the constable of France, a relative of the boys, complained to King Louis. The king ordered the lord of Coucy to appear in his court and when he refused and claimed trial by peers, had him seized and imprisoned in the Louvre until his trial. This seizure shocked the conservative barons, always jealous of their traditional privileges, because it was carried out, not by knights or barons, but merely by the king's armed sergeants, then too, it was also most unusual for a man of such standing to be imprisoned.

When the case was brought to trial Enguerrand of Coucy was supported by most of the important barons of France, while the king was left with only the members of his household. Enguerrand's spokesman insisted that the lord of Coucy did not want to submit himself to an inquest, because the case touched his person, his honour, and his inheritance, but that he was willing to defend himself in trial by battle. The king insisted that one could not proceed by the law of battle when the poor, the churches, or weaker people were concerned. He added that, after all, he was proposing nothing new, but was acting on precedent, and reminded them of Philip Augustus's action in holding an inquest on an accusation of murder against Sir John of Sully, and also seizing his castle for some twelve years. The king refused to listen to the barons' petitions for mercy, and passed a stiff sentence. Enguerrand was condemned to go overseas – this was later commuted to a fine of 12,000 pounds Paris; he lost to the abbey the wood where the boys had been found; he was deprived of high justice dealing with forests and fishponds, that is, he could not imprison or put to death for any infractions of his privileges there; and finally he had to endow several chaplaincies where masses would be said perpetually for the boys' souls.[18]

John of Thourotte, the castellan of Noyon, who had spoken for Enguerrand was appalled by the king's verdict, and said unguardedly that the king might as well have hanged all the barons. Louis heard of his words and sent his sergeants for the outspoken castellan.

> 'What is this, John? Did you say that I would hang my barons? Certainly I would not hang them, but I will chastise them if they misbehave.' John swore that he had not said it and had been betrayed by an evil-wisher, and would purge himself, and the king let him go.[19]

Louis certainly would not have gone so far: the death penalty was unheard of for a baron, except in cases of lèse-majesté or high treason. The weight of the king's verdict was still heavy enough to

11a. Louis reads his prayers while on a journey (from William of St-Pathus, *Life and Miracles of St Louis*)

11b. Death of Louis (from William of St-Pathus, *Life and Miracles of St Louis*)

12a. The scourging of Louis

12b. Louis gathers the bones for burial at Sidon (he is the only one not to hold his nose)

12c. Louis feeds the leprou monk of Royaumont (thes are three drawings of th windows of the sacristy c St Denis destroyed durin the Revolution, included i *Les Monumens de la Monarchi française* by the Benedictin monk, B. de Montfaucon Paris, 1730)

warn the barons that noble birth did not exempt them from the king's justice.

All the evidence shows that the king was particularly heavy-handed towards any who shared his responsibility for justice but did not share his delicate conscience in its proper administration. On several occasions he upheld those who appealed to him against the decision of his brother Charles. One particularly striking example was that of the knight who had lost his case in Charles's court and had then appealed to the king. Charles, angry at this rebuke to his power, had the knight put in prison. When the knight's squire came to the king to ask for justice, Louis called Charles to him and reprimanded him sharply. He reminded him that as king in France he would not in any way offend justice, not even for his brother, and he ordered Charles to set the knight free at once. When the case came up Charles was buttressed by all of his counsellors of Anjou and some of the best men of the law in Paris. The poor knight was overcome at this array of talent, but the king offered him counsel and lawyers equal to those of Count Charles. It was a long case, but the final sentence favoured the knight, and Charles's decision was overturned.[20]

Many of the king's decisions, and those of his trusted counsellors such as Simon of Nesle, illustrate the royal insistence on justice. They also make it clear that this was unpopular with the important and well-born, who felt it an inordinate reproach upon their family honour to have any relation publicly punished, however justifiably. The king was adamant, remembering the advice of his grandfather, Philip Augustus, who had said that 'no man could govern a country well if he could not refuse as boldly and bluntly as he could give'.[21]

The king's reforms were badly needed. A personal appeal, probably addressed to Louis's son, shows the appalling conditions. A poor knight of the county of Beaumont, who had followed Louis to Damietta and Tunis, and fought for Charles of Anjou in Sicily and at Marseilles, had been imprisoned by the provost of Beaumont for allegedly beating a clerk and stealing two of his horses. He had been condemned by the bailli of Senlis and then had appealed to parlement where John of Brienne, the Butler of France, had ordered that he should be let free or tried by the judgment of his peers. Despite this command, and clear proof of his innocence of the horse-stealing, the knight was kept in prison from mid-Lent to Christmas. When he fell desperately ill he requested the sacraments and was refused, so he escaped from prison and fled to sanctuary. He had then returned to prison on the promise of a quick trial, but after another long interval, was still awaiting judgment.[22]

Denial and delay of justice were only too common and difficult to eradicate; men rotted in prison at their own expense. The community of one small town complained that their local bailli 'wished to imprison them at his pleasure without petition, without knowledge of the case, without examination of witnesses, and without any judgment'.[23] No matter how efficient and equitable the king's justice was found to be in parlement or by his own intervention, the great body of Louis's subjects formed their opinion of him and his justice from the actions of the local royal officials and their courts. Louis realized that it was an important part of his responsibility to ensure that his men also gave fair and equitable administration.

XII

The King's Administration

Louis IX had inherited from Philip Augustus the nucleus of an administrative system. During the twelfth century a gradual development of the officials of the crown had kept pace with the enormous growth in the royal domain. At the same time, there remained considerable variations among the different parts of the realm.[1] Normandy especially had a highly organized central government, which in both its legal and financial practices was far more advanced than the rest of the kingdom. The guiding principle behind Louis's concept of administration was the medieval theory that the king's government, whether exercised directly by himself or indirectly by his officials, was an individual duty for which he was personally responsible. The king's conservatism often came into conflict with the nascent royal bureaucracy and the instinctive urge of royal officials to bend every possible effort to the extension of the royal power, using any available means. The possible excesses of his officials weighed heavily on Louis's conscience and his institution of the enquêteurs, merely put into practice his desire to acquit himself justly of his kingly duty.

By the beginning of Louis's reign the main responsibility for the local government of the kingdom was in the hands of royally appointed officials known as baillis or seneschals. The history of their development is long and complicated, since they sprang both from earlier seignorial officials and also from earlier, less supervised, royal officials such as the provosts, who now became subordinates. Generally speaking, the baillis were the chief local officials in the north, and the seneschals in the south, particularly in the newly acquired districts of Languedoc. The bailli or seneschal was the lynchpin of local administration, the visible symbol of royal power: he was appointed and paid by the king, and served as his direct representative. He united in his own person a host of functions since he was judge, chief of police, mobilization officer for the army, administrator of the royal domain in his district, and collector of the royal revenues. It is therefore not surprising to find Beaumanoir, the lawyer who had himself been a bailli, insisting that a bailli needed ten separate virtues, all ruled by wisdom and buttressed by loyalty to his lord.[2]

The baillis of the north had a slightly more peaceful assignment than the seneschals. In the south the nature and duties of the local officials were affected by the different laws and customs of these provinces but, most of all, by the residual bitterness arising from the Albigensian Crusade and the recent extension of the royal power. The seneschal was normally more important and independent than the bailli and, especially in the first half of the reign, was often insufficiently supervised by the distant royal court so that he acted with independent insolence. Peter of Athies, the seneschal of Beaucaire from 1239 to 1241, was the type of all a royal officer should not be. He figures luridly in many of the complaints brought before the enquêteurs and seems to have terrified the district he was supposed to administer. On one occasion a particularly brave bourgeois of Alais reminded him of his function as guardian of the king's justice; Athies turned on him fiercely, 'Say what you like. I would gladly give a hundred marks of silver never to hear the king or queen spoken of any more'.[3] Since the seneschal united the military, administrative, and judicial functions in his district, his use of these wide powers was of immediate concern to the king. After the pacification of the south and the failure of the last revolts, and particularly after the king's return from the crusade, the seneschals were less powerfully entrenched and more carefully supervised by the central curia.

The baillis and seneschals were not normally natives of the regions they administered: they came from the central government and often returned to duties there after their work in the provinces.[4] They were essentially lay career men who had worked their way up the service. Recruited mainly from the lower nobility and the rising bourgeois of the Ile-de-France, they were united by a fiercely aggressive loyalty to the king and his interests. Although they were supposed to administer the royal lands with due respect for the ancient customs and usages of each district, they, of course, attempted, not always successfully, to extend the methods and procedures preferred by the central government. Their annual salaries were generous, a necessary safeguard against corruption and bribery, but success in the king's service offered glittering prospects.

Under the bailli or seneschal were lesser officials whose titles and duties varied slightly in the different sections of the realm. Most were natives of the district they served and many of them, such as the provosts in the north and the bayles in the south, bought their offices at farm. The farming of offices was always an encouragement for graft and corruption, especially as much of the king's revenues passed through the hands of these men. The sergeant was the lowest and most oppressive official. He was an auxiliary and agent of the provost or the bayle and 'combined the duties of policeman and process-server.'[5] The difference between the country of the written, that is Roman, law in the south and the customary law in the north was also marked by a difference in officials. The bailli had a special clerk who served as his secretary: he was often a man of some importance but had no official standing. In the south, the seneschals had royal notaries as a recognized and necessary element in their court. Notaries had been important here since the twelfth century, for to be authentic, acts had to be written and signed by them. By the thirteenth century they were to be found serving all the various jurisdictions, seignorial, ecclesiastical, and municipal; it was in recognition of this tradition that the seneschals appointed specifically royal notaries for the work of the king's court.

During the early years of the reign the main preoccupation of local officials was frequently military. They called up the forces which the king had the right to demand to deal with strictly local revolts, or led contingents to the greater struggles against the count of Brittany, the rebels of Languedoc, or the English king. One of the frequent complaints brought against them was over these military summons, or *chevauchées*, for unscrupulous officials often called the men together when there was no military necessity and then exacted a sum of money in commutation of the service. One case before parlement even accuses the lord of Nesle of having summoned the men of Escuvell to a *chevauchée* and then used the body so gathered to make the lists and dig ditches for a tournament.[6]

The bailli or seneschal was also the chief financial officer of his district: one of his most important duties was to collect all the various revenues owed to the king and to render an accounting at Paris three times a year. These financial terms, usually All Saints, Candlemas, and Ascension, roughly coincided with the meetings of parlement. The bailli's or seneschal's accounts listed receipts as well as expenses. In receipts, the official distinguished between the *racheta*, sums paid by feudal lords to commute feudal obligations; *demesna*, the revenue coming from the king's domain land and his feudal rights there; and *expleta*, revenues from the royal justice, and especially the fines levied for offences. As well, he might have unusual receipts to report, such as the confiscation of the goods of condemned heretics or the returns from special levies. From these receipts the royal official was bound to provide for the necessary expenses of the region in his charge. These included *liberationes*, the wages of officers apart from the bailli or seneschal himself; *feoda*, rents assigned as fixed revenues (these were mostly pensions ordered at the king's pleasure); *elemosina*, alms to the poor and to religious houses; and *minuta expensa*, those miscellaneous and irregular charges which could not be listed elsewhere, After making up a complete balance sheet the official, at the time of his accounting, then remitted the excess of his receipts over his expenses.

The kingdom of France had at this time no one central official charged with finances. During the reign of Louis IX the Treasurer of the Paris Temple served as a banker for royal funds. He took in the receipts, and paid the expenses, but had no share in the administration. The Treasurer was overseen by a king's clerk who served as a rudimentary comptroller, acting in the king's interest. Not only the baillis and the seneschals had to present their accounts to the Treasurer; although they included within their overall account the accounts of their lesser officials, there were many other officials who had to account directly. Those sent on specific missions rendered an accounting for their expenses when they returned. The treasurer of the household, as we have seen, accounted at every term for the moneys received.

The mayors of royal towns also had to come to Paris to give an accounting for their year of office. The mayor had to state the funds as he found them when he entered office, and then the receipts and expenses of the year. These were very miscellaneous, including expenses for sending representatives to parlement or to deal with higher officials, as well as for ceremonial presents. The king wanted a strict supervision of the towns' accounts, because they were heavily taxed during his reign. They made lump sum payments for the crusade, for the king's ransom, for the expenses of the peace with England, and many of them found themselves heavily in debt and cumbered with the payment of interest[7] The financial difficulties of the town of Noyon (Oise), are typical. By 1260 Noyon had given the king 1,500 pounds for his first crusade and another 500 when it heard from the queen that Louis had need of money overseas. When the king returned Noyon lent him 600 pounds, but the king only returned 100, so – making a virtue out of necessity – the town gave him the rest. On the conclusion of the peace treaty with England Noyon had to raise another 1,200 pounds and all these sums were in addition to the 200 pounds they paid the king each year for their commune. Noyon had also been forced to shoulder further heavy expenses when Charles of Anjou campaigned in Hainault, as he had required their military support as well as provisions. Count Charles had also borrowed 1,200 pounds, and had only paid back 300 – this was not unusual as Charles owed money in many directions.[8]

Although the financial data on the reign of St Louis is fragmentary and incomplete there is enough to suggest the main lines of official practice and to show that there were gradual changes throughout the reign. As the revenues from royal justice constantly increased new local officials emerged who, though subordinate to the bailli or the seneschal, were specifically charged with financial affairs. Normandy had always been unusual among the great fiefs, for it was the only one with a specific Exchequer, which not only had clearly marked financial functions, but also served as the court for purely Norman cases. This highly organized administration was continued after Normandy was annexed to the royal domain. The Master of the Exchequer was the leading official of all Normandy: during Louis's reign he was usually non-Norman and trained at the central curia. During the latter years of the king's reign the Master was chosen from among the king's most eminent advisers, such as Archbishop Eudes Rigaud of Rouen; John of Brienne, Butler of France; and Matthew of Vendôme, the abbot of St Denis.[9]

But the most important function of the bailli or seneschal and the one which was to gain in prominence, was that of judge. Because he directly represented the king, his court was both a first court for royal cases, that is, cases where the nature of the offence or the status of the person came directly under royal jurisdiction; and the primary court of appeal in matters already decided in a seignorial court but referred for further judgment to the king. Besides decisions on matters originating in his own territory the growing use of inquests meant that the bailli or seneschal was often asked to carry out these inquiries for the king, for example in cases of inheritance and lordship. As the king's justice became more available and more popular, the work of these courts multiplied, and new officials were created. With the growing popularity of parlement as a court of appeal, the baillis and seneschals were also required to attend each session of parlement to defend the cases of their district. For prompt justice the king ordered special days for hearings of the cases of each bailliage and seneschalcy; this also shortened the absence of the officials from their district.[10]

It needs to be emphasized that these administrative and financial developments were the natural growth of a living structure, brought about by the pressure of events and duties, not planned in advance by a central official core. King Louis was perhaps less of a conscious innovator than other great medieval monarchs. His ideals of justice and feudal loyalty were static and, in a sense, old-fashioned; they often conflicted with his determination to extract the last iota of the royal rights. His treatment of the towns was strict and financially harsh. He did not encourage any development of municipal self-government, although he honoured the charters already granted.

The king's personal contribution to the improvement of the

royal administration was his determination that the machinery should run equitably as well as smoothly. One of the first things the king did after his return from the crusade was to act on the grievances his newly created enquêteurs had uncovered. They had harvested a fine collection of complaints. They had travelled widely over the realm in 1247 and 1248 in twos or threes, and among them were usually one or two friars and sometimes a secular clerk or knight as well. Their procedure is made clear in occasional reports. They allowed a statement by the complainant, then an examination of sworn witnesses for him on various points of fact. Sworn witnesses for the other side were then heard and both sets of witnesses were asked about their motives: were they inspired by love, hate, or hope of payment? Were they persons of good repute and not excommunicated or a known offender against the law? The enquêteurs also made it very clear that they were empowered to hear complaints against the king as well.[11] In a few cases the judgment on the complaint is given with the original statement and there are some lists of restitutions made, but these are scattered and show no consistent pattern.

The collection of complaints is one-sided for it contains only the grievances. It does not tell us how many of the accusations were unjustified or exaggerated. Its great value lies in the light it throws on contemporary reaction to events and people. The dislocations caused by the quartering of the king's forces in an unprepared town are shown by the poor widow of Chinon who complained that the sergeant of the king's bailli in Touraine and Anjou had taken her coverlet and pillow to the castle for the king's use at the time of the campaign in Poitou, and despite frequent pleas, she had never been able to recover them.[12] The aura of importance that surrounded even the lesser royal officials is illuminated by the appalled dismay of the Hospitallers at Compagnolles, near Béziers, who had been at dinner in the refectory when the *viguier*, Bernard Mabile, arrived at their convent. Not knowing of his arrival, they had not left the table to greet him, and for this affront they had been forced to give him an ox, a fat sheep, and thirty shillings.[13] The struggles against the king's enemies during the early years of the reign are echoed in the numerous complaints of destruction of goods by the king's army or his officials and of unnecessary summons for military service. In the south there were many more complaints, with more justification: some of the damages went back to the time of Simon de Montfort and the first fury of the Albigensian Crusade, others bore witness to the rapacity and independence of the various royal officials, as well as their determination to break the power of feudal lordships and independent jurisdictions.

The evidence these reports provide is very valuable for an understanding of the many specific details of the system of government, but it also abounds in vignettes which make these thirteenth-century common people extraordinarily real to us. There was the orphan girl who sought the withdrawal of the king's gallows from her one field, of which the rent was not sufficient to provide her with even the 'necessities of a miserable life'. The crowds coming to executions trampled her young grain and the bodies left to rot on the gallows, which had been put there 'against God and all reason', made it impossible for her to get anyone to work the field.[14] There was the case of Deodatus, a poor man, whose horses with their burden of bagged grain had been unlawfully seized by an official. The horses had been returned, but not the grain or the sacks. Deodatus was afraid to make his plea in public, because of reprisals, since he was a poor man burdened by a large family, but he begged 'the most illustrious king of France that for the love of God and the increase of piety, he should please have restored to him the grain and the sacks'.[15] In the case of Reginald the Apothecary of Poitiers, he claimed damages for unjust arrest and imprisonment. He had spent two years in gaol; his expenses there and gaining his freedom cost him fifty pounds, although no one could prove the truth of the accusation that he made deadly poisons.[16] Jacob Peter of Arles insisted that he was the guest in a house at Nîmes but was arrested on charges of adultery. Against a flurry of witnesses the royal official asserted stolidly that he had found the man's breeches under the coverlet and 'the mark of two heads on the pillow'![17]

Although Louis continued to send out occasional teams of enquêteurs during the remaining years of his reign, and his brother Alphonse did the same in his lands, their impact is already obvious in the ordinance of 1254 which was reissued and slightly rearranged in 1256. This royal enactment, often called the Great Ordinance, was intended to reform the administration of the realm. From the confused, petty, but often well-founded complaints of the aggrieved citizens, the king had learned the most common offences of his officials. By means of the ordinance he attempted to tighten his control over them, to insist on higher standards, and to preserve them from the most obvious opportunities for bribery and corruption.

All officials were required to take an oath, 'to swear to save and maintain our rights in good faith nor to take away nor diminish nor even impede the rights of others'. Those who broke their oath were liable to prosecution in the king's court, or by their immediate superior. To make the solemn nature of the oath even more evident, it was to be taken at a public court, so that officials would be constrained by fear of public shame as well as by good faith. Major restrictions were put on the freedom of action of the baillis and seneschals who so easily overawed the people within their power. They were not to accept gifts except fruit, or wine, or provisions to a value of not more than ten shillings. In turn, the baillis and seneschals were not to give gifts to the officials of the royal court or the enquêteurs, in hopes of avoiding punishment for their evil-doing. They were not to borrow more than twenty pounds, not to buy land within their district during their term of office, not to marry off their relatives or place them in religious houses there. When they had finished their term they were supposed to remain another fifty days in the district so that they could answer to any complaints.

Other articles dealt with abuses in the administration of justice. There were not to be too many sergeants: when these officials had to exercise their functions at a distance they were to have letters from their superiors, so that the people could know of their commission. No one was to be imprisoned for debt, except to the king, and no one was to be detained personally if he could give bail, except for flagrant crime. Officials were forbidden to use trickery or terror to force people to make a settlement: fines were only to be levied in open court. Officials were not to afflict subjects with new exactions, customs, or burdens, nor to order *chevauchées* as a way of raising money.

Other articles dealt with what we would consider matters of private morality, but the king, especially after the crusade, felt he should require them of his subjects by legislation. Royal officials were to abstain from blasphemy, from games of dice or chance, from fornication and the frequenting of taverns. They were to expel all prostitutes from the fields as well as the towns, and anyone who knowingly rented a house to a prostitute was liable to have it confiscated. No one was to take a horse against the owner's will, except for the king's business, and then he should not take the horse of a poor man, a merchant, or an ecclesiastic.

The Great Ordinance also reissued the regulations about the Jews made early in Louis's reign. It suggested, without requiring, the use of the inquest in criminal matters.[18] It covered an extremely wide field and its main clauses were reiterated throughout his reign. The ordinance enshrined many of Louis's ideals and made unmistakably clear that he wanted fair and just rule, and that even powerful officials would have to answer in the king's court for their misdeeds. The other great duty of a Christian king was peace, and it was to the settlement of outstanding quarrels that Louis turned next.

XIII

France and England 1254–1270

Peace with justice dominated Louis IX's ideal of kingship and his relations with England illustrate this. After his return from crusade the king felt that a firm treaty should replace the continuous series of temporary truces. Louis's desire for peace had previously been frustrated by the increasingly anachronistic English claims in France. Henry III had refused to recognize the conquests of Philip Augustus and the official royal style still proclaimed the king of England as duke of Normandy, count of Anjou and Maine, as well as duke of Aquitaine. Even the dismal failure of the English campaign in Poitou in 1242 had not forced Henry to abandon his groundless hopes for the return of his French lands, although it had stopped his attempts at open war.

An occasion favoured Louis's efforts to open negotiations with England for a permanent peace soon after his return. Henry III and Eleanor had been in Gascony during the autumn celebrating the marriage of their son Edward to Eleanor of Castile. Henry was anxious to arrange the formal burial of the remains of his mother Isabel, the fiery wife of Hugh of La Marche, in the Plantagenet chapel at Fontevrault. As an inveterate pilgrim, he was also hoping to visit the tomb of St Edmund Rich, the late archbishop of Canterbury, in the Cistercian abbey of Pontigny. Henry was always particularly interested in seeing any new developments in art or architecture – and was avid to see for himself the wonders of Paris. He sought and was granted Louis's permission to cross French territory on his way to Pontigny, and to return by way of Paris.

Louis surrounded by an elegant company, went to Orléans in November and then rode out to Chartres to meet the English retinue as they returned from St Edmund's shrine. The cathedral was practically complete and Henry must have been overawed by its majesty dominating the fertile plain. Even on a dark autumn day the brilliance of the windows and the magnificence of its sculptures would have fascinated and impressed him. This encounter of the two kings was really a state visit with the usual medieval additions: the towns and roads were decorated with branches and hangings, and the crowds turned out to greet the glittering cavalcade with songs, dances, and lighted candles. Slowly they rode back to Paris where Henry and the English company were installed in the Temple. The kings exchanged state banquets, dazzling affairs which Matthew Paris described in loving detail. They gave each other valuable gifts and Henry received the elephant which the sultan of Egypt had given Louis. Henry was profoundly impressed by the elegance of the many-storeyed plastered houses, as well as by the beauties of the Sainte Chapelle, which a contemporary song suggests that he would have liked to roll off in a cart.[1] The English scholars at the university of Paris joined in the celebrations. Freed from lectures and dressed in their best, they paraded through the streets with lighted candles, singing and playing musical instruments.

There was an atmosphere of a family reunion, especially since the widowed countess of Provence, Beatrice of Savoy, and her four married daughters were brought together. Like other family reunions, this one had undercurrents of jealousy and bad feeling. Marguerite, queen of France, and Eleanor, queen of England, were genuinely glad to see each other after the long years of separation. Sanchia, wife of Richard of Cornwall, and Beatrice, the youngest and the wife of Charles of Anjou, were a little piqued at their elder sisters' higher social position. The three older sisters joined in objecting to Beatrice's sole inheritance of the county of Provence, as they felt they had been unfairly treated by their father's will. But they concealed the bad feeling.[2]

King Louis had been motivated by more than simple courtesy and family feeling: his primary concern was for a firm peace and a legal settlement of the *de facto* French possession of Normandy, Anjou, Maine and Poitou. Louis emphasized to Henry that, because of their marriage to two sisters, they should be as brothers, and implied that he was open to some negotiation on the English claims. Whether or not Matthew Paris is accurate in his highly emotional rendering of the affecting parting scene between the two kings,[3] it is evident that a necessary first step had been taken. The two kings had met face to face, and Henry, generous and easily swayed, had been impressed by the charm and brilliant hospitality of his brother-in-law. The visit had created a climate of good feeling which helped to reinforce the pressure of outside events and finally produce a settlement.

The 'Sicilian Business', as it was known in England, was the real force which speeded the peace treaty. The pope was feudal overlord of the kingdom of Sicily. After the death of Frederic II, Innocent, and then Alexander, tried to bestow the Sicilian crown on any prince who would pay the expenses of the papal war against Frederic's heirs. The glamorous but empty offer was turned down by Richard of Cornwall, who foresaw the extremely high costs involved. Henry, less cautious and foreseeing, happily accepted the crown for his younger son, Edmund, thinking only of the prestige and glory. The English king neglected to consider the implied financial burden and failed to consult with his barons before his decision, but by 1257 he had begun to discover the enormously heavy bill which the pope was tendering along with the crown. The financial demands of Alexander IV for support in the war against Manfred were far beyond Henry's resources, unless he received generous aid from his barons, and this they were unwilling to give. The pope hoped that a settlement of the longstanding dispute between England and France might free English energies – and money – for the Sicilian affair.

There were several English embassies to Louis in the course of 1257; their members were distinguished, but no firm conclusions were reached.[4] The pope, anxious for success, encouraged new negotiations. Even when the last English embassy returned home at Candlemas 1258, it left behind the abbot of Westminster to observe directly the discussions of the French mid-Lent parlement. The specific terms suggested at this time have not survived, but they were probably similar to the later agreement and included the clause which was to delay the treaty's ratification drastically. The controversial clause included a demand for a separate, personal renunciation of any claims in France by Henry's brother and sister, Richard of Cornwall and Eleanor, countess of Leicester and wife of Simon de Montfort. The French terms were discussed at the English parliament of April 1258 when external pressures had become too strong for Henry to resist. The papal representatives had renewed Alexander's demands for military and financial contributions to the Sicilian campaign. They insisted that Henry should conclude a peace treaty with the French king and suggested that, as one of its terms, Louis might be asked to pay for the support of a certain number of knights, who could then be used in Sicily. Since the English barons had categorically refused to pay for the support of the Sicilian affair and they were now moving towards the formulation of the Provisions of Oxford, hostile to the king's interests, this suggestion looked tempting and Henry decided to negotiate on the basis of Louis's proposals.

On May 8 Simon de Montfort, Guy and Geoffrey of Lusignan, Peter of Savoy, and Hugh Bigod (brother of the Earl Marshal), or any three of them, were appointed to negotiate the treaty and take the required oaths. During the Middle Ages a king never swore personally to keep the terms of a treaty except in the actual presence of the other king. Instead the negotiators appointed were given letters of proxy empowering them to enter upon peace talks and to swear on the king's soul – the usual form of oath in such cases. The English negotiators were also given power to swear that the king would do his best to procure the desired renunciations by Richard of Cornwall and Eleanor. After receiving their instructions and powers the English envoys, accompanied by the archbishop of Tarentaise and other papal envoys who wanted to make progress reports to the pope from Paris, left London. The French Whitsun parlement was sitting during the last week of May,[5] and as it took about twelve days for envoys to travel from London to Paris, the English embassy should have arrived soon after its opening. They seem to have plunged immediately into their mission with their French counterparts, Alphonse of Brienne, count of Eu, and Simon of Clermont, lord of Nesle, who was particularly trusted by Louis. Discussions went well and within eight days the text of the articles of peace was agreed on by the two parties.

A copy of the articles was then deposited in the Temple under the seals of the archbishop of Tarentaise and Eudes Rigaud, archbishop of Rouen. The provisions called for the renunciation of the English claims to Normandy, Anjou, Touraine, Maine, and Poitou, not only by Henry and his two sons but also by his brother Richard of Cornwall, and his sister Eleanor and her two sons. At a formal meeting on May 28 Simon de Montfort, Peter of Savoy and Hugh Bigod took the oaths that Henry would keep the articles, while the French negotiators did the same for Louis. Before the peace could come into effect, there were still some stumbling-blocks. The agreement was not to become effective until Henry had done homage to Louis, and he and his sons had taken their personal oaths to keep the articles of the peace. Henry was committed to the observance of the peace if it was accepted by the French king before Candlemas 1259 and it was agreed that Louis, Henry and Richard of Cornwall, now king of the Romans, should meet at Cambrai on November 25 to ratify and publish the treaty. Although the first obstacles had been so easily overcome the remaining difficulties were to occupy another year and a half.

The treaty of Corbeil with Aragon, which was also negotiated during May 1258, was a much simpler and easier settlement. There had been several points at issue between King Louis and King James of Aragon. The Aragonese king held the lordship of the wealthy city of Montpellier by inheritance from his mother and used it as a pretext for involvement in the affairs of much of Languedoc. Aragon had also encouraged the Albigensians, and King James himself had helped Raymond of Toulouse and the other rebels during the campaigns in Poitou and the south. Louis was anxious to avoid further trouble in Languedoc by lessening the possible points of conflict. By the terms of the Treaty of Corbeil, Aragon gave up its claims to lands in southern France, including Carcassonne, Nîmes, and the counties of Milhau and Toulouse, while Louis renounced any French claims to the disputed district bordering on the Pyrenees, including Roussillon and the counties of Barcelona and Urgel. Although they would not have thought of it in such terms, both kings were returning to that natural frontier, the Pyrenees. At the same time as Aragonese proctors at Corbeil swore to observe the treaty, arrangements were made to seal the agreement by a marriage between Philip, Louis's second son, and Isabella of Aragon. Although she was to be handed over to the French that autumn at Montpellier, they were only to be married after she had reached the age of twelve.[6] In mid-July King James ratified the work of his proctors and at the beginning of December Alexander IV granted the papal dispensation for the marriage of Philip and Isabella, necessary because of relationship within the forbidden degrees.[7]

Meanwhile the peace treaty with England was becoming still further involved in the English domestic upheaval. Henry was not present at Cambrai to join in the solemn ratification and publication of the treaty, for the barons would not allow him to leave England and their surveillance. They sent their most distinguished envoys instead, Simon de Montfort, Roger Bigod, and the bishops of Worcester and Lincoln, but King Louis refused to meet them, and was not convinced that his brother-in-law was acting freely. Louis therefore sent envoys to the English court at the beginning of February 1259 to be assured both of Henry's good faith and of his agreement with the actions of his negotiators. The oath to keep the articles of peace was renewed in Henry's presence on February 9, and the following day the envoys received the solemn renunciations of Richard of Cornwall and his son. On February 24 King Henry himself, in the presence of the French king's envoys, renounced all his claims to Normandy, Anjou, Maine, Touraine, and Poitou.

There remained only two final stumbling-blocks – the renunciations required of Edward, Henry's oldest son, and of Eleanor, the king's sister. Edward, although reluctant, took the oath by the end of May 1259 but Eleanor continued intransigent. Henry, buffeted by his barons, plagued by the demands of the pope and the obstinacy of his sister, explained plaintively to Alexander and Louis that he had been unable to arrive at any settlement with Eleanor. She was using this clause of the peace treaty to advance her own financial claims. She felt that her brother had treated her unfairly for many years over her dower rights, and she would insist on compensation before she agreed to the treaty. She was so obdurate that finally two forms of the treaty were drawn up, one with her agreement and one without. The history of the wranglings and arbitrations of the summer of 1259 is confused and unilluminating, but by the end of October the treaty was ratified, although with the omission of the article concerning Eleanor. The formal meeting between the two kings was fixed for the end of November at Paris and Henry sailed from England on November 14.

The French parlement met from November 10 to 23[8] and had completed its business by the time Henry arrived at St Denis on November 25. Louis made every effort to mark Henry's visit with suitable formality. The French king, accompanied by the archbishop of Rouen who had been intimately involved in the treaty negotiations, went to meet the English king and his retinue at St Denis where Henry was honoured with a solemn procession by the monks. The following day both kings and their companies went on to Paris where Henry was welcomed by the citizens with another solemn procession at Notre Dame.[9] Louis was still not satisfied since agreement had not been reached with Eleanor, and he wanted to be quite sure that there was no legal loophole to cast doubt on the validity of the French title to these lands. With his help a compromise solution was finally reached on December 3: Henry agreed to leave in Louis's hands 15,000 marks of the money due him by the treaty as a pledge of his settlement of his debt to his sister. Eleanor now made her formal renunciation the following day, and her husband renounced any claims he might have to the Montfort family lands in Normandy or the conquests in Languedoc.[10] Archbishop Eudes Rigaud solemnly proclaimed the treaty in the orchard of the king's palace, in the presence of both kings and of a glittering assembly of the leading men of both kingdoms.

The final terms of the treaty provided for the abandonment by the English king, his heirs and relations, of all their rights in Normandy, Anjou, Maine, Touraine, and Poitou. In return, Henry received several conditional gifts – Saintonge south of the Charente, after the death of the count of Poitiers; the territory of the Agenais, if it escheated to the French king after the death of Jeanne of Toulouse, and until then a yearly rent; the French king's personal holdings in the dioceses of Limoges, Cahors, and Périgueux; and the territory of Quercy, if the English king could prove his claim to it. For these lands, and his holdings in Gascony, the English king was to do liege homage to the king of France and be recognized as one of the peers of France. In addition, Louis agreed to give Henry the sum of money necessary to support five hundred knights for two years: they were to be used for the service of God and the church, or to the profit of the kingdom of England.[11]

The treaty was greeted without enthusiasm by either side. The dream of the old territories in France died hard among the more ebullient English chroniclers, and Joinville recorded the complaints of the French councillors who accused their king of having given too much away. Louis's reasoning was idealistic, but it also had practical results. The king insisted that he wanted to have peace between his children and Henry's, for they were first cousins, and that he had also gained by the English king's acceptance of the tie of homage.[12] The old notion of homage as an essential personal link no longer compelled most men, but its importance remained in matters of law, since appeals could always be carried from the court of the vassal to the court of the lord. The terms of the Treaty of Paris unwittingly provided much material for legal quibbling: the continued appeal of cases from the English officials in the disputed territories to the parlement at Paris paved the way for the further increase of French influence and domination over the remaining fragments of English territory and also reinforced the pre-eminent position of the parlement of Paris.

In 1259 the situation in England between the king and the barons was uncomfortable. The king chafed at the control over his actions and extravagances which the baronial council insisted on exercising under the Provisions of Oxford, and the friendly atmosphere of the French court was a pleasant change. Henry gladly spent all of December there, arranging the final details of the marriage of his daughter Beatrice to John of Brittany, and the wedding was duly solemnized during his visit. Just after Henry had reluctantly begun his return journey early in January. Louis, the oldest son and heir of the French king, suddenly died, and Henry returned to express his sympathy. The body of the young prince was taken to Royaumont for burial and Henry helped to carry the coffin – a scene immortalized in the carving surrounding the young prince's tomb.*

It soon became obvious that the most immediately valuable article of the treaty for the hard-pressed English king was the money to be paid him for the support of the five hundred knights. Despite papal hopes Henry had no intention of sending them to Sicily. Even after the funeral of Prince Louis, Henry did not return to London where he was expected for the February parliament, but remained in France hiring knights to reinforce his position in England. He used the money promised him by the treaty and by the middle of April he had already received 25,000 pounds *tournois* of the sum owing him, adding another 15,000 pounds by summer.[14] Henry's finances were always chaotic and his struggles with the barons made them even more confused. Henry looked to Louis for help and support, moral as well as financial, and Louis was intimately concerned in the continuing struggle between Henry and his barons.

Nevertheless, Louis would not share Henry's spiteful attempts at vengeance against one of the leading barons. In the summer of 1260 when Henry endeavoured to have Simon de Montfort tried on a whole series of royal complaints, Louis sent Eudes Rigaud to London to see Henry and attempt to smooth the matter over. Louis had a real interest in Simon since the Montfort family were important barons of the Ile-de-France, and Amaury, Simon's older brother, had been Constable of France. Simon himself had frequently been at the French court, while he was seneschal for the English king in Gascony, as well as during the long-drawn-out negotiations for the treaty. The numerous personal ties which enlivened and complicated international relations during the Middle Ages trapped Louis, Henry, and Simon in a familiar net. Even in his attempt to resolve peacefully the issues between Henry and Simon the French king picked an ambassador who was a personal friend of Simon's, and knew all the complicated negotiations

*This particular section of the prince's tomb is now to be found in the Père Lachaise cemetery in Paris where, surprisingly, it forms a part of the tomb erected to Heloise and Abelard during the last century. The main part of the tomb with its handsome effigy was moved to St Denis from Royaumont after the French Revolution.[13]

over the peace treaty. Rigaud gave Simon's son Amaury a prebend in his cathedral at Rouen during this voyage, perhaps a mark of the French friendship and support.[15] The archbishop's intervention had some success, for Henry abandoned his case against Simon, at least for the time being.

Louis's involvement in English affairs continued throughout the barons' revolt: his aid was constantly sought by the parties, who valued his prestige and reputation for impartiality. Personal questions as well as state issues constantly demanded arbitration, the preferred medieval panacea for all disputes, and not only Louis, but also other members of his court, were called upon. For example, in January 1261 Henry agreed to submit to Louis's arbitration all the matters at dispute between himself and Simon and Eleanor. If Louis could not serve, then Queen Marguerite or Peter le Chambellan, one of Louis's most devoted and respected officials, could be substituted.[16]

The continuing intrusion of personal quarrels complicated and aggravated affairs of state. Louis held a remarkably even balance in his relations with England despite the emotional involvement of Queen Marguerite, and the presence of Queen Eleanor and other supporters of Henry at the French court. He was a brake on the high-handed petulance and secretive evasiveness of Henry and frequently exhorted his brother-in-law to deal fairly and openly with his barons, not prejudicing his case by disregarding his royal obligations. Louis also mitigated the wrath of Henry against Simon de Montfort when, in the autumn of 1262, the English king brought to the French court his complaints against his arrogant opponent. Although Henry's illness interrupted the case before any conclusion was reached, Louis once more urged Henry to come to some compromise with de Montfort, and he allowed Simon's wife to bring a suit in parlement against the count of La Marche and his Lusignan brothers over a disputed inheritance in Angoulême.

This equitable approach, and his continued efforts to make peace, resulted in 1263 in both Henry and the barons agreeing to submit all the disputes between them to Louis's final arbitration. But by now the personal quarrels in England had been engulfed in the struggle over the principles which divided king and barons, and which were embodied in the Provisions of Oxford. The Provisions were an extraordinary innovation. Under their terms the king was not left free to rule according to his own will and the dictates of the law, but was checked and controlled by a council of twenty-four of his barons who had the right to 'ordain, rectify, and reform the state of the realm according to what seemed expedient to the honour of God, the faith of the king, and the utility of the realm.'[17]

Looking back on the contemporary currents of thought and practice it is hard to understand what impelled the barons, led by Simon de Montfort, to insist so strongly on the arbitration of Louis. The ideal of limited monarchy, which the Provisions incorporated in a fumbling and incomplete way, was not then generally accepted. The theorists, Bracton, Beaumanor, and even Aquinas, all insisted that the king was subject to the rule of law but that his control was not in the hands of any of his subjects – he answered not to them, but to God. The Provisions had already been condemned by two popes, Alexander IV and Urban IV, as abridging the king's proper powers and rights, a concession he could not make. Louis's own ideal of kingship defined the duties of a king most strictly, but insisted equally firmly on the divine right of kingship and the king's essential and undivided responsibility for his subjects and the government of the realm. Louis had always dealt firmly with his own recalcitrant barons as well, he seems to have had a certain fondness for the improvident and incompetent Henry. There was the question too of the queen's influence. Louis had allowed the English queen and many of her followers refuge at the French court, and Marguerite continually pleaded her sister's cause, though Louis was accustomed to the ardent political partisanship of his queen, and had withstood it on many occasions. The king was undoubtedly more moved by the papal condemnation of the Provisions and particularly by the partiality of the papal legate appointed to settle the affair. Guy Fulcod had been one of Louis's own counsellors: a lawyer before he entered the church, Guy had served both the king and Alphonse of Poitiers. The legate, now the cardinal of Sabina and elected pope on February 5, 1265, was irrevocably opposed to the baronial party. His commission, issued by Urban IV from Orvieto at the end of

November 1263, gave him extraordinary powers and faculties, including even the right to call persons to appear before him overseas, and to preach a crusade against prelates and nobles of the realm who rebelled against the king or the legate.[18]

All these factors must have weighed with Louis as he listened to the appeals of the proctors on both sides. Because the parties had agreed to arbitration in a foreign court the procedure was not that of either the French or the English courts, but followed the new civil procedure just being defined for cases which really required some form of international law. On both sides the technical pleading was done by those trained in the universities in this new method. The chief of the baronial pleaders was Thomas of Cantilupe, who was well known to Louis, and possibly to the legate. He had been at the university of Paris, where Louis had come to visit him, studied law at the school of Orléans, and been named a papal chaplain at the Council of Lyons in 1245. But personal friendship was of no use, the baronial case was doomed.[19]

On January 23, 1264, King Louis gave his award at Amiens in all the matters disputed between Henry and the English barons. Louis upheld Henry in almost every particular. The Mise of Amiens declared the Provisions null and void, emphasizing that the pope had already declared them quashed, and annulled and absolved all concerned from their oaths to them. The king repealed and refused the claim of the barons that the kingdom of England should only be governed by natives, but allowed that the king of England might call to his council whatever natives or aliens seemed useful to him. Most important, for this was the cornerstone of royal power, Louis insisted that Henry had the right to name and remove officials at every level, from the chief justice and the chancellor to the sheriffs. In Louis's own words the king of England was to 'have full power and unrestricted rule within his kingdom'. There was only one cautious clause by which Louis claimed that he did not 'wish or intend in any way to derogate from royal privileges, charters, liberties, establishments, and praiseworthy customs of the kingdom of England existing before the time of the same provisions'.[20]

Controversy has continued to swirl over the exact meaning of Louis's award at Amiens and whether he really intended to deny so completely the validity of the barons' case. When Louis returned to his brother monarch the right to choose his own officials without consultation, he acted according to contemporary principles and it would have been unrealistic to expect him to ignore them. It has been suggested that the French king did not really set himself up as judge of the whole complicated controversy between the English king and his barons, which is summarized in the phrase *negotia regis et regni*, 'the business of the king and of the realm', and which dealt with the fundamental philosophy and practice of government. According to this view, when Louis admitted that the 'liberties, charters, and customs of England' should be respected, he merely denounced the form of the Provisions of Oxford, over which there was much controversy even in England, and did not attempt to deal with the root of the matter.[21] In any case, the Mise of Amiens was from the moment of its pronouncement a dead letter. King Henry rejoiced in the formal renewal of all his royal powers; Pope Urban was delighted with Louis's reinforcement of his own annulment of the Provisions; but the rebellious barons of England paid no attention at all to the award. The English chroniclers ascribed Louis's decisions to various causes, including the evil influence of the two queens working his sympathies. Whatever the reason the Mise of Amiens, far from settling the disturbed state of England, insured the outbreak of civil war in the early spring.

Despite Amiens Henry realized that his difficulties in his realm were by no means over. He was still relying heavily on the large sums of money that were being paid to him under the terms of the treaty of Paris. In January 1264 he stated that he had already received 76,000 pounds in advance for the money owed to him for the support of the knights, although the total sum had not been fixed. In February Henry designated his wife and his strongest supporters at the French court, Peter of Savoy and John Mansel, to receive the rest of the money for the knights, a sum which by then had been set at 58,000 pounds *tournois*. They were also to raise whatever money they could by pawning the king's jewels.[22] As the tempo of the civil war increased, and especially after the royal rout at Lewes, the royalist party sought desperately to raise further moneys in France. In August 1264 Queen Eleanor ceded to Louis for 20,000 pounds all the rights which the English king had gained in Limoges, Cahors, and Périgueux by the treaty of Paris. There was an added penalty of 10,000 pounds if King Henry did not ratify the act. The 20,000 pounds were paid back in the spring of 1266, but Louis reserved his right to the 10,000 pounds specified as penalty.[23]

The papal legate maintained his residence in France, for the rebellious barons refused to admit him or papal bulls. The French court also continued to shelter Eleanor of Provence, who tried desperately to rally an invasion force and to gather men and ships to rescue her husband. Louis did not aid her manœuvres when they went against his conception of justice, and he intervened on the other side, insisting that Alphonse of Poitiers should release some English subjects from Bayonne whom he had imprisoned on Queen Marguerite's demand and at Eleanor's request.[24] After their success at Lewes, the leaders of the barons also turned once more to Louis and his closest advisers to try and achieve peace, but with no success.

Even after the battle of Evesham had ended the rule of Simon de Montfort and re-established Henry on his throne, Louis's influence was used constructively to achieve reasonable treatment for the rebels and the successful pacification of England. Louis had learned from the conciliatory tactics of his mother. He continued to encourage Henry to be equally generous, but the English king was suspicious and vengeful. But the influence of Louis and the newly appointed legate Ottobuono, did have some softening effect, especially in one notable case. After the death of Simon de Montfort at Evesham, his wife and children were most bitterly pursued by Henry who could never forgo his rancour against them, and never forgave Eleanor for supporting Simon. When she and her daughter sailed from England as exiles they were warmly received in France. Eleanor retired to the Dominican convent at Montargis, where she died in 1275, but even in her widowhood she remained litigious and exacting. Louis was remarkably generous to her. In the summer of 1267 he sent two of his chief councillors, John of Brienne and the prior of Vauvert, to Henry and with their assistance Henry agreed to the release of the lands of Simon de Montfort the younger, and to an annual payment of 500 pounds sterling to Eleanor for her dower in England. Louis also saw to it that Eleanor's long-standing claims in the parlement of Paris were heard, and when they had been decided in her favour, he forced the lords of Lusignan to comply with the terms of the judgment. Over the years, even Queen Marguerite seems to have recovered sufficiently from her partisanship to plead with her nephew King Edward for the fulfilment of the Countess Eleanor's dying wish that he would show pity to her son and heir Amaury.[25]

Louis's settlement of the quarrel between France and England by the treaty of Paris was in its way a notable achievement. It finally put the seal of English acceptance on the French acquisition of Normandy, Anjou, and Poitou, but in his efforts to deal generously with Henry, Louis allowed legal loopholes which gave rise to intense squabbles over the next century and, in fact, helped to bring on the Hundred Years War. Insistence on the renunciation by the Countess Eleanor of her claims, dragged Louis into ever closer involvement in England's civil war. During the crucial years from 1259 to 1266 Louis aided Henry but, at the same time, he struggled to find a just and equitable solution for a conflict which admitted of no compromise. Although the intervention was welcomed by both sides it did not bring peace.

XIV

Louis of Poissy

Louis when he wrote secretly to his friends often called himself Louis of Poissy, from the little town where he was baptized. Those who were more formal rebuked him and wondered why he did not use his royal signature. He reminded them of the transitory nature of all kingship and compared himself to the King of Misrule at Twelfth Night, that king of the Bean 'who in the evening makes feast of his royalty: the next day, in the morning, he has no more royalty'.[1] The many accounts of Louis's life make it possible to draw a picture of the man beneath the royal trappings, even though the contemporary accounts tend to put an undue emphasis on pious platitudes. Happily, Joinville, though sincerely devoted to his king and proud of his friendship, retained his independent and secular attitude. The charm and individuality of Louis bridge the gap of centuries.

The influence of Blanche of Castile's practical devotion was strong throughout his life, like her he had a horror of mortal sin, which was not always shared by his barons. When Louis asked Joinville if he would prefer to be a leper or to have committed a mortal sin, the bluff seneschal did not pause: he knew he would rather commit thirty mortal sins than be a leper. The king tried to show him that this answer was foolish, for mortal sin was a spiritual leprosy more damaging and permanent than the earthly disease.[2]

Nevertheless, Louis's own remarks on spiritual matters are full of considerable common sense. The king considered the living of a Christian life of the utmost importance but he also understood it in terms that were intelligible to his contemporaries. He once asked Joinville: 'Do you want to learn how you can have honour in this world and please men and have God's grace and also have glory in the world to come?' Joinville was naturally anxious to hear how all this could be achieved. The king's answer was extremely practical: 'Don't do things or say things unless you would not do them otherwise even if all the world knew.'[3] When he advised his sons on clothes he told them to dress well enough to make their wives proud and fond of them, but not so extravagantly that the older men despised them.[4]

Louis's gestures of humility must be understood in the context of the medieval love of formal symbols. Every year he went to the abbey of St Denis on the saint's feast (October 9) and, on his knees and with his head bare, put four gold pieces on his head and then offered them on the altar. Serfs normally had to pay a four-penny tribute to their lord, and serfs of a church had the habit of putting the money on their head before putting it on the altar. By his act, the king declared himself a man belonging to St Denis,[5] and for a king to make such a gesture of subservience was almost unintelligible to his contemporaries. More in keeping with their views was Louis's reasoning when he and the king of Navarre and other great barons carried the relics of St Maurice and his companions in procession to a new church at Senlis. 'The king thought that it was a good thing that the saints who had been knights of Jesus Christ should be carried by knights.'[6]

Medieval hagiography observed rules: it was essential to emphasize the many mortifications, the generous charities, and the lengthy prayers of the individual acclaimed. Thus the friars and monks who wrote the first lives of Louis do not always tell us as much about the king himself as about the standards of his time. His alms, for example, were no greater than those of his brother, Alphonse of Poitiers, whose accounts are filled with generous gifts to churches and abbeys. The chroniclers also speak glowingly of the number of poor the king fed at his own table, or had fed from the fragments left in the hall, but this was an accepted obligation of the rich in the Middle Ages and those who attempted to avoid it were severely castigated by the preachers. Certain facts do stand out though as unusual. Louis's charity was given with personal effort and concern, even in his youth. Stephen of Bourbon tells of the young king disguising himself as a squire and going out early in the morning to give money to the poor who were waiting in the palace court. He was accompanied by only one servant who carried a big bag of pennies, from which Louis distributed the money with his own hands, taking special care to give the greatest amount to the most needy. The king then tried to slip back to his own chamber, but was waylaid by a friar who had been watching him.[7] Louis not only served the poor with his own hands and washed their feet, he also made his sons accompany him and share in these duties. Every Good Friday he gave alms to the poor with his own hand and insisted that his officials let the beggars approach him directly.

The king's charity was also practical. He was always particularly generous to the widows of crusaders, for whom he felt a particular responsibility, and gave them money through his almoner. He realized the difficulty of marrying a daughter when she had no dowry, and in such cases often gave a lump sum to provide one. If the girl could read, he was willing to arrange for her acceptance at a convent. Besides the sums spent on building religious houses, and here the orders of friars received the most, the king gave large amounts for houses for students,* a hospital for three hundred blind – the famous Quinze-Vingts – and many hospitals in the outlying towns.

He built the hospital at Vernon and furnished it with beds, cooking pots, and other necessities. He clothed the sisters in charge of the house every year and had a tunic made for the poor they cared for.[8] But always there was a characteristic emphasis on good sense and more important obligations. According to Joinville, Louis warned Theobald of Navarre not to spend too much money on the convent he built for the Dominicans at Provins, since a prudent man should only give in alms what is left of his estate after the claims of justice have been met.[9]

The royal biographers, with great edification, describes the king's lengthy prayers and frequent mortifications. Louis was always very precise in his observance of all the offices of the church. Also, in his time, it was general practice for everyone, however undevout, to hear mass in the morning before the

*Louis's generosity to his friend and clerk, Master Robert of Sorbon, who endowed a hostel for secular clerks studying at the university, was also the nucleus of the present Sorbonne.

beginning of the day's occupations: for many it was no more than this; while the chaplain droned through his mass his congregation chattered or carried on with their business. When Geoffrey of Beaulieu is enlarging on the king's great devotion he underlines as unusual the fact that Louis did not want to be interrupted by any conversation during services unless it was necessary, and even then it had to be brief.[10] Louis went to confession every Friday, and received communion six times a year – frequent for that period. He insisted on saying the office of the Blessed Virgin every day, even when travelling, and on solemn feasts had all the ceremonies carried out in such a solemn and leisurely fashion 'that he, like the others, got tired for the length of the service'.[11] His personal night prayers were so long that they wearied his chamberlains who waited impatiently for him outside the chapel. Sometimes Louis prayed so long that he lost track of place and time and would finally arise from his knees saying, 'Where am I?'[12] Louis never let fatigue or concern for the opinions of others turn him away from what he considered right. Talking to Joinville, he deplored the fact that some men were ashamed to do good because they might be called *papelards*, or hypocrites, a reproach he himself suffered gladly.[13] In one case, at any rate, the derogatory comment seems to have rebounded on the speaker. Thomas of Cantimpre tells the story, which he assures us is based on the account of an eyewitness, of the messenger of a German count who carried a letter from his master to the French court. On his return the count asked if he had seen King Louis. The arrogant messenger replied that he had indeed seen the miserable *papelard* king, who had a bent neck and a hood on his shoulder like a clerk. As the man spoke he grimaced and went through contortions trying to imitate the king's pose, only to find that his own neck remained permanently in the position he had mocked.[14]

Louis also had a special passion for sermons, even remembering the ones which had pleased him and reciting them to others.[15] He tried unsuccessfully to share his enthusiasm. He encouraged King Henry of England, whose almost obsessive attendance at mass was commented on by his contemporaries, to listen to some sermons instead. But, for once, Henry had the best of the argument: 'Is it not better,' he said, 'to see one's friend, than merely to hear him spoken of, even if good things are said?'[16] Louis's attitude reflected the enormous increase in preaching brought about in the thirteenth century by the new orders of the friars, who took over the neglected task of evangelising the poor and the city dwellers. Generally speaking, it was the friars who were asked to preach before the king, and he even came to their chapter houses and sat on the floor with them while they listened to the preacher of the day. Louis's passion for the friars was not always popular and, as we have seen, involved him in the bitter struggle within the university of Paris. One woman pleading in the king's court dared to reproach him as he passed by on his way to his room, saying that he should not be king of France because he was only king of the Franciscans and Dominicans, of the priests and clerks. The king answered her appeasingly, and told one of his chamberlains to give her money.[17] At the end of his life, he even discussed with Marguerite his desire to abdicate and enter either the Franciscans or the Dominicans. The queen reminded him that he was more useful to God keeping peace in the realm and encouraging the business of the whole church.[18]

His biographers unite in praise of his abstemiousness at table where he consistently watered his wine, refrained from salting his soup, and deprived himself of the special tender morsels which were presented to him. On Wednesdays and Fridays he fasted from both meat and fat, and even restricted himself to bread and water on the vigils of great feasts. Louis did not like ale, and though he frequently drank it during Lent his face showed his distaste.[19]

But the real change in the manner of his life came after his first crusade. From then on he attempted to wear a hair shirt, until he was discouraged from this by his confessors, although he continued to wear a hair belt next to his skin during Lent. During the last years of his life he even had himself beaten by his confessor after his Friday confession, and he sent the rod with its little chains and his hair belt to his daughter Isabel before his death.[20] The point which most needs to be underlined in our attempt to understand a life of pious practices which to us is unfamiliar and even in Louis's day unusual for a king is that Louis was, not merely for his hagiographers but for his contemporaries, a man of prayer and moderation. Queen Marguerite illustrates this in her remark to William of St Pathus, her confessor, that often the king would get up at night to pray and she would rise and cover him with a cloak lest he catch cold, while he never even noticed.[21]

Louis was more than a pious ascetic, he was a man of cultured tastes, probably the most cultured king of medieval France. He read both Latin and French but, in accordance with the growing use of the vernacular at all levels of society, he wrote only French. The king often liked to read or to be read to in the quiet hours after dinner or he would read in the evening until his three-foot candles burned down, but many times he would turn aside a suggested book with the comment that no book was as good as conversation where every man says what he pleased.[22] He listened too to the songs of minstrels after dinner but he did not really approve of the popular songs. One of his squires who sang the popular songs very well was made by the king to learn some of the old hymns to the Blessed Virgin and the king and the squire would sometimes sing the *Ave-Maris-Stella* together.[23]

The royal library owed its inception to Louis. When he was in Outremer he had been much impressed by the story of a Moslem sultan who had arranged for a supply of the books of the philosophers to be copied and stored so that they might be available to the educated who could not afford books. Louis decided that on his return to France he would follow this good example. He arranged for the book cupboards of the various abbeys to be ransacked, and the sacred scriptures and commentaries found there were transcribed at his own expense. The library was housed over the Sainte Chapelle with the chests, or *layettes*, of his charters. The king liked to study there himself. Practical as always, when buying for his library he preferred to have new copies written, rather than to acquire those already made, for in this way he increased the number of copies available.[24] Louis seems to have put into practice the counsel given by a twelfth-century abbot to the count of Flanders: 'For knighthood, or the profession of arms, does not preclude a sound knowledge of letters; indeed in a prince the union of both these things is useful as it is becoming.'[25]

The king's attitude to his household was strict, but generally fair. He loathed dice and games of chance and did not allow them in his household, and he also insisted that his men should live chastely. He was normally longsuffering with the mistakes of his servants and chamberlains, although it was a visible effort. For example, one afternoon Louis decided to go out to Vincennes and his chamberlain, hurriedly packing the chests, left in Paris the key of the chest which contained his master's surcoat (a sleeveless garment worn over the tunic). The king usually wore this at meals and called for it at suppertime. The worried chamberlain hunted through all the open chests without success, but Louis would not allow him to break into the locked one. Instead he dined in his long sleeved mantle, laughingly asking his knights how they liked this new fashion at table.[26] Another story concerns Jehan, a servant of Philip Augustus, who was kept to tend the fire in the king's chamber. Once when Louis's leg was inflamed and swollen he ordered the old man to bring a candle so that he could see the extent of the swelling. Jehan carelessly let a drop of hot wax fall on the swollen place and Louis reminded him that his grandfather had thrown him out of his household for merely putting wood on the fire which sparked when it burnt, but despite his annoyance, Louis kept him on.[27] His tongue could be sharp, as Joinville testified when Louis reproved Ponce, his squire, because he had not arrived at the right time at Hyères with the king's palfrey. Joinville reminded Louis that Ponce was an old man and faithful servant, who had served Philip Augustus and Louis VIII, and deserved some consideration. Louis retorted that in fact it was his forbearance in allowing a servant with bad habits to stay on that should be praised.[28]

There were other less sympathetic sides to Louis's personality and one of the unexplained contradictions of his private life is his relationship with Queen Marguerite. From the superficial evidence it is easy to claim, as Joinville did, that the king was lacking in a normal fondness and concern for his wife and children. The seneschal said that he had been with the king for five years and had never heard him mention the queen or the children, and that he did 'not think it was kindly so to be a stranger to his wife and children'.[29] An open profession of affection for one's wife was not frequent in thirteenth-century circles, where marriages were usually arranged to gain property or an alliance. Joinville himself, when he left for the crusade, admitted that he was afraid that if he looked back at Joinville his heart would weaken 'at the thought of the lovely castle I was leaving and of my two children'[30] but he never mentions his wife.

Some of this apparent coldness may have had religious reasons. Louis's avoidance of marital relations during periods of special prayer or penance was encouraged by his religious advisers. The theologians of the thirteenth century were generally opposed to marital relations except for the specific purpose of procreation, and sanctity was primarily defined as avoiding the urges of the flesh. Louis as king had to marry and produce children – he actually had a very large family – but that was all, and Marguerite suggests that this ascetism was not easy for him. The queen later told her confessor that the king, when tired with work, often used to come and sit with her and the children for a little recreation. Sometimes she noticed that while he was talking with her, he would not look at her, and she was afraid that she might have offended him. When she asked him if this was the case, he said no, but that a man should not look on that which he could not possess.[31]

Louis's deepest affection was reserved for his mother, and there were areas where Marguerite was never allowed to trespass, especially in the field of politics. She did all she could, but in vain, to bring Louis to an uncompromising support of Henry III and Eleanor. Her anger with Charles of Anjou, because of his possession of the county of Provence and his sustained refusal to release the remainder of her dower there, led to continual legal battles, but did not affect Louis's relationship with Charles. Most injudiciously, she attempted to bind her son Philip to obedience to continue even after his accession. When Louis learned of this he quickly procured papal absolution. On July 6th, 1263, Urban IV absolved Philip from the oath he had taken to his mother to keep the kingdom under her bail and wardship until he was thirty, not to take anyone on his council against her will, and – sign of the continued feud – not to make any treaty or alliance with Charles his uncle, the count of Provence. The pope said soothingly that the prince had been led more by youth than considered judgment,[32] but Marguerite had again been thwarted in her attempt to be another Blanche of Castile. It is perhaps a sign of the king's lack of confidence in her judgment that she was not named as a regent for the kingdom during his second crusade.

There are few stories which show Marguerite's character, particularly in the later years. As we have seen during the first crusade she was courageous and foresighted. She was determined in aiding her relatives and in pursuing her legal rights. But from the available evidence it would appear that the king and queen moved apart after the crusade and after the birth of their last child in 1260.

The most provocative gap in our knowledge of the relations between Louis and Marguerite is the extraordinary lack of any testimony from the queen at the inquiries for Louis's canonization. She lived till 1295, but, unlike Charles of Anjou, she was never called to give evidence. As was then usual, Marguerite spent her early widowhood in trying to further her legal claims and her old age in good works and pious foundation. In 1289 she founded a convent of the Sisters Minor of St Clare at Lourcens, just south of Paris, and lived there till she died on December 31, 1295. She had always been on particularly friendly terms with Edward her nephew, and when she died he asked for public prayers for her in England,[33] though he was then at war with France.

Louis's interest in his children seems to have been primarily didactic and in this he followed contemporary practice. A father, particularly, was meant to discipline his children, not to show affection. Louis himself taught them as much as he could and gave them competent teachers. Marguerite was interested in education for it was at her request that the famous Dominican Vincent of Beauvais wrote a treatise on the proper upbringing of the royal children, with special emphasis on the need for picking a good tutor.[34] Vincent was also royal librarian and chaplain, and had taught theology to the monks at Royaumont. His great *Speculum*, or 'mirror' was the best known encyclopaedia of the thirteenth century. Unfortunately, the title of his treatise, *Concerning the Instruction of Noble Children* is more interesting than its contents. Vincent presented a high-minded and somewhat monastic ideal, supported by a tissue of quotations from all the known authorities, but he tells us very little about practical matters. His work does show that both the boys and the girls were expected to read, although writing was considered more of an art. Vincent quotes approvingly the saying, 'An illiterate king is like a crowned donkey'.[35]

Louis relied more on his own personal example to train his children. After his sons had learned to read they had to come to compline with him, and afterwards they accompanied him to his chamber where he sat and talked with them. When he washed the feet of the poor on Holy Thursday his oldest sons had to do the same, and he taught them to join him in serving the poor.[36] The high moral tone of his teaching is strong in the texts of the *Enseignements*, or Precepts, which he is credited with having written by hand for Philip and Isabel. His advice to his daughter dealt primarily with private morality, encouraging the choice of good companions and religious observance and emphasizing the more feminine foibles which she should avoid.[37] His advice to his son and heir was more far-reaching, for besides extolling private virtue he instructed him to maintain the good customs of the kingdom, not to oppress his people, to maintain peace and justice, and above all to make sure that both the people and the customs which needed reform were reformed.[38]

This teaching was typical of Louis. He thought that the vocation of any Christian was to be a saint, but the vocation of a Christian king was to rule his realm in such a way that his people were also encouraged along the way to salvation. A religious aura surrounded all French kings.[39] It was partly attributable to the greater solemnity and ritual of their coronation, which set them apart from their subjects, and is further illustrated by the general and traditional belief in the 'king's touch', that is, the ability to cure scrofula merely by the imposition of the royal hands. Louis's predecessors had merely touched the place of the sickness and said some holy words, but Louis made the sign of the cross as well as saying a formula, for he was anxious that 'the cure might be attributed rather to the virtue of the cross than to the king's majesty'.[40] This was done in good faith, for Louis felt strongly the need for seeking God's help in his work as king. He sent special messages to the religious communities whenever parlement assembled, asking them to pray that God should give those present good counsel and an ability to make the right choice.[41]

His attitude towards heresy illustrates his intolerance of all error and sin, coupled with a real concern for any innocent victims. Heresy was both a religious and a secular issue, since those condemned by the church courts had their goods confiscated to the benefit of their secular lord. This provision encouraged some zealous officials to press the churchmen for condemnations and to deplore mercy on the part of the inquisitors. This excessive greed appeared time after time in the complaints made to the enquêteurs, and the king was anxious to make restitution. Louis insisted that the innocent wives and children of heretics should not suffer, and in many cases intervened to protect their dower or property rights.[42] In the later years of his reign he softened the provisions of the ordinance of 1229 against heresy, passed when the Albigensian Crusade had just ended. This did not mean that he had any sympathy with proved heretics for Louis, like most of his contemporaries, saw nothing unusual in using all the religious and secular power to combat the danger of heresy. Even Frederic II, personally tolerant, persecuted heresy within his domain because he felt it was a threat to his secular domination. Louis was further buttressed by his conviction that it was his duty to keep his kingdom Christian.

This duty determined his attitude to the Jews. Louis bitterly opposed usury and acted vigorously against the Jews who practiced it. He had no real understanding of the tenets of the Jewish faith or any great confidence in argument for he once told Joinville that only a very learned clerk should argue with the Jews: 'A layman, as soon as he hears the Christian faith maligned, should defend it only by the sword, with a good thrust in the belly, as far as the sword will go.'[43] Although he worked hard to cut out usury completely, he seems to have given the Jews some confidence in his justice, for several of them appear as plaintiffs before the enquêteurs. Louis too showed concern for the conversion of the Jews and, in his accounts, provided for the 'baptized' and the 'conversi'. The baptized were Jewish children who had been orphaned or abandoned: they were collected throughout the provinces and usually taken to the episcopal cities where they were fed and lodged at the king's expense, under the guardianship of the friars. The 'conversi' were adults, capable of instruction and they were given pensions and occasional alms of grain.[44]

The Jews had the monopoly of moneylending because usury was forbidden to Christians, but in the thirteenth century the Lombards and the Cahorsins (men from Cahors) joined them. The medieval rates of interest were appallingly high, the risks were great, and Christian moral theology had not kept pace with the conversion of the old agricultural economy based on barter to a new, more sophisticated commercial economy based on money and the longterm exchange of goods and credit. The taking of any interest was still denounced as usury even when the practice was generally accepted. At the end of his reign Louis continued to show his displeasure at the practice within his kingdom by an ordinance requiring the expulsion of all Lombard, Cahorsin, and other foreign usurers within three months. As in the original ordinances against the Jews, the people in debt to the moneylenders could get their goods back by the repayment of the simple debt without any interest. Lombards and Cahorsins engaged in business or legitimate trade were specifically exempted from the ordinance so long as they did not practise any kind of usury or indulge in other unlawful acts.[45]

Louis's most ardent anger seems to have been reserved for blasphemers. The medieval imagination produced some odd oaths and it was common for men to swear by various parts of the body of God, or the Blessed Virgin, or the saints. The king tried to counter such blasphemies with equally imaginative punishments, such as the time at Caesarea when the king had a blaspheming goldsmith put in the pillory with a heap of pig entrails around his neck and up to his nose.[46] The chroniclers talk of Louis ordaining that convicted blasphemers should be marked on the lips with a hot iron, but no such ordinance has survived.[47] The order which does remain provides a scale of punishments for those who blasphemed, depending on the seriousness of the blasphemy and the age of the offender. Between the ages of ten and fourteen, the transgressors were only to be beaten and not exposed in the pillory or put in prison.[48] Human nature is rarely changed by ordinance, no matter how high-minded, and there is no record that the people of France followed the sober example of their king whose most emphatic expletive was 'In truth it is so'.[49]

The picture of the king which emerges is that of a man of great private virtue who tried with unwavering effort to guide his people in the path of righteousness. He realized that his mortifications and prayers were not always popular among his court, or even among the people who would have preferred a gayer and more colourful figure. As he told Joinville, the court would not have complained if he had spent the time hunting that he spent on prayers and sermons.[50] Although he had always felt the weight of his responsibility for his kingdom as we have seen, it was after he returned from his first crusade that the style and focus of his life changed. He still gave feasts when the leaders of the realm met for the parlement, which were as impressive as any given by his ancestors, but his private life changed. This was most obvious in his clothes, his dress was now extraordinarily sober. Instead of scarlet and miniver, he wore only black or blue cloths and lamb's wool or squirrel. His saddles and stirrups were no longer gilded or blazoned.[51] As Pope Boniface VIII said in a sermon proclaiming Louis's canonization:

> After he was freed from prison he did not live nor was clothed as before, although his life and conversation before were honest enough. For afterwards the clothes he wore were religious not regal, not those of a knight but of a simple man.[52]

The crusading ideal continued to influence all his actions and the last ten years of his reign were dominated by his insistence that he must lead another expedition against the infidel to bring them to a knowledge and acceptance of Christ.

XV

The Final Years 1260–1270

Louis's conviction of the need for another crusade was heightened by his firsthand knowledge of the perilous condition of the Frankish states of Outremer, still further menaced by the renewed aggression of the Mongols and the Mameluk sultans of Egypt. His serious illness in October 1260,[1] and the fall of the Latin Empire of Constantinople to the Greeks in August 1261, warned him of his own weakness and the pressing problems of the east.

Obligations to his own realm were still pressing, for the death of Prince Louis in January 1260 meant that the new heir to the throne was only fifteen. Although most of the major ordinances of the reign had been enacted and the general pattern laid out, the king's work was not finished. The Great Ordinance had been promulgated and renewed, and was being enforced as far as possible. The thrice yearly meetings of parlement were established, they heard more and more cases as the king's reputation for justice and fair dealing spread. The practice of the inquest was making reluctant headway. There remained the need for currency reform.

All European medieval moneys were based on the weight of a pound of silver and during the period of greatest feudal strength many great lords, both religious and secular, had acquired the profitable right to coin money.[2] Ideally, all the moneys should have been of equal value but the various coinages fluctuated and depreciated in unequal ratios. A lord could enforce the use of his currency on his own lands but expansion of trade and travel increased the need for a general valid currency. Philip Augustus made a beginning in this, as in so many other things, for he concentrated the coining of money in the royal domain at Paris and established a standard worth for the Paris penny. When Philip conquered Normandy, Anjou, Maine, Touraine, and Poitou, he acquired territories where Paris money did not run and discovered a mixture of English, Angevin and other local moneys. After the conquests the second major coinage of the French kingdom was established as the money of Tours, it was struck there, and by the accession of Louis IX was worth four-fifths of the Paris money. In the royal accounting the pound Paris remained official until the fifteenth century, but commerce generally preferred the money of Tours.

Louis had been impressed during his stay in the east with the gold bezants of Constantinople and the Moslem maraboutins, which were then the only gold coins in general circulation. By the middle of the thirteenth century, Europe had regained its position of economic importance and the Italian city states' successful and extensive trade had once more made the Mediterranean what it had been in the great days of the Roman Empire: 'the centre of exchange, the motor of the economy, the heart of the civilization.'[3] Frederic II struck the first gold pieces, but in 1252 Florence began to coin the florin, the gold piece which was to have such great commercial acceptance for centuries. In 1266 Louis also struck a gold coin, the écu, but it was rare and bore no obvious relation to the normal moneys of account. The legend on the coin, *Christus vincit*, *Christus regnat*, *Christus imperat*, bears eloquent witness to Louis's own concerns and beliefs and was the forerunner of a whole series of royal coins bearing that device, which was considered a sacred prerogative of the crown of France.[4] But a more practical innovation was the production of the *gros tournois* in silver. This coin was worth twelve pennies, one shilling, and was most valuable since it was convenient, easily identified, within the ordinary commercial range, and also added to the penny another piece of real money which was also a money of account.

Louis's ordinance of 1262 emphasized his belief that the coining of money was a royal prerogative. Although Louis would not, and could not, deprive the great lords of their feudal right to strike money, he could limit it. The ordinance forbade any baron to let his money run except within the limits of his own lordship, but royal money was to run everywhere in the realm. The barons were forbidden to copy royal money or to make poor pieces of inferior worth, and the king reserved the right to forbid the use of foreign moneys not only in his own domain, but also in the lands of the barons. On this last issue, the king had to make some concessions, for in 1265 he allowed the *nantais* of Brittany, the *Angevins* and *esterlins* to run in his domain, but at a set ratio to the *tournois*.[5]

There were no exceptions to Louis's rules. Alphonse of Poitiers, who had the right to coin money in several centres in his lands, had been attempting to have all his money of the *tournois* type. This was against Louis's expressed wishes and in 1263 Alphonse was told, in no uncertain terms, that he must stop coining money in Poitou and must stop copying the royal money. Alphonse came to terms by gradually modifying his types of coinage and having a different coin for each of the great territorial divisions of his lands.[6] Other lords were less amenable. A general complaint was brought against the count of Angoulême in the Candlemas parlement of 1266 by the people of the city and diocese of Angoulême, claiming that the count frequently changed his money to his own advantage. After an inquest, the count admitted that he had in fact debased his money, but asserted that this was his right, and he could do as he pleased. Parlement did not agree and ordered the count to make good money, if he wanted to make money, and forbade him to let inadequate money circulate.[7] But it was not only secular lords who offended in this way. The bishop of Clermont excommunicated all those who would not accept some newly altered money at his own valuation and the king had to threaten to seize all his temporalities.[8]

Most of the serious royal problems of 1260–70 involved matters outside the realm. We have seen how even after the peace treaty Louis's involvement in English affairs during the Baron's War and its aftermath continued. It also took some time for the final settlements included in the treaty with Aragon to be worked out. The marriage arranged between Isabel of Aragon and Philip of France, now the heir to the throne, took place at Clermont at the end of May 1262, although James of Aragon had decided to marry his son Peter to Constance, daughter of Manfred. Manfred was the illegitimate son of Frederic II and the actual ruler of Sicily:

he was, as his father had been, hated by the pope, and Urban IV was much disturbed by this new and potentially dangerous alliance. Louis would only allow the marriage of Philip and Isabella after James had sworn that he would not uphold Manfred against the church, and that his son's marriage was not to the prejudice of the church or his alliance with France.[9] The king of Aragon also promised not to interfere in the affairs of the city of Marseilles, or to aid them in their revolt against Charles of Anjou, the count of Provence and one of their overlords.[10]

However, even after the marriage, points of discord remained; James struggled to maintain his rights in Montpellier, and even increase them despite French pressure. The bishop of Maguelonne had done homage to the French king's seneschal of Beaucaire for Montpellier and the bishop stated that in fact the king of Aragon held part of the town from the bishop.[11] A series of disputes over sovereignty were brought to Louis at Paris, and the Aragonese ambassadors claimed that the French king had no right to let his seneschal hear complaints from Montpellier, despite the bishop of Maguelonne's position.[12] The Aragonese complaints were listened to most politely, but they were not heeded, and the royal officials continued to maintain their usual tactic of insisting on every possible wisp of feudal claim in order to bolster the royal power.[13]

The king's prestige was further enhanced by other settlements which he made with less important neighbours. There was the inheritance of Flanders and Hainault and, according to Joinville, a dispute between Theobald II of Navarre and the duke of Burgundy over the abbey of Luxeuil.[14] In 1268 Louis served as arbiter in a whole series of disputes between some of his more turbulent lords. He established peace between the count of Bar and the count of Luxembourg, who disputed the possession of the castle of Ligny; between the king of Navarre and the count of Bar; and between the lord of Choiseul and the count of Bar.[15] Some of Louis's counsellors were not convinced of the wisdom of such peace-making efforts, feeling it would be safer to let potential enemies impoverish themselves by continued fighting. The king argued that both practical wisdom and religious precept required him to make peace and Joinville was convinced that the king's policy of reconciliation had worthwhile political results, since it brought many outsiders to his court to settle their affairs.[16]

The most serious external problem was the continuing struggle between the popes and the Hohenstaufen heirs of Frederic II.[17] Louis had originally maintained a position of careful neutrality, but the situation became more complicated after the death of Frederic in 1250. Conrad succeeded him and, despite the struggles of Innocent IV, had seemed well on the way to achieve what the pope most dreaded, the unification of the north and south of Italy. Suddenly Conrad died in May 1254, at the age of twenty-six, and the whole picture changed again. Conrad's legitimate heir was his son, the two-year-old Conradin, whose legitimate rights to Sicily were soon usurped by his uncle, the capable and ambitious Manfred. An attempted settlement between Manfred and Innocent collapsed almost as soon as it was made and Innocent died in December 1254 with the unhappy knowledge that the Sicilian problem was no nearer a satisfactory solution than when he had become pope ten years before. The new pope, Alexander IV, had been the cardinal-archbishop of Ostia and, unlike his predecessor, was known for his gentleness and his piety. Alexander approached the question of Sicily with less combative zeal but with an equally strong conviction that it was essential for the temporal interests of the papacy that Manfred should be crushed and Sicily should not be ruled by the Hohenstaufen.

The diplomatic manœuvres to dispossess Frederic's heirs had begun early. We have seen how in 1252 Pope Innocent had offered the Sicilian crown to Richard of Cornwall and almost simultaneously to Charles of Anjou, who wavered momentarily but, at Louis's insistence, turned it down. Louis felt that Conrad's rights should be respected and he particularly regretted the papacy's determination to turn the territorial war in Sicily into a crusade, when the lands of Outremer were struggling without western help. Louis's disapproval did not deflect the pope and, as we have seen, he then offered the kingdom to Henry of England for his younger son Edmund, a boy of only eight, and this was accepted. Although the offer went into abeyance, with the deaths of Conrad and Innocent, the project was reopened by Alexander IV, but foundered on the enormous papal fiscal demands and the firm refusal of the English barons to give financial aid. Alexander formally annulled the grant in December 1258 and nothing further was done before his death in 1261.

The college of cardinals had been reduced to eight members and it took much wrangling before a new pope was elected. After a three months' interregnum they agreed on Jacques Pantaleon, the Patriarch of Jerusalem. The new pope took the name of Urban IV, and the three years of his rule saw more action than those of his predecessor. Urban was in his sixties, but he had had a long career in ecclesiastical administration and wide experience on many fronts. A Frenchman born of poor parents at Troyes, he had been trained at the University of Paris and had come to the notice of Innocent IV at the Council of Lyons. He had done missionary work as legate in the Baltic and been bishop of Verdun before being appointed to the patriarchate of Jerusalem in 1255. There he had faced the quarrelling barons of Outremer, the continued feuding between the Venetians and the Genoese, and seen the dangerous onward sweep of Mongols and Mameluks. Energetic, dominating, and inflexible he has even been described as a 'sketch' for the ferocious Julius II.[18] Urban's own background and Louis's universal prestige encouraged the pope to turn to the French king for help, and the French point of view was strongly represented in papal councils since of the seven new cardinals Urban appointed three had been ministers of the French king.

Despite the many problems in Outremer, the Sicilian question was still central in the papal policy. Urban had decided that Charles of Anjou was certainly the most able prince available and Charles was ambitious for a throne. Louis was very dubious about the justice of such an offer weighing the rights of the young Conradin and his own previous support of Edmund. Louis's scruples were at first reinforced by the presence at his court of Baldwin, the defeated emperor of Constantinople. Baldwin took every possible opportunity to press the legitimacy of Manfred's claims in Sicily and to exploit Queen Marguerite's undisguised dislike of Charles of Anjou, but he also became involved in conspiracy with Manfred. When his intrigues came to light, Louis was shocked. Still somewhat dubious of the righteousness of the whole affair, Louis allowed himself to be persuaded by his brother and the pope and gave his consent to Charles's acceptance. This decision had important ramifications, for it meant that Charles's own strength and financial resources would be amplified by those of the kingdom of France, and that the count's insatiable ambition and arrogance would be masked by the irreproachable prestige and moral authority of Louis himself. In July 1263 Urban and Charles came to terms on a basis most favourable to the church, but the balance soon shifted. Once Charles had an unassailable legal position and had been accepted as the church's proper champion, he took every opportunity to improve the arranged terms, and before Urban's death in October 1264 had already forced major papal concessions.

Urban's death was followed by another disputed and long-drawn out conclave which finally brought another Frenchman to the papal throne. Guy Fulcod was elected pope taking the name Clement IV, while he was serving as papal legate to England, although in residence at the French court. His ties to the French king were long-standing, he had been one of Louis's trusted ministers for many years, and it was to be expected that the relations between the new pope and the French king would be close and warm. Clement immediately renewed his predecessor's arrangement with Charles of Anjou and begged him to take immediate measures against Manfred, whose strength in Italy seemed to be growing. The pope also renewed many of the special privileges which Louis enjoyed, such as freedom from excommunication for himself and his officials, special status for his chapels, and so on.[19]

Nevertheless, there was an innate tension between them which occasionally showed itself. When William of Charni was elected archbishop of Sens a conflict arose between Louis and Clement over who held the right to appoint to minor offices in the gift of a bishop when the see was vacant but was held under regalian right in the king's hands. The pope claimed that if a bishop had been consecrated or confirmed at Rome – as most bishops tended to be – his benefices were subject to papal provisions, that is, the right of the pope to name the next incumbent. On the other hand, Louis asserted, as he had been insisting firmly throughout his reign, that in these circumstances the right of appointment was the king's. The matter remained unsettled during Louis's lifetime, but both pope and king upheld their mutually exclusive authority equally firmly.[20]

Meanwhile, Charles of Anjou had taken advantage of Pope Clement's uneasy situation in Perugia and his fear of returning to Rome to improve his position once more. He also began to translate his legal title into practical power. In the spring and summer of 1265 Charles moved to counter Manfred's influence in the north and centre of Italy. His efforts were rapidly successful, and by June he had been formally made a senator of Rome. But Charles did not stop there: gathering his Provençal supporters and as much money as he could raise and borrow for the task, he set off in the autumn from Lyons at the head of an army. His force was specifically designed for the invasion of the kingdom of Sicily and a direct attack on Manfred himself. Despite a difficult passage over the Alps and through Lombardy Charles and his army arrived safely in Rome in the middle of January 1266. Both the desire to catch Manfred off his balance and the need to conserve his financial resources led Charles to embark on his campaign at once, without waiting for the more usual spring season. The count led his army out of Rome to the south, and was able to cross into the kingdom of Sicily by a bridge over the river Liri which had been abandoned but not destroyed. The opposing armies met at Benevento on February 26, and the battle was a decisive victory for Charles, a success crowned by the death of Manfred. By the beginning of March 1266 Charles and his wife, Beatrice of Provence, had made their solemn entry into Naples as king and queen of Sicily.

During the remaining years of Louis's life Charles was to continue from success to success in his new kingdom. Because of his new responsibilities Charles was somewhat removed from the French scene, but he was to play a decisive part in Louis's last crusade. Charles's ambitions were not satisfied with the kingdom of Sicily: the energetic prince dreamed of reconquering the Byzantine empire. By the treaty of Viterbo in 1267 he took over all the rights and claims of the deposed emperor Baldwin and with this long term objective worked for a foothold in the Balkan peninsula. His influence on his brother was considerable, since

13a. Agnes, youngest daughter of Louis d. 1327 – a detail of the early 14th century statue at Poissy, originally made for the Dominican priory built at Poissy for Philip the Fair, Louis's grandson

13b. Louis, eldest son of Louis, d. 1260 – a detail from his tomb in St Denis

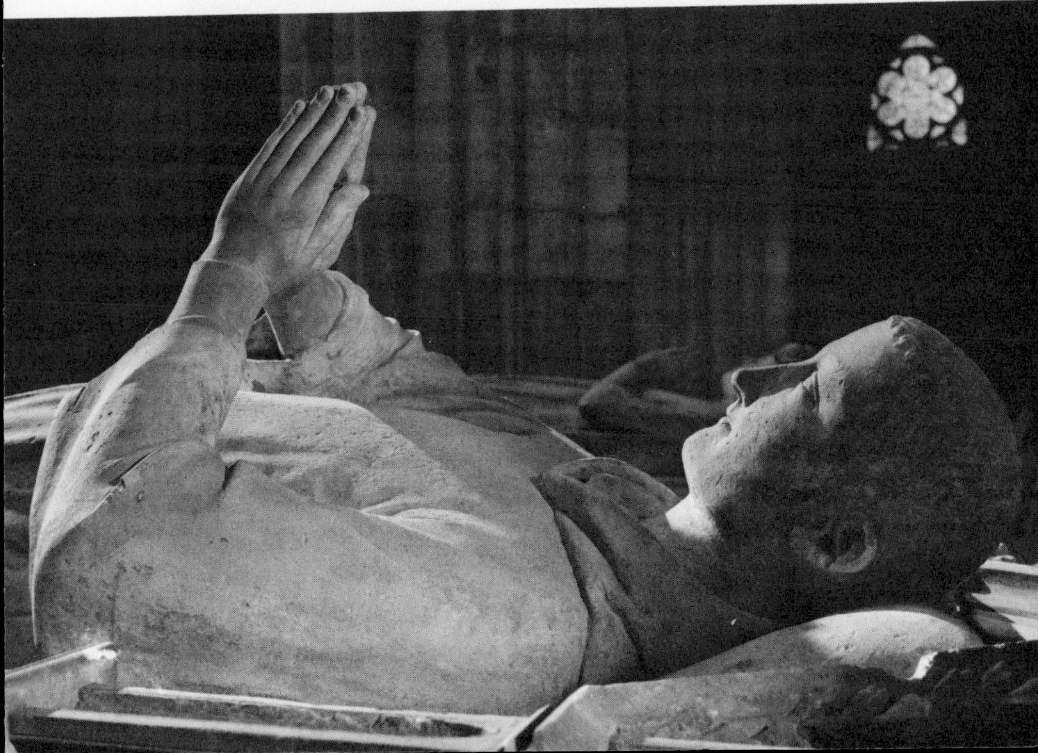

14. Louis – the statue now in the church of Mainneville (Eure) was originally made *c.* 1307 for the chapel of the Château de Mainneville, built for Enguerran de Marigny, favourite of Philip the Fair

Louis needed Charles's military support in the crusade, but Charles looked at the Mediterranean as merely a further problem in strategy to achieve greater goals: for Charles, another crusade was regarded almost as a business venture.

XVI

The Last Crusade 1270

The states of Outremer, always fragile and insecurely based principalities, had been temporarily strengthened by the fortifications Louis had constructed during his three-year stay, and also by the knights of his company, some of whom had remained. But these reinforcements counted for little when, within four years after Louis's return to France, both the newly resurgent Mongols and the Moslems were an imminent menace to the struggling Christian states.

The Mongols had been checked on their first great sweep into Europe in 1242 by the fortuitous death of the Great Khan and the subsequent need for Batu, the commander of the forces, to return to Karakorum for the council and the choice of a new khan. By the 1250s the Mongols were once again ready to move on into the near east, beyond the position they had already established in Armenia. The king of Armenia tried to build up a Christian alliance to aid the Mongols in their attempts to destroy the Moslems, but his efforts met little success among the suspicious Franks of Outremer, who preferred the Moslems they knew to these fierce and distant conquerors. The Mongols professed to be favourable to Christianity for many of the wives of the khans were Christians, although usually Nestorians, but they certainly did not share Louis's concept of their proper place within Christendom. The Mongols were firmly convinced of their call to world domination, and they would not recognize independent states which did not accept their overlordship, nor would they dream of being subject to the pope. In any case, their immediate objective was the destruction of the caliphate, the central religious power and focus of all Mohammedanism.

In 1256 a large Mongol army set out from central Asia under

the command of Hulagu, the brother of the Great Khan. It first wiped out the Assassins in Persia and then moved against Baghdad, which was besieged and captured in February 1258. The massacre was frightful: in forty days some eighty thousand inhabitants were slain, and when Hulagu withdrew he took with him the great accumulated treasure of the caliphate. The fall and destruction of both the city and the dynasty of the Abbasid caliphate had a widespread effect. The religious unity of the Moslem world and the middle east was finally broken beyond repair, though the Moslems soon regained their position of predominance over the the Mongol invaders. The fall of Baghdad was soon followed by that of Aleppo and Damascus. Attacks only ceased when Bohemond at Antioch felt it would be wise to contract an alliance with the Mongol conquerors and pay homage to Hulagu, despite the humiliating conditions required.[1]

By the spring of 1260 the Christians of the near east were in a more desperate situation than ever before. Acre had become the centre of Christian resistance and the leaders there wrote pleadingly for assistance to the princes and prelates of Europe. Among their letters was one to Charles of Anjou, begging his help and describing the perilous state of the kingdom of Acre, since the Christians were now surrounded by the onrushing wave of Mongols and saw no possibility of deliverance.[2] Once more the invasion was dramatically halted by the death of the Great Khan. Mongka had died in August 1259 while campaigning in China, and the succession was disputed. Hulagu had to return to the council, withdrawing his own leadership and some of his troops and leaving a subordinate in command. The Egyptian army, led by the Mameluk Baibars, then moved to attack the Mongol forces, whose first tentative raids into Palestine had proved them a danger to Egyptian security. The weak Christian communities found themselves in even deadlier peril, caught between the two opposing forces, and again they appealed for help.

The danger from the Mongols was soon removed, for on September 2, 1260, the battle of Ain Jalud marked the decisive defeat of the Mongol power. The Egyptian army under Baibars practically wiped out the Mongol forces which had penetrated into eastern Galilee, and Egypt remained the chief power in the near east till the rise of the Ottoman Turks. The destruction of their army and the conflict over the election of the Great Khan prevented the Mongols from attempting to make good their loss, or even holding Damascus, Aleppo, and Baghdad. The Christian hopes for a great alliance against the Moslems, which had been encouraged by the Christian sympathizers among the Mongols, evaporated with their defeat. The general fear of invasion by the fierce Tartars died away, only to be replaced by the realization among the thoughtful that the Christian situation in Outremer was no better. The crusader states had merely exchanged the threat of the Mongols for that of the Egyptians, whose religious fervour against the Christians was once more aroused.

On Passion Sunday (April 10) 1261, Louis called a great council of the bishops and magnates of his realm to discuss a papal bull of the previous November, begging for aid for Outremer. In view of the defeat of the Mongols, which Alexander had not known of when he wrote, the men of France did not see their way to any immediate action. The council compromised by ordering increased prayers and processions, the punishment of blasphemers, and the repression of excess in food and clothing. In hopes of encouraging knights to go overseas to fight in earnest, tournaments were forbidden for two years and no games, except practice with the bow and the crossbow, were allowed.[3] But 1261 provided still another shock for the continually weakening Christian position. In August the Latin Empire of Constantinople, that fragile creation presided over by the impecunious and incompetent Emperor Baldwin, was overthrown by the troops of the Greek claimant, Michael Paleologus. Baldwin fled to the west seeking financial and military help. The influence of the king's advisers and the many problems occupying Louis at home made him realize that his presence was necessary in France, but his desire to come to the aid of Outremer remained. When most of the affairs of France were settled and Charles had succeeded in subduing the Sicilian kingdom, Louis could prepare for another crusade. The pope could no longer temporize by putting forward the struggle for Sicily as a holy war, and Louis bent every effort to the achievement of his dream.

The king called a great council of his barons in Paris at the end of March 1267 and on the feast of the Annunciation (March 25) he and his sons took the cross. Louis's decision was not popular, as Joinville shows. Many of the barons were undecided: afraid to offend the king if they did not vow to accompany him, and yet seriously ill at ease about the value of another crusade. Joinville records his own outspoken refusal to the pressure of his overlord, the king of Navarre, and of Louis himself, who begged him to go.

> I answered that while I was in the service of God and the King overseas and after my return the officers of the King of France and the King of Navarre had so ruined and impoverished my people that the day would never come when they and I would not suffer the effect. I told them, too, that if I wished to do God's will I should stay at home to help and protect my people; for were I to endanger my person in the pilgrimage of the Cross, knowing full well that it would be at the expense of my people's well-being, I should incur the anger of God, who gave His life to save His people.[4]

Joinville merely puts into rather limited and high-minded terms a current of feeling that was steadily becoming more powerful. Anti-crusading sentiment was exceedingly strong by the middle of the thirteenth century and contemporaries have described the various arguments used. The crusades now seemed to many a waste of Christian blood, and many felt that the Christians violated the rights of the Moslems by invading their lands. The original zeal for a holy war against the infidel had died down, moderated by a growing secularization of outlook as well as a greater knowledge of the many complicating factors involved. A popular argument was that the crusades did not make for the conversion of the Saracens, but only aroused them further against the Christians. The preachers, as well as the poets, almost seemed to wonder if the crusade was against the will of God since He allowed such dreadful misfortunes to befall those Christians who went to fight the Moslems.[5]

There were other, less high-minded reasons for opposing the crusade too. In a *Collection of the Scandals of the Church* made by Gilbert of Tournai, a Franciscan who was known to Louis IX, public opinion was shown as vigorously disapproving of the financial abuses carried on in the name of a holy war. It was considered a sinful abuse to tax the poor and the church to provide money for the crusade – and this had been done for both Louis's crusades. Another continuing scandal was the growing practice of the redemption of crusading vows at fixed rates. Unscrupulous collectors and fraudulent preachers often used this trick for personal gain. Crusading vows were also imposed as a form of penance or as a punishment for criminals and then redeemed at fairly high rates.[6] A more secular voice raised against the crusade was that of the poet Rutebeuf, who especially hated the mendicant orders and their influence at the king's court and in the University of Paris. *Renart le Bestourné*, one of the most venomous of his poems against the king, may well have been written at the time of the king's decision to go on crusade.[7] It seems obvious that Louis's insistence on a second crusade was not a popular decision at any level of society.

Louis was not to be dissuaded, despite the perilous state of his health. In 1267, when he took the cross, Joinville had found him so weak that he could not bear either to ride or to go in a carriage, and Joinville had to carry him in his arms from one house to another.[8] Louis suffered from recurring fevers and inflammation of his leg, for he had never really regained his strength after the hardships of the first crusade, but his health was not normally as poor as Joinville describes it.

Louis wrote almost immediately to Charles of Anjou about his plans and sent as his messengers John of Valenciennes, Peter le Chambellan, and Master Nicholas of Chalons, his most trusted and familiar officials. They presented the message to Charles at the papal court in the first few days of May. Louis urged his brother to take the cross, 'to give example and encouragement to other men and to further dismay the enemies of the Faith by your renown'. If Charles could not go, his brother asked him for aid with ships and armed men, as well as any possible supplies of provisions and animals. Still more necessary was the return of the various sums which Charles owed the king. There were 8,000 marks still unpaid of Queen Marguerite's dower; 7,000 marks given Charles to pay the obligations contained in the will of his father-in-law, Raymond Berenger of Provence; 30,000 pounds which Louis had lent Charles in the Holy Land; and 5,000 marks which the king had given Charles when he was married, but which were to be repaid if Charles received greater dignities, as he certainly had. Louis reminded Charles that he needed the money for his crusading plans and also to arrange the marriages of his children and the knighting of his eldest son Philip.[9]

Charles delayed in answering, hoping to have the advice and aid of the pope. The advice that Clement gave him is not recorded, but the pope conceded to Louis for the crusade a tenth of all the ecclesiastical goods in France for three years, a twentieth of the cities and dioceses of Liège, Metz, Toul, and Verdun, and the proceeds from the redemption of crusading vows and pious legacies for the aid of the Holy Land.[10] Louis needed the money for he had already sent considerable financial aid to the Holy Land. Just before he took the cross he had responded to the pleas of the beleaguered Christians at Acre by authorizing loans up to 44,000 pounds *tournois*. The sum was quickly absorbed for by the end of June all the letters of authorization had been handed over to a company of Sienese merchants in payment of already contracted debts.[11]

The king's family affairs also made heavy inroads on his finances. The knighting of Philip was held at Pentecost (June 5) 1267, and was notable for its elegance. It is interesting to note that, despite the complaints of such poets as Rutebeuf, who deplored the king's lack of generosity to his household and implied his avariciousness, the expenses for Philip's knighting were rather more than those for Robert of Artois, the king's brother, thirty years before. The increase probably reflects a rise in prices in the interval but the expenditure illustrates that the king's asceticism did not make him overlook his secular obligations. He even allowed himself to be splendidly dressed; Philip was even more gorgeously dressed than his uncle had been, as was only suitable for the heir to the throne. The fifty-two young men who were knighted with him were given their robes and a warhorse and palfrey each, at a cost of 4,000 pounds. The total expenses of the feast, which include the miscellaneous items of twelve pounds for the trumpeters and twelve pounds seven shillings for compensation for the young wheat destroyed by the great company riding between Paris and Vincennes, was 13,758 pounds, some 4,000 pounds more than the earlier feast.[12]

Before his departure the king also wished to settle the marriages of as many as possible of his large family. Some were already provided for: Isabel, the oldest, had been married to King Theobald of Navarre in 1255, and Philip had married Isabella of Aragon in 1262. The marriage of John Tristan had been arranged some years previously with Yolande, daughter of the count of Nevers and the lord of Bourbon, and they had been married by January 1266 and Yolande's dowry assigned to her.[13] John Tristan quickly entered on his wife's inheritance as Yolande's father, Eudes, died on crusade at Acre in early August 1266.* Negotiations had also been started, and the necessary dispensation obtained, for the marriage of Blanche to Ferdinand of Castile, which took place at Burgos at the end of 1269. Marguerite, born in 1254, was married just before her father's departure to John, duke of Brabant, and received 10,000 pounds as her marriage portion.[15] Preliminary negotiations for the marriages of Peter and Robert had begun, while Agnes, at ten, was still very young. The king chose the partners for his children with skill and discretion, encouraging friendship and ties of alliance with the princes and great feudal lords who ringed his kingdom.

Another of the king's remaining duties was the assignment of appanages to his sons. Louis VIII had given dangerously generous appanages to his younger sons, and Louis IX could still not be positive that royal good luck and the absence of direct heirs would bring back to the royal domain and control Poitou, Toulouse, and ultimately Anjou. Louis may have been doubtful of his father's wisdom for the appanages he assigned to Peter and John were very modest, only sufficient for their subsistence.[16]

The king was also busy with the preparations for the crusade. The detail of the many preliminaries appears most clearly in the administrative correspondence of Alphonse of Poitiers. Alphonse

*The inventory of his estate is particularly interesting for the light it sheds on the nature of the establishment of an important magnate overseas. Included among his followers, whose wages were paid by his executors, were knights, sergeants, squires, grooms, and his group of Turcopoles, or light horsemen. The executors found two great warhorses and fifty-one large black palfreys in his stable, as well as three mules and a donkey to carry the water. Perhaps the most surprising item of all is the list of books, for the count had copies of the *Roman des Lorrains*, several romances on Outremer, and a *chansonnier*, or song-book, probably written by Theobald of Navarre.[14]

was by nature a worried and conscientious administrator and his letters to his officials in the south are full of exact, and often stupefying, detail. As he had joined his brother in taking the cross he wanted to be sure that all the preparations were properly made. For example, in June 1267 he wrote to his leading lieutenant in the south, Sicard Alaman, concerning the bows and arrows that he had ordered. It appeared that the arrows already ordered by Sicard were too long and not sufficiently reinforced with iron. Alphonse sent him four samples: he wanted 100,000 like them for eighteen shillings *tournois* the thousand – or less, if possible. Before they went too far with the provision of arrows the count wanted to see a sample.[17] By the next year Alphonse was writing to his seneschal in Toulouse concerning the terms of service and the rates of pay for men accompanying him overseas. In June Alphonse only proposed to pay 180 pounds *tournois* at the most to a knight for all his expenses, that is, his passage, food, and reimbursement for lost horses. However, by September the count had had to increase his offer to 200 pounds, as knights could not be had for less in either Poitou or France.[18] In May Alphonse had tried to hire Master Assaut, a 'most expert' engineer, to go overseas with him and was willing to pay him five shillings a day, but Assaut was unable to get permission to go from his master, the king of Castile.[19]

The basic need was for ships. Louis had made a provisional arrangement with Venice for fifteen ships, but, as in 1248, this fell through, and the king turned once again to Genoa and Marseilles. Louis appointed two commissioners in October 1268 to deal with the Genoese over the construction and leasing of ships. By the beginning of December the contracts and leases had been arranged, and the Genoese had promised to build several good-sized ships for the king's passage overseas and to rent him the *Paradise*.[20] These were the first ships ever actually owned by a king and Louis really deserves to be considered as the founder of the French navy. Another innovation was the king's appointment of a Frenchman, Florent of Varennes, as admiral.[21] By February 1269 the king's debts to the Genoese shipbuilders were already being paid at the Temple in Paris, and at Vincennes, when the Italians received 10,880 pounds *tournois* for the work done so far.[22]

But there were still not enough ships and the king's correspondence for the spring of 1269 reflects the urgency of his requirements. At the beginning of April 1269 Louis sent his commissioners back to Genoa and added another knight to rent and contract for more ships.[23] Louis obviously hoped that they could, on their journey south, take with them some of the money already collected for the crusading tenth, in order to increase their funds on hand. The collectors of the tenth in the diocese of Maguelonne wrote to Louis in the middle of May that, on the authority of his letter, they had sent 470 pounds *melgorien* with William of Mora, the leading commissioner, as the first payment for the second year. They apologized to the king for the small amount, but assured him that there were many crusaders in the diocese who were exempt.[24] That the king's envoys must have had enough money is shown by the many letters at the end of May and the beginning of June which mention their numerous contracts and part payments for the building and leasing of ships. The king rented the *Saint-Suaveur*, the *Charity*, the *Saint-Nicholas*, and the *Saint-Esprit*, and the *Bonaventure* for varying sums between 850 and 2,400 pounds *tournois*. Five relatively small ships, at a cost of 1,700 pounds each, were to be built for the king and the whole fleet was to be at Aigues-Mortes by May 8, 1270, when the remaining obligation would be paid.[25]

Louis's financial resources were further strained by his desire to be joined by a representative of the English king. Henry III had long ago promised to go on crusade but he was too old and weak, and Edward agreed to take his father's place. The kingdom had been sufficiently pacified after the final collapse of the baronial revolt but the young prince's main problem was financial. Edward went to Paris in August 1269 to discuss the crusade with his uncle and, as a result of this meeting, Louis agreed to advance Edward 70,000 pounds *tournois* to enable him to participate in the crusade. Edward was to repay the loan from the revenues of Bordeaux at the rate of 10,000 pounds a year, beginning in 1274. The prince also agreed to be at Aigues-Mortes before August 15, 1270, ready to embark with the French king. The agreement was ratified by Louis, and in September by Henry III. By November 1, 1269, Edward had already received 45,000 pounds from the treasurer of the Temple. The remaining 25,000 were paid to Edward by William de Mora, the real treasurer of the crusade, after Louis's death, when the prince arrived at Tunis.[26]

All was ready for a departure early in the spring of 1270. During the last few months Louis completed the last details and visited his favourite places. The Christmas season was divided between Paris and Vincennes, and in January the king went once more to Chartres. Back in Paris Louis drew up his will and decided on the regents for the kingdom during his absence. Louis's will is characteristic. It is, first of all, most generous in its charities. There were specific legacies for the royal foundations Royaumont and Lys, and a large number of small legacies to religious houses, especially those of the Franciscans and Dominicans. The largest sums of money, however, were reserved for the most practical forms of charity: 2,000 pounds for the 200 poorest hospitals; 2,000 pounds to 800 leper-hospitals; 1,000 pounds for dowries for poor women; 210 pounds to the poor scholars of Paris; and 2,000 pounds to the orphans, widows, and lesser poor. These charities, although generous, are on much the same scale as those of his father. In more secular matters Louis IX also showed a sense of responsibility for those around him. He left 2,000 pounds to be distributed by his executors among his sergeants who had not yet been rewarded, 'or not enough', and ordered also that the clerks and chaplains of the household who had not yet been provided with a benefice should have twenty pounds a year until they received one. But it is interesting to note that Louis IX was far less generous with his own family than his father had been. Where Louis VIII had left Blanche of Castile 30,000 pounds, Marguerite of Provence received only 4,000. His sister Isabel had been given 20,000 pounds while Agnes, his only unmarried daughter, received 10,000 pounds, the same sum given to her sisters as their marriage portions. In a personal bequest, his library was to be divided equally among the Dominicans and Franciscans of Paris, the abbey of Royaumont, and the Dominicans of Compiègne. His executors were all clerics: the bishop of Paris, the bishop-elect of Evreux, the abbots of St Denis and Royaumont, and two of the king's clerks.[27]

The abbot of St Denis, Matthew of Vendôme, was also appointed one of the regents of the kingdom, a duty he shared with Simon of Nesle, a king's knight who was enthusiastically described by William of Nangis as 'wise and faithful'.[28] To make sure that there were no difficulties with the regency Louis also made careful provision for substitutes if necessary. The bishop-elect of Evreux was to substitute for the abbot of St Denis, if Matthew should die; John, count of Ponthieu was to substitute for Simon of Nesle, if Simon died.[29] As we have seen Louis did not probably trust Marguerite's political judgment enough to include her among the regents, but this decision combined with the small amount left her in his will seems rather ungenerous.

By the middle of March the king and his sons were ready to depart. Louis visited St Denis and took down the great oriflamme from above the altar, and was given his insignia of pilgrimage by the abbot. Together with his sons he went to the chapter to ask for prayers and placed his kingdom under the protection of St Denis. When the party came out from the church they were surrounded with 'rivers of tears'.[30] Certainly many must have felt as dubious about this venture as the outspoken Joinville who thought that

> all who advised him to go committed a mortal sin, for while he was still in France the whole Kingdom enjoyed peace at home and with all its neighbours, but after his departure its condition grew constantly worse.[31]

The first night the king and his sons spent at Vincennes where they parted with Queen Marguerite, and then the procession moved sluggishly towards the south.

The stages were painfully slow, probably because of the king's weakness. It took ten days to reach Sens, only seventy miles away; from there the king went on to Vézelay where he had recently enriched the church with a generous gift of relics and reliquaries studded with precious stones.[32] Louis also visited Cîteaux, was at Mâcon for Easter (April 13), and reached Lyons only by the end of the month. The king paused for ten days in Nîmes and then remained at St Gilles, some twenty-five miles from Aigues-Mortes, until the middle of June. This slow progress was disappointing, and was to prove fatal. Alphonse of Poitiers had set off from Paris at about the same time as his brother, but had travelled south through his Poitevin lands. On March 26 he wrote to

Brother John the Templar about the last items to be purchased for the expedition and warned him most emphatically that he must be at Aigues-Mortes by the first week in May at the very latest.[33] Alphonse must have heard of his brother's delay, for he too paused on his journey spending the first two weeks of May in Toulouse, and arriving at Aimargues, a small settlement near Aigues-Mortes, after the middle of May. Even with this delay the ships were not ready to receive them at once, so many of the barons and their armies turned aside to wait in the nearby towns.

Aigues-Mortes was neither popular nor comfortable. When Clement IV wrote to Louis about the project of fortifying the town with walls, the pope described with reminiscent clarity 'the persecution of the winds which, from every side, beat on the place with a free will, making it uninhabitable with growing piles of sand'.[34] Louis and his immediate company celebrated Pentecost (June 1) at St Gilles and held a last solemn court there. St Gilles had been the original family home of the counts of Toulouse and had inspired one of the most lyrical outbursts of the 12th century traveller, Guy of Bazoches.

> Here smile cultivated and fertile fields, and here the sides of the hills are adorned with vineyards. The pleasing aspect of the shrubbery and the beauty of gardens meets the eye, and oh! how the sweet smell of grass fills the air! Fruit trees groan under their load and lament their fertility, and the warbling birds in the branches send forth rich harmonies. If we look in a different direction we see the plain stretching out its level lap covered with green meadows and alluring us with its beauty. The Rhône, disdainfully cutting through the midst of the fields, rolls down proud waters and, reaching its place of birth, flows forth into the neighbouring sea.[35]

The fertility of St Gilles would have impressed the practical king, but natural beauty was rarely commented on by medieval men.

Unfortunately, the bored common soldiers, left to themselves in Aigues-Mortes without the supervision of the great lords, were soon embroiled in fights. The Provencals and Catalonians, never on the best of terms with the men from the north, rose against the French, and in the ensuing fighting many were chased into the boats or up to their necks in the water, and more than a hundred men were killed. As soon as the news reached the king, he moved quickly from St Gilles to Aigues-Mortes and ordered the leaders of the uprising to be hanged.[36]

In the last few days before the king took ship, his mind turned once more to affairs in his kingdom. His last letter to the regents on June 25 sums up Louis's continuous efforts to push his people into the Christian mould and adequately to discharge his royal duties. The letter begins with a statement of Christian principles which is more than just a formality, and it goes on to order the regents to make sure that the ordinance against blasphemy is enforced. The regents were also to check on the amounts received by the baillis as fines for this offence, but the king's portion of the money was to be given to the poor. Prostitutes were to be chased out of the towns, while criminals and malefactors were to be driven from the realm. Churches and ecclesiastical persons were to be protected against violence, the rights of the king and his subjects were to be defended, and the complaints of the poor were to be heard. Any judges who were known to have received presents, and those defamed of notorious crimes, were not to be admitted to the king's council. The king also reminded the regents that the oaths taken to the king by the members of his council were no longer in force, and they should require new oaths from all, except the prelates and bishops.[37] Concerned with settling all his affairs equitably, the king also ordered an extra allowance for the master-chaplain of his Sainte Chapelle, and insisted on the need for his chapel to possess in peace the rents he had given it.[38]

The king and his sons entered their ships on Tuesday, July 1, and the following day they sailed for Cagliari, the point of reunion for the fleet.[39] Despite a great storm which made most of the crusaders seasick and slowed their passage, the king's ships arrived off Sardinia by July 8 and Louis waited there for the other great barons. By Friday the ships of Alphonse of Poitiers, Theobald of Navarre, John of Brittany and the count of Flanders had arrived. A great council was held on Saturday to settle the place of the attack. Although no word appears in the chronicles to suggest that the king had decided on the actual point of attack before this council, it is obvious that the decision had already been made, and probably some time before. Louis, although not a great general, was a very cautious planner and did not believe in leaving things to chance. In his previous crusade he had arranged for great supplies of foodstuffs to be stockpiled in Cyprus to await the coming of the crusaders, and to provide their supplies for the second half of the expedition. On this occasion, no such arrangements had been made. The contracts for the Genoese ships were also made with considerable flexibility, specifically allowing the king to stop at one port and then re-embark and head for a further port without any further charge. All these straws point towards Louis's own decision to attack first at Tunis. Certainly, Tunis was an odd place for an ardent crusader to launch his attack. The emir of Tunis was no menace to the beleaguered Christians in the Frankish states. In order to help them, any full scale attack should be launched against the Mameluk sultans of Egypt and be primarily designed to aid Acre. Baibars had already conquered Jaffa, Beaufort and Antioch in 1268 and Acre despairingly awaited the final blow.

The argument which continues to rage in every discussion of Louis's second crusade is who was responsible for deflecting the crusade to Tunis? Was it due to the considered policy of Charles of Anjou, whose interests in Sicily also gave him a lively interest in Tunis just across the straits? Or was Louis actually convinced by the rumour that the Tunisian king wished to become Christian and was merely awaiting a Christian presence to facilitate the change? Those who believe that Charles of Anjou was not responsible lay most of the blame for the attack on Tunis on the naïvety of the king in believing the rumour of the emir's conversion, and over-emphasizing the effect it might have on the deliverance of all the Christians of North Africa. They argue that Charles of Anjou was primarily interested in regaining the Latin Empire of Constantinople, and that he was not anxious for any crusade that would turn crusaders in another direction. As well, they advance the hypothesis that Louis's knowledge of geography was so poor that he did not even realize the actual distance of Tunis from Egypt and the beleaguered Christians of Outremer. None of these reasons seems strong enough to support their case.

Charles of Anjou was twelve years younger than his brother Louis: he was full of health and strength, and flushed with his triumphs at Benevento and Taliacozzo. His kingdom of Sicily was now subdued and could serve as a stepping-stone to a great empire in the east. This incurably ambitious prince admired and respected his brother, but Charles's advice about a crusade would tend to be self-seeking: after all, he was bound to such an expedition only by family feeling and the need to ensure Louis's aid and continued assistance in his other projects. However, Tunis was, at this time, a thorn in Charles's side. The emir of Tunis had been a staunch supporter of the Hohenstaufens and, even after Charles's victories, sheltered his enemies. The emir had also refused to make the annual payments which he had been accustomed to make to the Hohenstaufen rulers for free access to the Sicilian ports and markets. Under these circumstances, Charles was anxious to settle his account with this annoying prince.

Both Louis and Charles needed each other's help. If Louis was to have even an adequate army, he needed the troops that Charles could bring. On the other hand, Charles was anxious to have French crusaders to help him in his dream of reconquering the empire of Constantinople. He felt that if a rapid and decisive stroke could be made against the Tunisians he would then be able to determine the ultimate destination of the crusaders, while having gained, in any case, a practical advantage. It would appear that, during the five years the crusade was actively considered, Louis's burning sense of mission was stronger than his considered judgment. If the present interpretation of Rutebeuf's poem, *Renart Bestourné*, is correct, Rutebeuf, who represented one current of popular opinion, saw Charles of Anjou as the wily fox who used for his own ends the pious obstinacy of the king and his dependence on the friars.[40] The extraordinarily precise detail of the ship's contracts, the absence of stockpiles of provisions in any of the islands, the extreme secrecy which was maintained as to the target for the crusade; all these seem to point to the conclusion that the decision to attack Tunis may have been taken as early as 1268 or 1269.

There is also the possibility that Louis may have been influenced towards the western Mediterranean by the renewed hope that there was a chance of reunion between the Greek and Roman church, and of some assistance from the Mongols. In the summer of 1269 an embassy was sent to Louis by Michael Paleologus, the

15. Reliquary head of Louis from the Sainte Chapelle – the frontispiece of Du Cange's edition of Joinville (1668). The reliquary was destroyed during the Revolution

16a. First seal of Louis made at his accession *c.* 1223

16b. Later seal of Louis made after his illness of 1244

16c. Elephant presented to Henry III by Louis IX, 1255

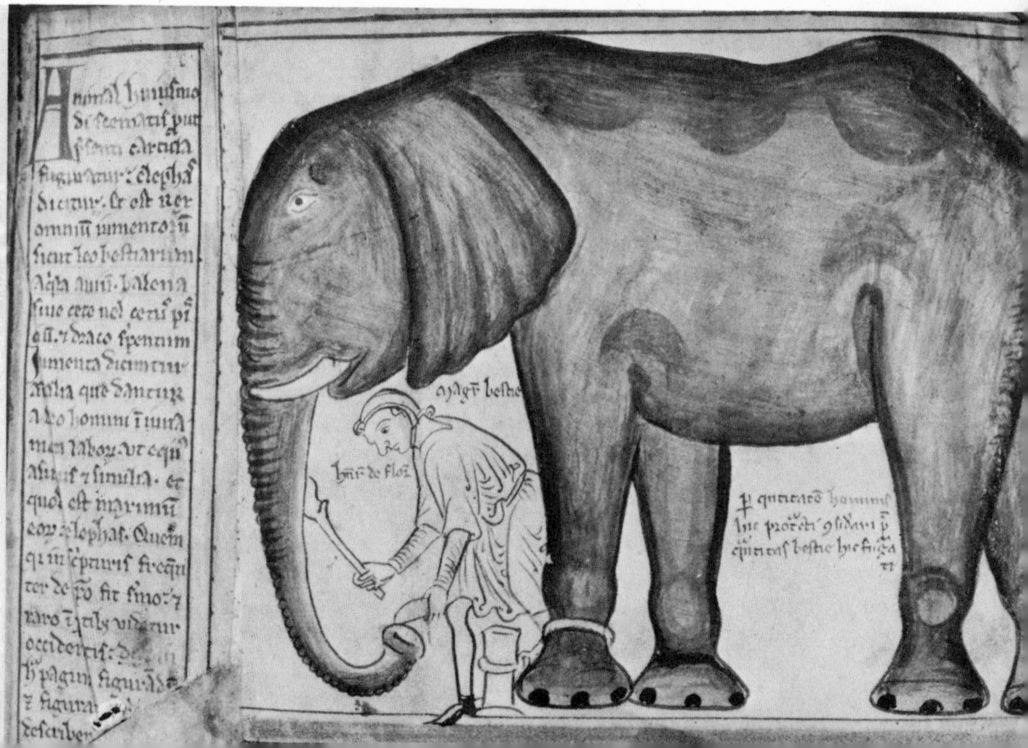

Greek emperor of Constantinople, to discuss reunion. The following winter, another envoy from Michael told Louis of the marriage of Apagan, the son of the khan Hulagu, to Michael's daughter, and his baptism as a Christian.[41] Louis's earlier hopes for the conversion of the Mongols, discouraged by the reports of the friars he had sent to the khan's court, may well have risen again. The king may have been convinced that the Christians in the east would be aided by this Christian Mongol leader, and that the diversion to the west would assist by drawing off a valuable source of supplies and reinforcements for the Egyptians. Whatever the reasons which were brought forward to justify the decision, it must be recognized that Louis's physical weakness and overmastering desire to fight the infidel did not improve his judgment, or his ability to withstand his brother's partisan pleading. Nevertheless, the king's prestige was so great that few dared to oppose him, and the second crusade headed for Tunis, after the barons and the Genoese had been encouraged by tales of the riches and the possibility of booty.[42]

It was particularly unfortunate that the crusaders had not been able to sail at the beginning of May or June, as originally planned. Their departure in July meant that they arrived in North Africa at the peak of the summer heat, a time when campaigning was incredibly difficult. The ships left Cagliari on Tuesday, July 15 and arrived at Tunis, after an easy passage, on Thursday. The French captured the harbour and landed with little difficulty, setting up their tents on a peninsula, but there was no fresh water and on the following Monday they moved on and pitched their camp in a valley below Carthage, a few miles away.[43] At first all seemed to go well. Despite desultory Moslem attacks the crusaders made their camp safe with ditches, and then attacked and captured Carthage. The king was waiting for the arrival of Charles of Anjou and his army before proceeding further, a fact which seems to reinforce the estimates of the small size of Louis's own army on this occasion. From the amount of shipping used, it would appear that the king had a total army of less than 10,000 men, a force much smaller than the one he had led in 1248.[44] Louis attempted to maintain his full strength by issuing strict orders that no one was to leave the battle line for individual sorties. In this brief campaign the king seems to have succeeded in enforcing this necessary but unpopular discipline.

As July turned into August and the king of Sicily had still not arrived, all the foreseeable disasters of a campaign conducted in such heat descended upon the French. In the country around Tunis a heat of a hundred degrees is common in August and the earth is sunbaked and scorching with little respite at night. It must have been most oppressive for soldiers clad in heavy wool and chain mail. Since there was also a lack of both fresh water and healthy food – the army relied on a heavy meat diet made up primarily of salt pork – the camp was soon afflicted by fever and dysentery. Many of the great barons died: two of the notables mentioned by the king in a codicil to his will as his executors died before the king and had to be replaced.[45] Among the first victims was the king's own son, John Tristan, a boy of only twenty who had been born at Damietta at the time of his father's capture, and who died on board his ship on August 3. Although John does not seem to have been any holier than his brothers, contemporary opinion treasured the circumstances of his birth and death and set him apart for special veneration. During the following seventy years he became a hero of legend, transformed into a king of Tarsus who almost suffered martyrdom but was rescued in time to marry the heroine and provide a happy ending.[46]

John's death was followed in a few days by that of the papal legate. Then Louis himself fell desperately ill, and so did his son and heir Philip. Louis knew he was dying, and that the crusade as a military venture was doomed, but with his failing strength he concentrated on his own immediate duties. Louis's last days mirrored the concerns of his whole life. According to a very early tradition, he called Philip to his side and gave him his instructions dealing with private morality and royal duties, his *Enseignements*, to respect as he would his will. The king then gave himself up to prayer and preparation for death. He received the sacraments devoutly and his son, Peter of Alençon, later described to Joinville how his father had called on the saints as death approached, especially the patron saints of France, St Denis and St Genevieve.[47] According to William of St Pathus his last words were a prayer for his people:

> Gracious good God, have mercy on this people who stay here and lead them to their country, that they do not fall into the hands of their enemies and are not constrained to deny Thy holy name.[48]

Then, in the pious tradition of the time, the king had himself laid on ashes arranged on the floor in the form of a cross, where he died in the middle of the afternoon on August 25.

There was no time to indulge in private sorrow, no pause to praise Louis's virtues or to mourn the effect of his death on the kingdom of France. As the king lay dying, the fleet of Charles of Anjou was sighted off the coast, and his landing brought new hope to an army that was cast down and confused, as well as decimated by illness. The new king, Philip III, was weak from the fever and inexpert in war, so that the arrival of the experienced and capable Charles was of immeasurable assistance. Charles hurried to the king's lodging and found his brother's body still warm: affection, and perhaps remorse, brought him to his knees to weep and pray. This moment of feeling soon passed and Charles took effective command of the expedition. He ordered his brother's body to be prepared for return to France, since it ought to be buried at St Denis with the other kings of France. The army too was desperately anxious to keep this last souvenir of their holy king, feeling that his relics might ward off further ill fortune. The tremendous heat, and the absence of embalming, meant that the whole body could not be preserved, so in the accepted medieval method the corpse was boiled with water and wine to separate the flesh from the bones and make them suitable for the long trip back to France. Charles asked for the heart and entrails for himself, and had them buried in the Benedictine abbey of Monreale near Palermo.[49]

For all practical purposes the crusade wasted away with Louis's death. The army, never enthusiastic, was too much discouraged by the prevalent illness and death, and there was no inspiring leader determined to carry on. The French won some small successes and the sultan of Tunis, whose army had also suffered from the general contagion, offered peace. Charles suggested that Philip should accept. After all, it was wise for Philip to return to France as soon as possible and, since the sultan was disposed to make large concessions, the peace offer gave the new king the opportunity to conclude honourably an ill-conceived expedition. The treaty, drawn up at the end of October, strongly favoured the Christians, especially Charles of Anjou who obtained all the concessions he had desired. The French received 210,000 ounces of gold to pay the expenses of the war, the exchange of prisoners, and the right for Christians to live, do business, and practise their religion in the sultan's lands.[50]

Edward of England arrived during the final peace negotiations, and would have preferred a campaign to a peace treaty. Under the circumstances, he had no choice but to join the French army and the troops of Charles of Anjou when they re-embarked on November 15, 1270. They set sail for Sicily, since it was very late in the season to attempt the direct, but dangerous, voyage across the Mediterranean. Ill fortune still dogged the crusaders, for the fleet had scarcely reached Trapani when it was struck by a heavy storm, which sank many of the ships and drowned their passengers. Only Edward's ships were unscathed, and many of the pious connected this miraculous deliverance with his determination to carry on the crusade. Edward did, in fact, go on to Acre with a small band of supporters only returning to England after his father's death and his own accession to the throne. Meanwhile Philip III led the sad remnants of his army on the long land journey up the Italian peninsula. The last of the great crusades was over.

XVII

Apotheosis

The Most Christian King of France was dead. His flaming faith and luminous certainty of belief died with him. The religious idealism which had led Louis to describe his army before Tunis as under the orders of 'Our Lord Jesus Christ and his sergeant Louis, king of France'[1] had lost its compelling public force with the death of its outstanding exemplar. No man came forward to raise again the banner the king of France had let fall. The surviving crusaders were depressed and disillusioned with the value of a war which had been perverted to his own ends by the insatiable ambition of Charles of Anjou. The teasing mirage of a new Latin empire of Constantinople, with himself at its head, determined most of Charles's later actions but it always eluded his grasp. Despite the efforts of some of the succeeding popes, the age of the crusades was over and the fall of the last Christian strongholds in Outremer unavoidable.

The general mood of disillusion and cynicism was especially marked in France where the roll-call of Louis's last crusade was a vast necrology. Besides the loss of the king, John Tristan, and other magnates at Tunis, Philip and his army only regained France after suffering other heavy casualties. Theobald of Navarre, husband of Philip's sister Isabel, had been ill when they left Tunis: he died at Trapani in the beginning of December. His wife also died before returning to France. Isabella of Aragon, Philip's queen, fell from her horse in January while fording a stream in flood near Cosenza. This resulted in the birth of a stillborn son, and her own death a few days later.* The last of the

*An early deathmask appears to have been taken from Isabella, as her monument at Cosenza (reproduced at the Musée des Monuments Historiques) depicts the young queen with a roughly stitched cut on her face and a haggard and drawn expression.

victims were Alphonse of Poitiers and his countess, Jeanne of Toulouse, who died in August 1271, just before they reached France. Philip had returned to Paris by May 1271 and he fulfilled his final sad, filial duty by leading the great funeral procession to St Denis. The funeral marked the end of an era for France, it had lost its holy king, but it had gained a legend.

Louis IX had dominated the religious imagination of his contemporaries. Almost immediately there was talk of the miracles that were worked at his tomb at St Denis and the new pope, Gregory X, instituted an inquiry. Gregory was inclined in Louis's favour, in any case, since he was a determined proponent of another crusade, and he named as the legate in charge of the inquiry Cardinal Simon of Brie, the devoted Frenchman who had already served Louis himself during the planning of the last crusade. The pope also asked Geoffrey of Beaulieu, Louis's confessor for many years, to prepare a summary of the king's virtues. Gregory died in 1276 before he received the legate's report, although Geoffrey of Beaulieu had completed his task before his own death in 1274 or 1275. Gregory X was followed by a series of short-lived popes, mainly Italians, whose struggles with Charles of Anjou did not encourage them to look for sanctity in the members of the French royal house. Finally, in 1280 Simon of Brie became pope himself, under the name of Martin IV; he was for patriotic reasons convinced of the piety of the Capetian monarchs. Having been involved in the first abortive inquiry, Martin was anxious to see the case for canonization pushed forward actively. The pope ordered a public inquiry, headed by the archbishop of Rouen, the bishop of Auxerre, and the bishop of Spoleto, to hear the cause at St Denis. The sessions opened in May 1282, and during the next ten months the commissioners heard a series of thirty-eight witnesses on the king's life and more than three hundred and thirty on the miracles. Charles of Anjou, in a last moment of glory before the Sicilian Vespers robbed him of half of his kingdom, made a special deposition in Naples in February 1282 on his brother's virtues.[2] The dossiers of these inquests were so full that at the time of the canonization Pope Boniface remarked that the process had required more documents than an ass could carry. Even one of the notaries merely charged with receiving information made 200 pounds *tournois* in a year.[3] Unfortunately, the dossiers have been lost and only odd fragments remain, although William of St Pathus in his life of Louis summarized the evidence and listed the witnesses who testified to the king's character.

William also reported the miracles brought forward at the inquiry; they were characterized by a domestic touch and a strongly local flavour.* Primarily they concerned people of St Denis or Paris, or those from other parts of the realm who had known the king personally. A shoemaker from Lincoln, who had lived in St Denis for thirty years, did not share the local feeling for Louis. He mocked those who came to pray at the king's tomb, claiming, in a burst of patriotism, that Henry of England had been a better man than Louis. The sceptic was struck down by a malady in his leg and knee and was only cured by praying at Louis's tomb and repenting his mocking words.[4] More characteristic was the story of Master Dudes, canon of Paris and a doctor of medicine. He had voyaged to Tunis with Louis and continued to serve his son. In 1282 Dudes fell ill with an ague and a fever, and the physicians of Paris despaired of his recovery. Having made his confession and settled his affairs, Dudes, as a last resort, thought of Louis and prayed to his old master, 'as I have served you, I beg that you will help me'. In a dream he was transported to Louis's tomb and saw the king, dressed in white embroidered with gold, bearing crown and sceptre. The king touched his head and removed the 'evil humour' that was the cause of his illness. The next morning he awoke cured, and confounded his doctors by insisting on a chicken and some wine.[5]

There was the very practical miracle too, brought forward by the wife of a man who had once been one of Louis's squires. Her cellars in Paris were flooded, and she remembered that Louis had given her husband some of his old peacock feather hats. Secretly, and against the advice of the monks she had consulted, she sent a young servant down to the flooded cellar to make the sign of the cross over the water with one of the hats. Before the evening

*Perhaps it should be noted here that the liberation of Paris in 1944, accomplished with few casualties and only minor destruction, also took place on the feast of St Louis, August 25th, the day of his death.

curfew the water had gone down so much that they could draw wine from the wine casks which had been floating around the cellar, and by the next day only some mud marked the great flood. Her neighbours' cellars did not dry out so fast.[6]

Despite the weight of the evidence and the miracles, the final achievement of Louis's formal canonization only came some years later and after the death of Pope Martin. At the beginning of August 1297, Benedict Cajetan, who as a cardinal had received the deposition of Charles of Anjou seventeen years before, and had now become Pope Boniface VIII, attempted to smoothe his unhappy relations with Philip the Fair and proclaimed Louis among the confessors of the Church. The following year on the day of Louis's feast Philip the Fair and the archbishop of Sens presided at the exhumation of the saint's body which was transferred to the Sainte Chapelle. Before it was returned to St Denis Philip the Fair had had a magnificent reliquary made for the skull. Designed in gold by one of the finest goldsmiths of the time and decorated with many jewels, it was kept at the Sainte Chapelle and reverenced with the relics of the Passion which the holy king had enshrined there. It did not survive the Revolution, although the skull itself was saved and now rests in the treasury of Notre Dame. In 1308 Philip, Louis's grandson, presided over a partition of the relics among various religious houses and royal relations. Over the years small fragments of his bones have come to rest in many places, including many of the innumerable churches dedicated to St Louis of France.[7]

The canonized king became both the glory and the symbol of the French monarchy. Joinville, with a typical old man's love of moralizing, draws a lesson from the canonization for the king's descendants.

> For this there was, and should still be, great rejoicing throughout the Kingdom of France; great will be the honour to all of his house who strive to resemble him in well-doing, and great the reproach to all those who refused to imitate him in good works; great reproach, I say, to those of his house who seek to do ill, for fingers will be pointed at them, and it will be said that the holy King from whom they are sprung would have scorned to do such wrong.[8]

It is only an aprocryphal story that Louis XVI's chaplain at the guillotine addressed his king with the cry of 'Son of Saint Louis, go up to heaven',[9] but the pride in the unique inheritance which the legend enshrines was a valuable part of the French myth of royal grandeur. The French monarchy exploited the prestige and reputation of its saintly forebear to its own advantage. Louis's persistent concern for justice and peace, his continued efforts to give good government to his realm, had masked the rapid centralization of the kingdom and the growing personal power of the king exercised through his officials. Louis had felt deeply his personal responsibility for his people, and they repaid him with their description of the time of 'the good king Louis' as a golden age of peace and justice. Even his brave but fruitless crusading attempts gained him prestige among his contemporaries, both Christian and Moslem, and surrounded the slight figure of the king with a halo of romance and adventure. Over the years the myth of Louis has become so powerful that the practical, dryly humorous, sometimes intolerant accents of the living king have become almost submerged in a wave of pious sentimentality and nationalistic emotion.

It is Joinville who comes closest to summing up the whole man as his contemporaries knew him. The seneschal tells of the time that Louis set Joinville and Master Robert of Sorbon disputing over the superiority of a *prud'homme* to a devout man, and then gave his own decision on the question. 'I would dearly love to have the name of a *prud'homme,*' Louis said, 'so long as I deserved it, and you would be welcome to the rest. For a *prud'homme* is so great and good a thing that even to pronounce the word fills the mouth pleasantly.'[10] Louis shared the opinion of his grandfather, Philip Augustus, who described with admiration a *prud'homme* as one who was both brave in body and also the faithful servant of Christ. The word, with its untranslatable nuances of meaning, embodies a whole range of medieval virtues which demanded the respect of all, knights and common people as well as the clerks and the pious. Louis wholeheartedly admired this balanced ideal and sought to achieve it: his unshakable Christian faith flowered in an equally firm conviction of the monarch's duty and right to maintain untouched 'the rights of his subjects, the prerogatives of his crown, and the safety of his realm'.[11] The extent of his success in harmonizing these often contradictory objectives is witnessed by the plaintive tone of a contemporary memorial verse.

> I say that justice is dead and loyalty extinct
> Since the good king, the holy creature, died
> Who did justice to each upon his complaint . . .
> To whom can the poor people now cry
> Since the good king is dead?[12]

APPENDICES

APPENDIX I

The Sources

NARRATIVE SOURCES

CONTEMPORARY LIVES

John of Joinville. The most important of all sources for a life of Louis is Joinville's biography of his king. It was composed in two parts: the circumstantial and vivid memoir on the crusade was probably written around 1272, while the introductory and concluding sections were added at the specific request of Queen Jeanne of Navarre, Louis's granddaughter. The queen was dead before the book was concluded in 1309 and Joinville presented it to the future Louis X. The added sections are of less interest and value than the crusading narrative, because much of them were copied from other lives, but there are occasional original and revealing anecdotes. Joinville's portrait of his king is delightfully personal, intimate, and secular, and illustrates the accepted ideals of the noble society of the time.[1]

Geoffrey of Beaulieu. Geoffrey was a Dominican who served as Louis's confessor, and accompanied him on both crusades. His *Life and holy conversation of Louis of pious memory late king of France* is what might be expected from its title and the fact that it was commissioned by the pope. It celebrates the Christian virtues of the private man, but is almost completely uninterested in the work of the king. The *Life* is arranged according to virtues, rather than any chronological plan, and its value lies in Geoffrey's intimate knowledge of Louis.[2]

William of Chartres. Another Dominican and royal chaplain who had been with the king on his crusades, William's avowed intention in writing his life was to extend and complete the work of

Geoffrey of Beaulieu. His work is of the same type, and although there are a few different stories William's is the more verbose and repetitive.[3]

William of St Pathus. William of St Pathus had not been a personal associate of the king but he served for eighteen years as the confessor of Queen Marguerite of Provence, and also as confessor of their daughter Blanche. William wrote a two-part description of the king's life and miracles at Blanche's request, using the evidence included in a resumé of the inquiry for Louis's canonization in 1282. The life is based on the deposition of the various witnesses at the inquiry, and is headed by a valuable list of those who were called upon to testify. This analysis of the evidence is all the more interesting because the original records have disappeared. The value of the section on the king's miracles is not primarily historical, although it illustrates the obvious official encouragement of the king's cult at St Denis and Paris. William of St Pathus was less immediately concerned than Geoffrey of Beaulieu or William of Chartres, but he is a more sober and credible reporter who had also profited by the memories of Queen Marguerite. We have his text in French, but it was originally written in Latin about 1303, and was perhaps translated into the vernacular by the author himself. In any case, the translation was made almost immediately.[4]

William of Nangis. The official historiographers of the French kings were drawn from the monks of the abbey of St Denis, which had many close links with the royal house. William of Nangis was a monk there, and the custodian of its charters between 1285 and 1300. He compiled the *Deeds of King Louis* during the reign of Philip III, drawing primarily on the works of Geoffrey of Beaulieu, Gilon of Rheims (whose chronicle has vanished), and Primat. The only original section of William's work deals with the period between 1226 and 1248, and this was probably borrowed from Gilon of Rheims. William also wrote a *Chronicle* which carried his account as far as 1300 and which provides some useful details on the events following Louis's death at Tunis.[5]

CHRONICLES

Primat. Primat was also a monk of St Denis and wrote a universal chronicle in Latin which originally stopped at 1278. His work deals more fully with Louis's last crusade than does that of William of Nangis, and was probably drawn up under the supervision of Abbot Matthew of Vendôme, who had served as regent.[6]

Vincent of Beauvais. The learned Dominican's four-part encyclopaedia includes a section known as the *Mirror of History.* It is primarily a compilation of extracts from other chroniclers and deals with universal history to 1250. It was a most popular patchwork, and was read and quoted for several centuries. The recently discovered Vinland Map, as well as a previously unknown description of the first journey to the Mongols in 1245 were found attached to a fourteenth-century copy of a part of Vincent's *Mirror of History.*[7]

Baldwin of Avesnes. Baldwin was the son of Bouchard of Avesnes and the Countess Marguerite of Flanders. This useful chronicle which deals particularly with affairs in Flanders and the north cannot be positively attributed to him, although he was known by reputation as one of the wisest knights of his time, though very small and thin.[8]

Alberic of Trois-Fontaines. Alberic was from Champagne, a monk of the Cistercian abbey of Trois-Fontaines, and his chronicle is a valuable contemporary source for the affairs of Champagne till about 1240. Alberic had access to a large number of historical works and charters to be found in the abbeys of Champagne, and used his material carefully. He loved genealogical details, and carefully described natural catastrophes such as floods, as well as the more apocryphal flights of dragons.[9]

William of Puylaurens. His *Chronicle of the Albigensians* is remarkably impartial, recording events reported by others with such enormous partisanship. He deals fully with the Albigensian troubles and the affairs of the count of Toulouse, and more briefly with general events. William is favourable to Count Raymond, but not to the heretics.[10]

Minstrel of Rheims. The Chronicle known as the *Récits d'un Menèstrèl de Reims* was certainly composed for oral recitation by a travelling minstrel, and was written by an inhabitant of Rheims in the thirteenth century. The author was probably a layman, for he was outspoken in his criticism of the pope and the clergy. Although the *Récits* is essentially a chronicle of France and Outremer, written in the vernacular, it needed dialogue and stories to hold the attention of the audience and to make the tale seem vivid and convincing. Under such circumstances, it is not surprising that a plausible fiction was often preferred to the sober truth, and that the Minstrel of Rheims must really be described as a teller of tales rather than a sober chronicler.[11]

Matthew Paris. Matthew Paris, Benedictine monk of St Albans, is the best known – and most enjoyable – chronicler of the thirteenth century. Although his first interest is in English affairs, his *Chronica Majora* is a valuable source for affairs of France and the Empire, and also for the crusades and the invasions of the Mongols. In his *Liber Additamentorum* he also provides copies of documents illustrative of the later sections of the *Chronica Majora*, and which are not available elsewhere. Matthew is vivid, racy, full of prejudices, especially against the pope and the friars, and rather more enthusiastic about Louis than about his own king in England. Unfortunately his chronicle does not extend as far as the period of the Barons' War, but ends in the spring of 1259.[12]

Salimbene. This Italian Franciscan of good family wrote a very personal chronicle about his wanderings as a friar. He was in France in 1247 and 1248 and met the king and his retinue on their way to the crusade. Salimbene encountered most of the great men of the day who had any contact with the Franciscans, and described them with gusto.[13]

Grandes Chroniques. The large compilation known as the *Grandes Chroniques*, or that part of it which deals with the reign of Louis IX, is a fourteenth-century translation of the Latin works of Vincent of Beauvais and Primat, with some additions from the *Chronicle* of William of Nangis and some interpolations by the translator, John of Vignay.[14]

Continuation of William of Tyre. William of Tyre, the brilliant twelfth-century historian of the crusades, had many copyists and continuators. This work, often referred to as the Bothelin MS., is one of the most useful narrative sources for Louis's first crusade. It was written by a subject of the French king and is somewhat partisan.[15]

Miscellaneous. Other minor French chronicles, such as that of Philip Mousket, have been collected in volumes XX-XXIII of the *Recueil des Historiens des Gaules et de la France,* and occasionally add some interesting detail. Other English annals, particularly those of Burton, add to the knowledge of the crusade and the relations with France. The Moslem chroniclers who describe Louis's crusades, Djamal ad-Din and Maqrisi, present an opposite point of view, but testify to the general prestige of King Louis. Letters are also particularly informative sources for both crusades. Louis himself described events from the fall of Damietta to his departure for Acre,[16] and John Sarrasin wrote to Nicholas Arrode a detailed account of the taking of Damietta.[17] There is also a most informative letter of Peter of Condé to the regent, Abbot Matthew, on the terms of peace arrived at with the sultan of Tunis.[18] These are in addition to the many letters included in Matthew Paris's chronicle or his *Liber Additamentorum.*

GOVERNMENT RECORDS

FRENCH

Ordonnances. An eighteenth-century collection known as the *Ordonnances des rois de France de la troisième race,* attempted to include all the legislative activity of the French kings from the time of Hugh Capet. That part of the collection which deals with Louis's reign is very miscellaneous, and includes many items which cannot be called legislation, as well as the accepted ordinances.[19]

Layettes. The *Layettes du Trésor des Chartes* are the undifferentiated collection of documents from Louis's chancery. The early administrative and legal records of France were not subdivided as early or as continuously maintained as those of England. After the loss of his registers and charters at the battle of Freteval, Philip Augustus decided to settle his archives at Paris. When Louis ordered the building of the Sainte Chapelle, he also had constructed a new building for the royal archives. This small three-story structure, next to the Sainte Chapelle, had sacristies on the first two floors, corresponding with the upper and lower chapels. The third floor was designed for the exclusive use of the king, was entered by a special spiral staircase, and housed the royal archives and library. This location for the royal records corresponded to the practice in the monasteries, where the archives were put above their sacristies, or treasuries, in which the relics and valuable ornaments were kept. Both documents and valuables were thus given the added protection of a religious building. The king's records were kept in small chests, or *layettes*, and the place and nature of the storage gave the collection its name. The *Layettes*, as they are commonly referred to, are a collection taken from three main sources. First, there are documents arising from the king's relations with foreign princes, great feudal lords, and royal vassals, especially those which might be used to enforce a legal claim. Secondly, there is the correspondence addressed *to* the king, and occasionally copies of letters *from* the king. Thirdly, there are the collections of documents acquired from seignorial archives when new territories entered the royal domain. For example, all the documents concerning the conquest of the Albigeois were deposited in the *Layettes* during Louis's reign, and those which dealt with the county of Toulouse were added after the death of Alphonse. Unfortunately, no general inventory was made till 1318, and all during Louis's reign there was no principle of order or arrangement. The published edition does not separate the different topics, but is purely chronological.[20]

Olim. The registers of the decisions of parlement were nicknamed the Olim, from the opening words of the second book. The register for the last years of Louis's reign was compiled by John of Montluçon, a notary attached to parlement.[21]

Financial Records. The thirteenth-century financial records of France have only survived in fragments. Most of the medieval accounts were destroyed in 1737 when the building of the Chambre des

Comptes was destroyed by fire. The destruction of most of the remainder was accomplished by the revolutionaries, who sent the old parchments to the arsenals to be used as cartridges. The surviving sparse and fragmentary accounts have been collected in volumes XXI and XXII of the *Recueil*, and commented on by the scholarly editors. This material can occasionally be supplemented by now destroyed documents quoted by such seventeenth-century scholars as Du Cange and Le Nain de Tillemont.[22]

Registers of the Enquêteurs. The surviving registers of the complaints heard by Louis's enquêteurs have been published in volume XXIV of the *Recueil*. They are an invaluable source for the local history of the reign, and an aid in tracing the careers of the royal officials.[23]

Administrative Correspondence of Alphonse of Poitiers. Alphonse had systematic registers kept after 1263, although the earliest one is lost. Since Alphonse lived in the Ile-de-France, almost all his relations with the lords of the south and his own local officials were carried on by correspondence. His letters throw valuable light on the methods and problems of government in the conquered south. Their businesslike tone and emphasis on clarity, brevity, and intelligibility make them models of administrative prose.[24]

FOREIGN

Papal Registers. The papal registers of Innocent IV, Alexander IV, Urban IV and Clement IV are full of letters to Louis on various matters of general interest. They include not only privileges and concessions, but also a good many polite disputes over jurisdiction.[25]

English Governmental Records. From 1254 on the Patent and Close Rolls contain many letters from Henry to Louis. Read in conjunction with the French documents, they chart the gradual warming of relations, the negotiation of the peace treaty, and Louis's deepening involvement in attempts at arbitration during and after the Barons' War.[26]

MISCELLANEOUS

Because Louis was such a towering figure, there are many incidental sources of information about him and his methods of government. Such popular lawbooks as the *Etablissements de Saint Louis* and Philippe of Beaumanoir's *Coutumes de Beauvaisis* give an almost contemporary picture of the accepted law and legal theory in the northern part of the realm.[27] *The Register of Eudes Rigaud* describes the episcopal visitations and daily journeys of the archbishop of Rouen from 1248 to 1269. Rigaud was one of the king's closest councillors and friends after Louis's return from the crusade and so his register dates, and occasionally describes, his meetings with the king.[28] The works of such poets as Rutebeuf give some hint of the current of popular feeling, while the sermons of Stephen of Bourbon frequently include stories of Louis himself and of those surrounding him.[29] The stories may not be true, although the Dominican Stephen knew most of the great men of Europe of his day and was a fund of historical anecdote, but they illustrate the friars' view of Louis which they were busy preaching throughout the kingdom. A much later work on King Louis, which should, nevertheless, be included among the sources because of its use of now vanished information, is the *Vie de Saint Louis* by Le Nain de Tillemont.[30] Written in the seventeenth century and drawing on many documents since destroyed, Tillemont's life is an excellent biography and a scholarly storehouse which many other later biographers have plundered.

Finally, it seems only right to include the work of the contemporary artists among the sources which provide our knowledge of King Louis. Such achievements as the Sainte Chapelle, the stained glass windows, the sculptures, and the illuminated manuscripts often have the king and his exploits as their subject, and also illustrate the new and triumphant style of architecture and decoration which Louis himself encouraged and which influenced all of Europe. The artists put into an idealized form the values and concerns of the thirteenth century, and they illustrate the leading role played by the holy and cultured French king.

APPENDIX II

Notes

INTRODUCTION

page 20 1. Lorgnon, *Documents Parisiens*, 55.

CHAPTER I–THE YOUNG KING'S INHERITANCE

page 21 1. Joinville, 69. (All the references to Joinville are to the numbered paragraphs of the De Wailly edition. The Hague translation follows the same system of numbering and the English quotations are normally taken from that translation.)

2. Beaulieu, 19e.

22 3. Gerald of Wales, *De principis instructione*, *Opera* VII, 6–7, quoted in Thompson, *Literacy of the Laity*, 130 and 154, n. 165.

23 4. Berger, *Blanche de Castille*, 7–8.

5. *Magna Vita S. Hugonis*, II, ed. D. L. Douie and H. Farmer (London, 1962), 156.

24 6. Etienne de Bourbon, 389, n. 1.

7. *Recueil* XXII, 595.

8. *Ménéstrel de Reims*, 157–8.

9. St Pathus, *Vie de Saint Louis*, 18.

10. *Recueil* XXIII, 16.

11. Joinville, 71.

25 12. *Layettes* II, 1710.

13. *Layettes* II, 1828, 1811.

27 14. De Pange, *Le Roi très chrétien*, 262–3.

33 15. *Layettes* II, 1710.

CHAPTER II – BLANCHE OF CASTILE AND THE REGENCY 1226–1234

page 34 1. *Layettes* II, 1823–7.
35 2. *Layettes* II, 1909. Borrelli de Serres, *Récherches sur divers services publics*, 183.
36 3. Chronicle of Philip Mousket, *Recueil* XXII, 241, ll.27495–502.
4. *Layettes* II, 1850.
5. *Layettes* II, 1895.
6. Berger, *Blanche de Castille*, 69.
37 7. Borrelli de Serres, *Récherches*, 183.
8. *Layettes* II, 1922, 1926.
38 9. *Grandes Chroniques* VII, 38.
10. Joinville, 73.
11. Nangis, *Life*, 314c.
40 12. Nangis, *Life*, 316e. *Grandes Chroniques* VII, 3–4.
13. *Recueil* XXIV, 18–20, nos. 117, 126, 130.
14. Paris, *Chron. Maj.* III, 191.
41 15. *Layettes* II, 2056–8
42 16. *Recueil* XXIV, 730.
17. *Recueil* XXIV, 58, n. 439.
18. Berger, *Blanche de Castille*, 205–6.
43 19. *Recueil* XXI, 220–26.
44 20. Paris, *Chron. Maj.* III, 204. *Layettes* II, 2141.
21. *Layettes* II, 2144.
22. *Layettes* II, 1992. *Histoire Générale de Languedoc* VIII, cc. 883–93.
45 23. *Chartularium universitatis Parisiensis* I, 129–31, n. 72.
46 24. *Ordonnances* I, 50–2.
25. Hefele-Leclerq, *Histoire des Conciles* V, pt. II (Paris, 1913), 1496–1501.
26. Puylaurens, *Recueil* XIX, 223.
47 27. Campbell, 'Ecclesiastical Censures in the Reign of Saint Louis', *Speculum* XXXV (1960), 535–41.
48 28. Nangis, *Chronicon*, 547.
29. Pontal, 'Le différend entre Louis IX et les évêques de Beauvais', *Bibl. de l'éc. des Ch.* CXXIII (1965), 5–34.

page 49 30. Paris, *Chron. Maj.* III, 166–9. *Grandes Chroniques* VII, 60–1.

50 31. *Ordonnances* I, 47–8.

32. *Layettes* II, 2083.

51 33. Berger, *op. cit.*, 341.

34. Duclos, *Histoire du Royaumont* I, 37–42.

52 35. St Pathus, *Vie*, 71.

36. *Ibid.*, 94–5.

37. Duclos, *op. cit.* I, 210.

38. *Ibid.*, 109.

CHAPTER III – THE KING COMES OF AGE 1234–1240

page 55 1. Nangis, *Life*, 322c.

56 2. *Recueil* XXI, 246–8.

3. Joinville, 607.

57 4. Paris, *Chron. Maj.* III, 477.

5. Lecoy de la Marche, *Saint Louis, son gouvernement et sa politique*, 347.

6. Etienne de Bourbon, 388, n. 1.

58 7. Joinville, 81.

8. *Layettes* II, 2312–14, 2322.

59 9. *Layettes* II, 2432.

10. *Layettes* II, 2443.

11. Chron. St Denis, *Recueil* XXI, 111. Alberic of Trois-Fontaines, *Recueil* XXI, 616.

60 12. Chron. St Denis, *Recueil* XXI, 111–12. *Grandes Chroniques* VII, 67–8.

13. *Layettes* II, 2320.

14. Paris, *Chron. Maj.* III, 298.

15. *Layettes* II, 2705.

61 16. *Recueil* XXII, 580.

62 17. *Ibid.*, 580–3.

18. Miracles of St Genevieve, *Recueil* XXIII, 136–7. Paris, *Chron. Maj.* III, 387.

19. Nangis, *Chronicon*, 547.

63 20. Cabrol and Leclerq, *Dictionnaire de l'archéologie chrétienne*, VII, Instruments de la Passion.

21. *Recueil* XXII, 27–32.

page 65 22. *Recueil* XXII, 601.
66 23. Theophilus, *De Diversis Artibus*, trans. with intro. and notes by C. R. Dodwell (London, 1961), 63.
24. Le Roux de Lincy, *Paris et ses historiens*, 47.
25. *Layettes* II, 2776.
67 26. *Recueil* XXII, 583–615.
68 27. Chenon, 'L'hérésie à La Charité-sur-Loire', *Nouvelle Revue historique de droit français et étranger* XL (1917), 299–345. Haskins, 'Robert le Bougre', *Studies in Medieval Culture*, 193–244.
28. Puylaurens, 765.
69 29. *Recueil* XXI, 741.
30. Puylaurens, 766.
31. Paris, *Chron. Maj.* IV, 22–4. Nangis, *Life*, 328.
70 32. *Recueil* XXIV, 554, n. 133; 552, n. 109; 661, n. 66.
33. Puylaurens, 767. There is a very detailed account of the siege of Carcassonne in a letter from William of Ormes to Queen Blanche: Douet d'Arcq, 'Siège de Carcassonne', *Bibl. de l'éc. des Ch.* VII, 363–79 and also in *Hist. Gén. de Lang.* VIII, cc. 1042–5.

CHAPTER IV – CAMPAIGN IN POITOU 1242

page 73 1. Joinville, 93–7.
2. *Layettes* II, 2928.
74 3. Delisle, 'Mémoire sur une lettre inédite adressée à la reine Blanche', *Bibl. de l'éc. des Ch.* XVII, 526.
4. Paris, *Chron. Maj.* IV, 178–9, 184.
5. Charles Bemont, 'Le Campagne en Poitou', *Annales du Midi* V, 289–314, gives the best and most coherent account of the whole campaign, with reference to all the sources.
75 6. Lot, *L'art militaire et les armées au moyen age*, 236.
7. Paris, *Chron. Maj.* IV, 195.
8. Nangis, *Life*, 336a.
76 9. Paris, *Chron. Maj.* IV, 213.
10. *Layettes* II, 2980, 2981.
11. Chron. St Denis, *Recueil* XXI, 113. Nangis, *Life*, 334e. Paris, *Chron. Maj.* IV, 253.

page 77 12. *Layettes* II, 2995–6, 3013.
13. Paris, *Chron. Maj.* IV, 230–3.
78 14. *Ibid.*, 232–42.
15. *Ibid.*, 242.
79 16. Runciman, *The Medieval Manichee*, 144–7.

CHAPTER V – THE KING, THE POPE AND THE EMPEROR 1235–1247

page 81 1. This attitude is strongly upheld by Powell, 'Frederic II and the Church', *Cath. Hist. Rev.* XLVIII, 487–97.
2. Rome, 'Henri II de Braisne, archevêque de Reims', *Travaux de l'Académie Nationale de Reims*, CLIV, 71–92. Pontal, *op. cit.*, 19–30.
82 3. *Layettes* II, 2404.
4. *Registres Greg. IX*, 2961, 2964.
83 5. Joinville, 670–71.
84 6. Nangis, *Life*, 324e–6a.
85 7. Paris, *Chron. Maj.* III, 626–7.
8. Nangis, *Life*, 330–2.
86 9. Paris, *Chron. Maj.* IV, 392.
10. Nangis, *Life*, 344, 346. Joinville, 106–7. Paris, *Chron. Maj.* IV, 397–8.
87 11. *Layettes* II, 3380.
88 12. Nangis, *Life*, 352, 354.
13. Paris, *Chron. Maj.* IV, 484.
89 14. *Layettes* II, 2719.
90 15. Paris, *Chron. Maj.* IV, 546. Nangis, *Life*, 354. Puylaurens, 770–1.
91 16. Paris, *Chron. Maj.* IV, 591–3.
17. Berger, *Saint Louis et Innocent IV*, 251–3.
18. Paris, *Chron. Maj.* IV, 608.
92 19. Paris, *Liber Additamentorum*, 131–2.
20. *Ibid.*, 99–112.
21. Campbell, 'Protest of Saint Louis', *Traditio*, XV, 405–18.
93 22. Boutaric, *Saint Louis et Alphonse de Poitiers*, 216, n. 3–217.

page 93 23. *Ordonnances* I, 97–9.
24. Langlois, 'Saint Louis', in *Histoire de France*, ed. Lavisse, vol. III, pt. II, 63–4.

CHAPTER VI – PREPARATIONS FOR THE CRUSADE 1245–1248

page 97 1. Nangis, *Life*, 342c.
98 2. Southern, *Western Views of Islam*, 34–66.
99 3. Lecoy de la Marche, 'Prédication de la croisade', *Revue des questions historiques* XLVIII, 5–28
4. Etienne de Bourbon, 91–2, n. 101.
5. Anonymous Chronicle of Caen, *Recueil* XXII, 23. Etienne de Bourbon, 89–90, n. 98.
100 6. Nangis, *Life*, 352. Paris, *Chron. Maj.* IV, 490.
7. Paris, *Chron. Maj.* IV, 502–3.
101 8. Strayer, 'The Crusades of Louis IX', *History of the Crusades:* II, The Later Crusades, collects and analyses on pp. 490–1 the figures in *Recueil* XXI, 512–15.
9. Joinville, 112. Louis's use of credit is described in Servois, 'Emprunts de Saint Louis', *Bibl. de l'éc. des Ch.* XIX (1857) and Sayous, 'Les mandats de Saint Louis sur son tresor', *Revue Historique* CLXVII, 254–304.
102 10. Philoon, *The Early Economic and Commercial Development of Aigues-Mortes, 1246–1314.*
103 11. *Layettes* II, 3522.
12. Philoon, *op. cit.*, 56.
13. Byrne, *Genoese Shipping*, 8.
104 14. *Layettes* II, 3537. Jal, 'Pacta Naulorum', *Documents Historiques Inédits*, 605–9. Philoon, *op. cit.*, 169–74.
15. Joinville, 112. Paris, *Chron. Maj.* V, 92. Puylaurens, 771.
16. Tillemont, *Vie de Saint Louis* III, 174, 111.
105 17. Joinville, 130–1.
106 18. *Recueil* XXIV, 4*.
19. *Enquêtes Administratives d'Alfonse de Poitiers*, i.
20. Joinville, 110–11.

page 106 21. *Layettes* III, 3715.
22. *Layettes* II, 3534.
107 23. *Ménéstrel de Reims*, 190–2.
24. Salimbene, 317.
108 25. Salimbene, 318–21.
26. Salimbene, 322.
27. Joinville, 123–4. Nangis, *Life*, 356.
109 28. Puylaurens, 771.
29. Joinville, 127.
30. Reinaud, *Extraits des historiens arabes*, 476.
31. Both Strayer, 'The Crusades of Louis IX', 493–5, and Runciman, *History of the Crusades* III, 257–261 give comprehensive narratives of the events during Louis's stay in Cyprus, with the relevant references.
110 32. Joinville, 136.
111 33. Salimbene, 301, 304.
112 34. Joinville, 146. Foulet, *Lettre à Nicholas Arrode*, 19–20.
35. Continuation of Wm. of Tyre, *Recueil des historiens des Croisades, Historiens Occidentaux* II, 571.
113 36. Strayer, *op. cit.*, 493–4.

CHAPTER VII – THE CRUSADE: VICTORY AND DEFEAT 1249–1250

page 114 1. Strayer, *op. cit.*, 495–504. Runciman, *op. cit.*, 261–74. Also Grousset, *Histoire des croisades* III, 438–93.
115 2. Wright, *Geographical Lore of the Time of the Crusades*, 300, 206–7.
116 3. Du Cange, *Joinville*, Dissertation, 18, 244–6.
118 4. *Rec. Hist. Crois.*, *Hist. Occ.* II, 595.
5. Paris, *Liber Additamentorum*, 152–4, 165–70.
6. *Ibid.*, 167–9.
119 7. Berger, *Blanche de Castille*, 373.
8. Joinville, 183.
121 9. *Ibid.*, 206.
123 10. *Ibid.*, 228.
124 11. Riant, 'Déposition de Charles d'Anjou', *Notices et Documents* . . . 171.

page 125 12. *Song of Roland*, trans. D. L. Sayers (London, 1957), 123, ll.1863–5.
126 13. Joinville, 397–8.
14. *Ibid.*, 399–400.
15. Maqrisi (trans. Blochet), 227.
127 16. St Pathus, *Vie*, 112–13.
17. Nangis, 376
18. Joinville, 403.
19. *Ibid.*, 322.
20. Riant, 'Déposition', 171–2.
21. Strayer, 'Crusades of Louis IX', 490–2, 504.
129 22. Riant, 'Déposition', 172–3.
23. Joinville, 366–7.
130 24. Riant, 'Déposition', 174.
25. Joinville, 381–5
26. *Ibid.*, 386–7. St Pathus, *Vie*, 127–8.
131 27. *Rec. Hist. Crois.: Hist. Orientaux* II, 214.

CHAPTER VIII – THE YEARS IN OUTREMER 1250–1254

page 132 1. Joinville, 405.
133 2. *Ibid.*, 430–4.
3. Duchesne, *Historiae Francorum Scriptores* (Paris, 1649) V, 428–32. Translation in Joinville, Hague edition, 247–54.
134 4. *Chart. Univ. Par.* I, 317–18, n. 279.
135 5. A comprehensive narrative of events during the king's presence in Outremer is to be found in Runciman, *History of the Crusades* III, 274–81 and Strayer, 'Crusades', 504–8.
136 6. Baldwin of Avesnes, *Recueil* XXI, 164a.
7. Joinville, 451–63.
137 8. Beaulieu, 14.
9. Joinville, 554–7.
138 10. *Layettes* III, 3956.
11. Joinville, 516.
139 12. *Ibid.*, 551–2.
13. Fedden and Thomson, *Crusader Castles*, 32–5.
14. Joinville, 565–6.

page 140 15. *Ibid.*, 569–81.
16. St Pathus, *Vie*, 100–2.
17. Beaulieu, 17c.
18. Joinville, 605.
141 19. *Ibid.*, 617.
20. Beaulieu, 18, 14–15.
142 21. Joinville, 618–29.
22. *Ibid.*, 630–3.
143 23. *Ibid.*, 645–9.
24. *Ibid.*, 640–4.
145 25. Paris, *Chron. Maj.* V, 465–6.
26. *Ibid.*, 459–60.

CHAPTER IX – RETURN TO FRANCE 1254

page 146 1. Paris, *Chron. Maj.* V, 170.
2. *Recueil* XXIV, 313.*
147 3. *Enquêtes Administratives d'Alfonse de Poitiers*, xix.
4. *Registres Innocent IV*, 5329, 5294–8.
148 5. Paris, *Chron. Maj.* V, 260.
6. *Grandes Chroniques* VII, 162–6. Paris, *Chron. Maj.* V, 246–52.
149 7. *Chart. Univ. Par.* I, 222–4, n. 197.
8. *Layettes* III, 4030.
9. *Layettes* III, 4055.
10. Webb, 'Roger Bacon on Alphonse of Poitiers', *Essays . . . to Reginald Lane Poole*, 292–300.
11. *Grandes Chroniques* VII, 168–9.
150 12. Bloch, 'Les Serfs du Chapitre de Paris', *Mélanges Historiques* I, 462–90.
151 13. Riant, 'Déposition', 175.
14. Rigaud, *Register*, 167.
15. Anonymous Chronicle, *Recueil* XXI, 83. Nangis, *Life*, 316.
152 16. *Layettes* II, 3534.
17. *Layettes* II, 3552.
153 18. Paris, *Chron. Maj.* V, 537, 439–40.
19. Salimbene, 322–3.
154 20. Joinville, 659.

CHAPTER X – PARIS: THE KING'S CAPITAL

page 155 1. Poete, *Une vie de cité*, *Paris de sa naissance*, I. Hillairet, *Connaissance du Vieux Paris*.

157 2. Fontette, 'La vie économique de la region parisienne', *Revue historique de droit français* XXXVI, 525.

3. *Ibid.*, 485–540.

4. *Ibid.*, 499.

5. Paris, *Chron. Maj.* V, 481.

158 6. Borrelli de Serres, *Récherches*, 45, n. 3.

7. Joinville, 114–18.

159 8. Guy de Bazoches, quoted in Wright, *Geographic Lore*, 332.

9. Guerout, 'Le Palais de la Cité', *Mem. des Sociétés Historiques et Archéologiques du Paris et de l'Ile-de-France* I, 57–183.

161 10. Du Cange, *Joinville*, 108–12.

162 11. Joinville, 726.

12. Douet d'Arcq, *Comptes de l'hôtel des rois de France*, v-vi.

163 13. *Life of St Thomas*, ed. Kenelm Foster (London, 1959), 45.

164 14. Little, 'Saint Louis' Involvement with the Friars', *Church History*, XXXIII, 141–2.

15. *Ibid.*, 142–3.

165 16. Poete, *Vie de cité*, 122.

166 17. *Grandes Chroniques* VII, 186–8.

18. *Recueil* XXIV, 25*. Borrelli de Serres, *Récherches*, 547–9.

19. Borrelli de Serres, 'Une legende administrative', *Récherches*, 531–72.

167 20. *Le Livre des Métiers d'Etienne Boileau*, ed. de Lespinasse and Bonnardot, 56–61.

21. *Ibid.*, 198–207.

168 22. *Ibid.*, 26.

23. *Ibid.*, 14.

24. *Ibid.*, 21–4.

CHAPTER XI – THE KING'S JUSTICE

page 170 1. Beaumanoir, *Coutumes de Beauvaisis*, II, 264.
2. Viollet, *Les Etablissements de Saint Louis* I, introduction.
171 3. *Les Olim ou registre des arrêts*, ed. A. Beugnot, I.
4. Quoted in Langlois, 'Les origines du parlement de Paris', *Revue Historique* XLII, 91 n. 1.
172 5. Anonymous Chronicle, *Recueil* XXI, 84g.
6. Viollet, *Etablissements* I, 265–73.
7. Le Roux de Lincy, 'Chansons Historiques', *Bibl. de l'éc. des Ch.* I, 372–4.
173 8. Guilhermoz, 'Saint Louis, les gages de bataille et la procédure civile', *Bibl. de l'éc. des Ch.* XLVIII, 111–20.
9. *Ordonnances* I, 86–93.
10. Chenon, 'Les jours de Berry au Parlement', *Nouvelle Revue Historique de droit français et étranger* XLIII, 81–2.
11. *Olim*, I, 35, ix.
12. *Actes du parlement de Paris*, ed. E. Boutaric, I, n. 518.
174 13. *Olim* I, 431, xxv.
14. *Actes* I, n. 1300.
15. *Olim* I, 497, xix.
16. Joinville, 66–7.
175 17. *Ibid.*, 59–60.
176 18. Nangis, *Life*, 398. St Pathus, *Vie*, 136–9. *Layettes* IV, 4697. Tardif, 'Enguerrand de Coucy', *Bibl. de l'éc. des Ch.* LXXXIX, 5–14, 414–54.
19. St Pathus, *Vie*, 139.
177 20. *Ibid.*, 140–2.
21. Joinville, 662.
178 22. Berger, 'Requête adressée au roi de France', *Etudes . . . à Gabriel Monod*, 343–9.
23. *Recueil* XXIV, 291–2, n. 127.

CHAPTER XII – THE KING'S ADMINISTRATION

page 179 1. Although there are still not enough studies of local administration in the time of Saint Louis there are three valuable ones: Strayer, *The Administration of Normandy under Saint Louis;* Waquet, *Le bailliage de Vermandois aux XIIIe et XIVe siècles;* and Michel, *L'administration royale dans la senéchaussée de Beaucaire.*

page 180 2. Beaumanoir, *Coutumes de Beauvaisis* I, 17–27.
3. *Recueil* XXIV, 394a, n. 21.
4. *Recueil* XXIV, introduction.
181 5. Strayer, *Administration of Normandy,* 103.
182 6. *Actes* I, n. 233a.
183 7. *Layettes* III, 4609–10, 4629, 4634, *inter alia.* Stephenson, 'Les "Aides" des villes françaises', *Moyen Age* XXXIII, 313–18.
8. *Layettes* III, 4598.
184 9. Strayer, *Administration of Normandy,* 92–3.
10. Chenon, 'Les Jours de Berry', XLII, 143–4.
185 11. *Recueil* XXIV, 519–20, n. 250; 483, n. 123; 386.
12. *Recueil* XXIV, 97, n. 18.
13. *Recueil* XXIV, 374–5, n. 66.
186 14. *Recueil* XXIV, 363–4, n. 14.
15. *Recueil* XXIV, 337, n. 78.
16. *Recueil* XXIV, 114, n. 167.
17. *Recueil* XXIV, 407–8, n. 14.
188 18. *Ordonnances* I, 65–81. *Hist. Gén. de Lang.* VIII, cc. 1345–52. Joinville, 693–719. Nangis, *Life,* 392–8.

CHAPTER XIII – FRANCE AND ENGLAND 1254–1270

page 190 1. *The Political Songs of England,* ed. and trans. T. Wright (Camden Series, 1839), 67.
2. Paris, *Chron. Maj.* V, 475–81.
191 3. *Ibid.,* 481–3.
4. The slow stages which ultimately brought about the treaty of Paris are traced in Gavrilovitch, *Etude sur le Traité de Paris, 1259,* and Chaplais, 'The Making of the Treaty of Paris (1259)', *English Historical Review* LXVII, 235–53.
192 5. Rigaud, *Register,* 351–2.

page 194 6. *Layettes*, III, 4411, 4412.
7. *Layettes* III, 4433–5.
195 8. Rigaud, *Register*, 396.
9. *Ibid.*
10. *Layettes* III, 4564–5.
196 11. *Layettes* III, 4416, 4466. Gavrilovitch, *op. cit.*, 23–5.
12. Joinville, 65.
197 13. *Saint Louis à la Sainte Chapelle*, 79, n. 149.
14. Gavrilovitch, *op. cit.*, 61, n. 1.
198 15. Labarge, *Simon de Montfort*, 186–8.
16. *Calendar of Patent Rolls* 1258–66, 145.
199 17. Walne, 'The Barons' Argument at Amiens 1264', *English Historical Review* LXIX, 421.
200 18. *Registres Urban IV* II, 581, 588–98, 600–1.
19. Walne, 'The Barons Argument', *English Historical Review* LXIX, 418–25; LXXIV, 453–9.
20. Wilkinson, B., *The Constitutional History of England* I (Toronto, 1948), 175–7.
201 21. *Ibid.*, 147–8.
22. Gavrilovitch, *op. cit.*, 62–3.
202 23. *Ibid.* Pièces Justificatives V, 121–3; VI, 123–4.
24. Boutaric, *Saint Louis et Alphones de Poitiers*, 110.
203 25. *Calendar of Patent Rolls* 1266–72, 140–1. *Olim* I, 263. Labarge, *Simon de Montfort*, 264, 271.

CHAPTER XIV – LOUIS OF POISSY

page 204 1. Chron. de St Denis, *Recueil* XXI, 119a.
2. Joinville, 27–8.
205 3. St Pathus, *Vie*, 72–3.
4. Joinville, 38.
5. St Pathus, *Vie*, 44 and n. 1.
6. St Pathus, *Vie*, 16.
206 7. Etienne de Bourbon, 443.
8. St. Pathus, *Vie*, 87.
9. Joinville, 34.
207 10. Beaulieu, 13e.
11. *Ibid.*, 54–5.
12. St Pathus, *Vie*, 37.

page 207 13. *Ibid.*, 73.

14. *Histoire littéraire de France* XXIII, 159.

15. Beaulieu, 13.

208 16. Rishanger, *Chronica et Annales*, ed. by H. T. Riley (Rolls Series, 1865), 75.

17. St Pathus, *Vie*, 118–19.

18. Beaulieu, 7

19. St Pathus, *Vie*, 121.

20. Beaulieu, 10d. St Pathus, *Vie*, 63.

209 21. Delaborde, 'Une oeuvre nouvelle de Guillaume de Saint-Pathus', *Bibl. de l'éc des Ch.* LXIII, 286.

22. Joinville, 668.

23. St Pathus, *Vie*, 19.

24. Beaulieu, 15.

25. Quoted in Thompson, *Literacy of the Laity*, 140.

210 26. St Pathus, *Vie*, 114–15.

27. St Pathus, *Vie*, 116–17.

28. Joinville, 661–2.

29. *Ibid.*, 594.

211 30. *Ibid.*, 122.

31. Delaborde, 'Une oeuvre nouvelle', 285. J. T. Noonan, *Contraception, a History of its Treatment by the Catholic Theologians and Canonists* (Cambridge, Mass., 1965) gives a useful summary of the contemporary attitudes, 246–57.

32. *Layettes* IV, 4859.

212 33. Boutaric, 'Marguerite de Provence', *Revue des Questions Historiques* III, 457.

34. Vincent of Beauvais, *De Eruditione*, 3, 8–9.

213 35. *Ibid*, 8, 176.

36. St Pathus, *Vie*, 63–4. Beaulieu, 7.

37. St Pathus, *Vie*, 59–63.

38. Joinville, 740–54. St Pathus, *Vie*, 64–71.

39. Bloch, *Les rois thaumaturges*, 89–97, 185–215.

40. Beaulieu, 20.

214 41. St Pathus, *Vie*, 58.

42. *Hist. Gén. de Lang.* VIII, cc. 1440–5.

43. Joinville, 53.

page 215 44. Bruel, 'Notes de Vyon d'Hérouval', *Bibl. de l'éc. des Ch.* XXVII, 612–15.
45. *Ordonnances* I, 96.
46. Joinville, 685.
47. St Pathus, *Vie*, 27. Beaulieu, 19. Nangis, *Life*, 398. Joinville, 685.
48. *Ordonnances* I, 99–103.
216 49. Joinville, 686.
50. Beaulieu, 13d.
51. Joinville, 667. St Pathus, *Vie*, 111.
52. *Recueil* XXIII, 150.

CHAPTER XV – THE FINAL YEARS 1260–1270

page 217 1. Rigaud, *Register*, 427.
2. Lot and Fawtier, *Histoire des Institutions françaises : II, Institutions royales*, 209–13.
218 3. Bautier, 'Les grandes problèmes politiques et économiques de la Méditerranée médiévale', *Revue Historique* CCXXIV, 20.
4. Kantorowicz, *Laudes Regiae*, 3–4.
219 5. *Ordonnances* I, 94–5.
6. Boutaric, *Saint Louis et Alphonse de Poitiers*, 188–91.
7. *Olim* I, 638–9.
8. Infra, 93.
220 9. *Layettes* IV, 4775.
10. *Layettes* IV, 4774.
11. *Layettes* III, 4156, 4312.
12. *Hist. Gén. de Lang.* VIII, cc. 1519–26.
13. Rouquette, 'Saint Louis et le comté de Melgueil', *Revue d'histoire de l'église de France* V, 182–99.
14. Joinville, 681.
15. *Layettes* IV, 5357–71 ; V, 831, 835, 838–9 ; IV, 5471–5480.
221 16. Joinville, 687.
17. Runciman, *The Sicilian Vespers*, 65–95, gives a detailed account of Charles's acquisition of the kingdom of Sicily.
222 18. Hefele-Leclerq, *Histoire des Conciles* VI, 31.

page 223 19. *Registres Clement IV*, 412, 419.

224 20. Tillemont, *Vie de Saint Louis IV*, 412–15. *Registres Clement IV*, 1332, 1379–80.

CHAPTER XVI – THE LAST CRUSADE 1270

page 227 1. Runciman, *History of the Crusades* III, 293–314.

2. Delaborde, 'Lettre des Chrétiens de Terre-Sainte', *Revue de l'Orient Latin* II, 213–14.

228 3. Nangis, *Life*, 412.

229 4. Joinville, 735.

5. Throop, *Criticism of the Crusade*, 147–83.

230 6. *Ibid.*, 69–104.

7. Ham, *Rutebeuf and Louis IX*; cf. Rutebeuf, *Oeuvres Complètes*, ed. Faral and Bastin, I, 543.

8. Joinville, 737.

231 9. *Layettes* IV, 5286 bis.

10. *Registres Clement IV*, 464–6.

11. *Layettes* IV, 5255–62, 5291–3, 5295.

12. *Recueil* XXI, 393–7; XXII, 580–7.

232 13. *Layettes* IV, 5132.

14. 'Inventaire et comptes', ed. E. M. Chazaud, *Mem. de la Société nationale des Antiquaires de France*, v. 32, 164–206.

15. *Layettes* IV, 5639.

16. *Layettes* IV, 5495, 5498.

233 17. Alphonse de Poitiers, *Correspondance Administrative*, I, 167–9.

18. *Ibid.*, 521–2, 565–6.

19. *Ibid.*, 505–6, 603–4.

20. *Layettes* IV, 5418, 5435–8, 5443–4, 5468. Jal, 'Pacta Naulorum', *Documents Historiques Inédits* I, 516–42.

21. La Roncière, *Histoire de la Marine Française* I, 184.

22. *Layettes* IV, 5483–6. Jal, 'Pacta Naulorum', 542–6.

234 23. *Layettes* IV, 5504.

24. *Layettes* IV, 5518.

25. *Layettes* IV, 5514, 5521–5, 5538–9, 5543–4. Jal, 'Pacta Naulorum', 551–98.

235 26. Trabut-Cussac, 'Le financement de la croisade

anglaise de 1270', *Bibl. de l'éc. des Ch.* CXIX, 114–20; documents 1–3, 123–4.

page 235 27. *Layettes* IV, 5638. Will of Louis VIII, *Layettes* II, 1710.

236 28. Nangis, *Chronicon*, 562.

29. *Layettes* IV, 5662–3.

30. Nangis, *Life*, 440.

31. Joinville, 736.

32. *Layettes* IV, 5297–8, 5301.

237 33. Alphonse de Poitiers, *Corr. Admin.* II, 411–12.

34. *Layettes* IV, 5209.

35. Guy de Bazoches, quoted in Wright, *Geographic Lore*, 237–8.

238 36. Nangis, *Life*, 440–2.

37. *Ordonnances* I, 104–6.

38. *Layettes* IV, 5710.

39. The best account of the crusade is given by Strayer, 'Crusades of Louis IX', 511–18.

240 40. Ham, *Rutebeuf and Louis IX*, 24–7.

241 41. Berger de Xivrey, 'Notice d'un manuscrit grec', *Bibl. de l'éc. des ch.* XXIV, 99–102.

42. Nangis, *Life*, 446–7.

43. Nangis, *Life*, 448–52.

44. Lot, *L'art militaire*, 196–7.

242 45. *Layettes* IV, 5730, 5734.

46. Foulet, 'Jehan Tristan, son of Saint Louis', *Romance Philology* XII, 235–8.

47. Joinville, 756–7.

243 48. St Pathus, *Vie*, 155.

49. Nangis, *Philip III*, 466, 468.

244 50. *Spicilegium* III, 667–8.

CHAPTER XVII – APOTHEOSIS

page 245 1. St Pathus, *Vie*, 28.

246 2. Delaborde, 'Enquête faite à St Denis', *Mém. de la société de l'histoire de Paris et de l'île-de-France* XXIII, 2–4.

247 3. Riant, 'Déposition', 155.

page 247 4. St Pathus, *Miracles*, 150–1.
5. *Ibid.*, 113–17.
248 6. *Ibid.*, 140–2.
7. *Saint Louis à la Sainte Chapelle*, 86–7.
8. Joinville, 761.
249 9. *Butler's Lives of the Saints* (ed. Thurston and Attwater, London, 1956) III, August 25.
10. Joinville, 32.
250 11. Berger, *Saint Louis et Innocent IV*, 2.
12. De Pange, *Le Roi très Chrétien*, 399.

THE SOURCES

page 253 1. Joinville, *Histoire de Saint Louis*, ed. and trans. into modern French by N. de Wailly, 1874. English trans. R. Hague, London, 1955.
2. Beaulieu, *Life*, *Recueil* XX, 3–27.
254 3. William of Chartres, *Life*, *Recueil* XX, 28–41.
4. William of St Pathus, *Vie de Saint Louis*, ed. H. F. Delaborde, Paris, 1899. *Les Miracles de St Louis*, ed. P. B. Fay, Paris, 1931.
5. Nangis, *Life* (in both French and Latin), Recueil XX, 312–463. *Chronicon*, *Recueil* XX, 544–82.
255 6. Primat, *Recueil* XXIII, 8–88.
7. Vincent of Beauvais, excerpts from the *Speculum Historiale*, *Recueil* XXI, 71–5. *The Vinland Map and the Tartar Relation*, New Haven, 1965.
8. Baldwin of Avesnes, *Chronicle*, *Recueil* XXI, 161–81.
9. Alberic of Trois-Fontaines, *Chronicle*, *Recueil* XXI, 595–630.
10. Puylaurens, *Historia Albigensium*, 1230–72, *Recueil* XX, 764–76. Some excerpts of earlier events are in *Recueil* XIX.
256 11. Ménéstrel de Reims, *Récits*, ed. de Wailly, Paris, 1876.
12. Paris, *Chronica Majora and Liber Additamentorum*, III-VI, ed. H. R. Luard, Rolls Series, 1876–82.
13. Salimbene, *Cronica*, ed. F. Bernini, Bari, 1942.
14. *Grandes Chroniques* VII, ed. J. Viard, Paris, 1932.

page 257 15. Continuation of William of Tyre, *Recueil des Historiens des Croisades, Historiens Occidentaux* II, 566–629.

16. Duchesne, *Historiae Francorum Scriptores* (Paris, 1649), V, 428–32; translation in Hague edition of Joinville, 247–54.

17. Sarrasin, *Lettre à Nicholas Arrode*, ed. A. Foulet, Paris, 1924.

18. Peter of Condé, *Spicilegium*, ed. d'Achery (Paris, 1723) III, 667–8.

19. *Ordonnances des rois de France de la troisième race*, ed. M. de Laurière, I, Paris, 1723.

258 20. *Layettes du Trésor des Chartes*, 4 vols. Introduction in vol. I.

21. *Les Olim ou registre des arrêts*, ed. A. Beugnot, vol. I, 1254–73.

259 22. *Recueil* XXI, 220–6, 236–51, 252–84, 286–392, 393–403, 404, 513–15, 533–6, 542, 556; XXII, 583–615, 623–72.

23. *Recueil* XXIV, ed. and with a valuable introduction by L. Delisle.

24. Alphonse de Poitiers, *Correspondence Administrative*, ed. A. Molinier, 2 vols. Also his *Enquêtes Administratives*, ed. by P. E. Fourmier and P. Guebin, Paris, 1959. The introduction includes a list of Alphonse's journeys and places of residence.

25. The papal registers for the popes of Louis's reign have been published by the Bibliothèque des Ecoles Françaises d'Athènes et de Rome, with various editors.

26. The last three volumes of the *Calendar of Patent Rolls*, Henry III, and vols. VIII-XIV of the *Close Rolls*, Henry III are the most useful.

260 27. *Etablissements de Saint Louis*, ed. P. Viollet, 4 vols., Paris, 1881. Beaumanoir, *Coutumes de Beauvaisis*, ed. A. Salmon, 2 vols., Paris, 1899–1900.

28. *The Register of Eudes of Rouen*, trans. S. M. Brown and ed. J. J. O'Sullivan, New York, 1964.

page 260 29. Etienne de Bourbon, *Anecdotes Historiques, légendes et apologues*, ed. A. Lecoy de La Marche, Paris, 1877.

30. Tillemont, *Vie de Saint Louis*, ed. J. de Gaule, 6 vols., Paris, 1849.

APPENDIX III

Bibliography

PRIMARY WORKS

Actes du parlement de Paris I, 1254–99, ed. E. BOUTARIC. *Inventaires et documents*. Paris, 1865.

ALBERIC OF TROIS-FONTAINES, *Chronicle*, *Recueil* XXI, 595–630.

Alphonse de Poitiers. Correspondance Administrative. ed. by A. MOLINIER. 2 vols. Paris, 1894–1900.

——— *Enquêtes Administratives d'Alfonse de Poitiers: Arrêts de son Parlement tenu à Toulouse*, ed. P. E. FOURNIER and P. GUEBIN. (*Documents inédits sur l'histoire de France.*) Paris, 1959.

BALDWIN OF AVESNES, *Chronica. Recueil* XXI, 161–81.

BEAULIEU, GEOFFREY OF. *Life and Holy Conversation of Louis of pious memory late king of the French. Recueil* XX, 3–27.

BEAUMANOIR, PHILIPPE DE. *Coutumes de Beauvaisis*, ed. A. Salmon, 2 vols. Paris, 1899–1900.

CHARTRES, WILLIAM OF. *Concerning the Life and Acts of Louis king of the French. Recueil* XX, 28–41.

Chartularium universitatis Parisiensis I, ed. H. Denifle. Paris, 1889.

Continuation of William of Tyre, known as the Rothelin Ms. *Recueil des Historiens des Croisades: Historiens Occidentaux* II, 483–639. Paris, 1859.

DELABORDE, H. F. 'Enquête faite à St-Denis en vue de la canonisation de saint Louis', *Mémoires de la société de l'histoire de Paris et de l'Ile de France* XXIII (1896).

——— 'Instructions d'un ambassadeur envoyé par Saint Louis à Alexandre IV', *Bibliothèque de l'école des Chartes* XLIX (1888).

——— 'Lettre des Chrétiens de Terre-Sainte à Charles

d'Anjou', *Revue de l'Orient Latin* II (1894).

——— 'Une oeuvre nouvelle de Guillaume de Saint-Pathus', *Bibliothèque de l'école des Chartes* LXIII (1902).

DELISLE, L. 'Mémoire sur une lettre inédite adressée à la reine Blanche par un habitant de La Rochelle', *Bibliothèque de l'école des Chartes* XVII (1856).

DE WAILLY, N. 'Récits du treizième siècle sur les translations faites en 1239 et 1241 des saintes reliques de la passion', *Bibliothèque de l'école des Chartes* XXXIX (1878).

DOUET D'ARCQ, L. *Comptes de l'hôtel des rois de France aux XIVe et XVe siècles.* (Société de l'histoire de France, vol. 130). Paris, 1865.

——— 'Siège de Carcassonne 1240', *Bibliothèque de l'école des Chartes* VII (1845).

DUCHESNE. *Historiae Francorum Scriptores*, V. Paris, 1649.

Etablissements de Saint Louis, ed. P. VIOLLET. (Société de l'histoire de France) 4 vols. Paris, 1881.

ETIENNE DE BOURBON. *Anecdotes Historiques, Legendes et Apologues*, ed. A. Lecoy de La Marche. (Société de l'histoire de France) Paris, 1877.

Grandes Chroniques de France, ed. J. VIARD, VII. (Société de l'histoire de France) Paris, 1932.

Histoire Générale de Languedoc, C. DEVIC & J. VAISSETE, revised by A. MOLINIER, VIII. Toulouse, 1904.

'Inventaire et comptes de la succession d'Eudes, comte de Nevers', *Mémoires de la société nationale des Antiquaires de France*, XXXII (1871).

JOINVILLE, JOHN OF. *Histoire de Saint Louis*, ed. and trans. N. de Wailly. Paris, 1874.

——— *Life of St Louis*, trans. R. HAGUE. London, 1955.

LANGLOIS, C. V. *Textes relatifs à l'histoire du Parlement depuis les origines jusqu'à 1314*. Paris, 1888.

Layettes du Trésor des Chartes, ed. TEULET, DE LABORDE, & BERGER, vols. II-V. Paris, 1866–1902.

LE ROUX DE LINCY. 'Chansons Historiques des XIIIe, XIVe, et XVe siècles', *Bibliothèque de l'école des Chartes* I (1839).

LE ROUX DE LINCY & L. M. TISSERAND. *Paris et ses historiens aux XIVe et XVe siècles.* (*Histoire Générale de Paris*) Paris, 1867.

Livre des Métiers d'Etienne Boileau, ed. R. DE LESPINASSE & F. BONNARDOT. (*Histoire Générale de Paris*: Collection de documents) Paris, 1879.

MAQRISI. 'Histoire d'Egypte', trans. with notes E. Blochet, *Revue de l'Orient Latin* XI (1905–8), (449–96), 192–239.

MÉNÉSTREL DE REIMS. *Récits d'un Ménéstrel de Reims au XIIIe siècle.* (Société de l'histoire de France) Paris, 1876.

The Mongol Mission, ed. CHRISTOPHER DAWSON. London, 1955.

MONTFAUCON, B. DE. *Les Monumens de la monarchie française qui comprennent l'histoire de France*, II. Paris, 1730.

NANGIS, WILLIAM OF. *Chronicon, Recueil* XX, 544–82.

Life of Saint Louis (in Latin and French), *Recueil* XX, 312–463.

Les Olim ou registre des arrêts, ed. A. BEUGNOT, vol. I, 1254–73. (Collection des Documents Inédits) Paris, 1839.

Ordonnances des rois de France de la troisième race, ed. M. DE LAURIÈRE, I. Paris, 1723.

PARIS, MATTHEW. *Chronica Majora and Liber Addimentorum*, ed. H. R. Luard, III-VI. (Rolls Series) London, 1876–82.

PRIMAT. *Chronique*, trans. Jean de Vignay, *Recueil* XXIII, 8–88.

PUYLAURENS, WILLIAM OF. *Historiae Albigensium*, 1230–72, *Recueil* XX, 764–76. *Historiae Albigensium*, to 1230, XIX, 193–225.

Recueil=*Recueil des historiens des Gaules et de la France.* XX, ed. Daunou and Naudet: XXI, ed. de Wailly, Guiniaut; XXII, de Wailly, Delisle; XXIII, de Wailly and Delisle and Jourdaint; XXIV, ed. L. Delisle. Paris, 1855–1904.

Registres des Papes. Bibliothèque des écoles françaises d'Athènes et de Rome.

Alexander IV (ed. DE LA RONCIÈRE), 3 vols.
Clement IV (ed. E. JORDAN), 2 vols.
Gregory IX (ed. AUVRAY, CLEMENCET, & CAROLUS-BARRE), 4 vols.
Innocent IV (ed. BERGER), 4 vols.
Urban IV (ed. GUIRAUD & CLEMENCET), 4 vols.

REINAUD, J. T. *Extraits des historiens arabes relatifs aux guerres des croisades*. Paris, 1829.

RIANT, COMTE. 'Déposition de Charles d'Anjou pour la canonisation de Saint Louis', *Notices et Documents publiée pour la Société de l'histoire de France à l'occasion du cinqantième anniversaire*, 155–76. Paris, 1884.

RIGAUD, EUDES. *The Register of Eudes of Rouen*, trans. S. M. Brown, ed. J. J. O'Sullivan. New York, 1964.

RUTEBEUF. *Oeuvres Complètes*, ed. E. Faral and J. Bastin, 2 vols. Paris, 1959–60.

ST-PATHUS, WILLIAM OF, *Les Miracles de Saint Louis*, ed. P. B. Fay. Paris, 1931.

——— *Vie de Saint Louis*, ed. H. F. Delaborde. (*Collection de textes pour servir à l'étude et à l'enseignement de l'histoire*) Paris, 1899.

SALIMBENE. *Cronica*, ed. F. Bernini. Bari, 1942.

SARRASIN, JOHN. *Lettre à Nicholas Arrode*, ed. A. L. Foulet. (*Lettres françaises du XIIIe siècle*) Paris, 1924.

Spicilegium, ed. LUC D'ACHERY, III. Paris, 1723.

THOMAS, A. 'Les plaintes de la Comtesse de La Marche', *Bibliothèque de l'école des Chartes* LXVIII (1907).

——— 'Une chanson française sur la bataille de Taillebourg', *Annales du Midi* IV (1892).

TILLEMONT, LE NAIN DE. *Vie de Saint Louis*, ed. J. de Gaule. 6 vols. Paris, 1849.

VINCENT OF BEAUVAIS. *De Eruditione Filiorum Nobilium*, ed. Arpad Steiner. Cambridge, Mass., 1938.

——— *Speculum Historiale*, excerpts in *Recueil* XXI, 71–5.

SECONDARY WORKS

ATIYA, A. S. *The Crusade: Historiography and Bibliography*. Bloomington, Indiana, 1962.

BAUTIER, ROBERT-HENRI. 'Les grandes problèmes politiques et économiques de la Méditerranée médiévale', *Revue Historique* CCXXXIV (1965).

BELPERRON, PIERRE. *La Croisade contre les Albigeois et l'union du Languedoc à la France* (1209–49). Paris, 1942.

BEMONT, CHARLES. 'Le campagne en Poitou', *Annales du Midi* V (1893).

BERGER, ELIE. 'Les dernières années de Saint Louis', *Layettes du Trésor des Chartes* IV. Paris, 1902.

Histoire de Blanche de Castille, reine de France. (Bibliothèque des écoles françaises d'Athènes et de Rome, vol. 70) Paris, 1895.

'Requête adressée au roi de France', *Études d'histoire du Moyen Age dédiée à Gabriel Monod.* Paris, 1896.

Saint Louis et Innocent IV. Paris, 1893.

BERGER DE XIVREY. 'Notice d'un manuscrit grec du XIIIe siècle', *Bibliothèque de l'école des Chartes* XXIV (1862).

BLOCH, MARC. 'Blanche de Castille et les serfs du Chapitre de Paris', *Mélanges Historiques* I. Paris, 1963.

Les Rois Thaumaturges. Strasbourg, 1924.

BORRELLI DE SERRES, L. L. *Récherches sur divers services publics du XIIIe au XVIIe siècle*, I. Paris, 1895.

BOURQUELOT, F. 'Fragments de Comptes du XIIIe siècle', *Bibliothèque de l'école des Chartes* XXIV (1862).

BOUTARIC, EDGARD. 'La guerre des Albigeois et Alphonse de Poitiers', *Revue des questions historiques* II (1867).

'Marguerite de Provence, son caractère, son rôle politique', *Revue des questions historiques* III (1867).

Saint Louis et Alphonse de Poitiers. Paris, 1870.

BRANNER, ROBERT. *St Louis and the Court Style in Gothic Architecture.* London, 1965.

BRUEL, A. 'Notes de Vyon d'Hérouval sur les baptisés et les convers', *Bibliothèque de l'école des Chartes* XXVII (1866).

BYRNE, E. H. *Genoese Shipping in the Twelfth and Thirteenth Centuries.* Cambridge, Mass., 1930.

CAMPBELL, GERARD J. 'The Attitude of the Monarchy towards the use of ecclesiastical censures in the reign of Saint Louis', *Speculum* XXXV (1960).

'The Protest of Saint Louis', *Traditio* XV (1959).

CAROLUS-BARRE, LOUIS. 'Consultation du cardinal Pietro Colonna sue le Ile miracle de saint Louis', *Bibliothèque de l'école des Chartes* CXVII (1959).

CHAPLAIS, PIERRE. 'The Making of the Treaty of Paris (1259) and the Royal Style', *English Historical Review* LXVII (1952).

CHENON, E. 'L'hérésie à La Charité-sur-Loire et les débuts de l'inquisition monastique', *Nouvelle Revue Historique de droit français et étranger* XL (1917).

——— *Histoire Générale de droit français public et privé.* 2 vols. Paris, 1926–9.

——— 'Les jours de Berry au Parlement de Paris de 1255–1328', *Nouvelle Revue Historique de droit français et étranger,* XLII (1918), 143–91; XLIII (1919), 71–111.

CIPOLLA, CARLO M. *Money, Prices and Civilisation in the Mediterranean World, fifth to seventeenth century.* Princeton, 1956.

DARLINGTON, OSCAR G. *The Travels of Odo Rigaud, archbishop of Rouen* (1248–75). Philadelphia, 1940.

DE LAGARDE, GEORGES. *La Naissance de l'esprit laique au declin du Moyen Age.* vol. I: Bilan du XIIIe siècle, 3rd ed. Louvain, Paris, 1956.

DELISLE, LEOPOLD. 'Chartes du sire de Joinville pour le prieuré de Remonvaux', *Bibliothèque de l'école des Chartes* XVIII (1856).

——— 'Le Clergé Normand au XIIIe siècle', *Bibliothèque de l'école des Chartes* III (1846).

——— 'Fragment d'un registre des enquêteurs de Saint Louis', *Académie des Inscriptions et Belles Lettres: Comptes Rendus.* Paris, 1889.

DE PANGE, JEAN. *Le Roi très Chrétien.* Paris, 1949.

DE WAILLY, NATALIS. 'Sur la date et le lieu de naissance de Saint Louis', *Académie des Inscriptions et Belles Lettres; Comptes Rendus.* Paris, 1865.

DIMIER, ANSELME. *Saint Louis et Cîteaux.* Paris, 1954.

DU CANGE, C. DU FRESNE, ed. Joinville, *Histoire de S. Louys.* (With several dissertations on the reign of Louis IX.) Paris, 1668.

DUCLOS, H. *Histoire du Royaumont, sa fondation par Saint Louis et son influence sur la France,* vol. I. Paris, 1867.

FARAL, EDMOND. *La Vie quotidienne au temps de Saint Louis.* Paris, 1938.

FAWTIER, ROBERT. *The Capetian Kings of France,* trans. L. Butler and R. J. Adam. London, 1960.

FEDDEN, R. & THOMSON, J. *Crusader Castles*. London, 1957.

FONTETTE, F. DE. 'La vie économique de la région parisienne d'après des actes de vente immobilière du XIIIe siècle', *Revue historique de droit Français* XXXVI (1959).

FOULET, ALFRED L. 'Jehan Tristan, son of Saint Louis, in history and legend', *Romance Philology* 12 (1959).

GAVRILOVITCH, M. *Étude sur le Traité de Paris de 1259*. Paris, 1899.

GRODECKI, LOUIS. *Sainte-Chapelle*. Paris, n.d.

GROUSSET, RENÉ. *Histoire des croisades et de royaume franc de Jerusalem*, vol. III: La Monarchie Musulmane et l'anarchie franque. Paris, 1926.

GUEROUT, J. 'Le Palais de la Cité des origines à 1417', *Mémoires des Sociétés historiques et archeologiques du Paris et de l'Ile-de-France* I (1947).

GUILHERMOZ, P. 'Saint Louis, les gages de bataille et la procédure civile', *Bibliothèque de l'école des Chartes* XLVIII (1887).

HAM, EDWARD B. *Rutebeuf and Louis IX*. University of North Carolina, Studies in the Romance Languages and Literature 42. Chapel Hill, 1962.

HASKINS, C. H. 'Robert le Bougre and the Beginnings of the Inquisition in Northern France', *Studies in Medieval Culture*. New York, n.d.

HEFELE, C. & LECLERQ, H. *Histoire des conciles*. vol. V, pt. II; vol. VI, pt. I. Paris, 1913–14.

HILLAIRET, J. *Connaissance du Vieux Paris: Rive droite, rive gauche*. Paris, 1957.

Histoire littéraire de la France. Paris, 1733.

HUBERT, JEAN. 'Les Routes de Moyen Age', *Les Routes de France depuis les origines jusqu'à nos jours*. (Colloques, cahiers de civilisation). (Association pour la diffusion de la pensée française) Paris, 1959.

JAL, A. 'Pacta Naulorum', *Documents Historiques Inédits*, vol. I, ed Champollion-Figeac. (*Collection des Documents Inédits* LXX.) Paris, 1841.

KANTOROWICZ, ERNEST. *Frederick the Second, 1194–1250*. London, 1931.

——— *Laudes Regiae*. Berkeley, 1958.

KOHLER, CHARLES. 'Deux projets de croisade en Terre-Sainte', *Revue de l'Orient Latin* X (1903–4).

LABARGE, M. W. *Simon de Montfort.* London, 1962.

LANGLOIS, C. V. 'Doléances recueillies par les enquêteurs de Saint Louis', *Revue Historique* XCII (1906), 1–41; C (1909), 63–95.

'Une lettre adressée à Alphonse de Poitiers', *Bibliothèque de l'école des Chartes*, XLVI (1885).

'Les origines du parlement de Paris', *Revue Historique* XLII (1890).

Le Règne de Philippe III le Hardi. Paris, 1887.

'Saint Louis, Philippe le Bel, les derniers Capétiens directs (1226–1328)', in Lavisse, *Histoire de la France depuis les origines jusqu'à la révolution*, vol. III, pt. II. Paris, 1901.

LA RONCIÈRE, CHARLES BOUREL DE. *Histoire de la marine française*, vol. I; Les origines. Paris, 1899.

LECOY DE LA MARCHE, A. *La France sous Saint Louis et sous Philippe le Hardi.* Paris, 1893.

'La prédication de la croisade au treizième siècle', *Revue des Questions Historiques* XLVIII (1890).

Saint Louis, son gouvernement et sa politique. Tours, n.d.

LITTLE, C. K. 'Saint Louis' Involvement with the Friars', *Church History* XXXIII (1964).

LONGNON, AUGUSTE. *Documents Parisiens sur l'iconographie de Saint Louis.* (Société de l'histoire de Paris et de l'Ile-de-France, Documents, n.8.) Paris, 1882.

LOT, FERDINAND. *L'art militaire et les armées au Moyen Age*, 2 vols. Paris, 1946.

LOT, F. & FAWTIER, R. *Histoire des Institutions françaises au Moyen Age*, vol. II: Institutions Royales. Paris, 1958.

LUCHAIRE, ACHILLE. *Les Communes françaises à l'époque des Capétiens directs.* Paris, 1890.

MEYER, PAUL. 'Les derniers troubadours de la Provence', *Bibliothèque de l'école des Chartes* XXX (1869).

MICHEL, R. *L'Administration Royale dans la Sénéchaussée de Beaucaire au temps de Saint Louis.* Paris, 1910.

MILLER, EDWARD. 'The State and Landed Interests in Thirteenth Century France and England', *Change in Medieval Society*, ed. Sylvia Thrupp. New York, 1964.

MIROT, L. *Manuel de géographie historique de la France*, vol. I: L'unité française. Paris, 1948.

MOLINIER, A. 'Étude sur l'administration de Louis IX et d'Alfonse de Poitiers', *Histoire Général de Languedoc* VII. Toulouse, 1879.

'Les Grandes Chroniques de France au XIIIe siècle', *Études d'histoire du Moyen Age dédiée à Gabriel Monod.* Paris, 1896.

Les Sources de l'histoire de France, vol. III. Paris, 1903.

PAETOW, L. J. 'The Crusading Ardor of John of Garland', *The Crusades and Other Historical Essays presented to Dana C. Munro*, ed. L. J. Paetow. New York, 1928.

PELLIOT, P. 'Les Mongols et la Papauté', *Revue de l'Orient Chrétien*, 3rd ser., vol. III.

PETIT-DUTAILLIS, C. *Étude sur la vie et règne de Louis VIII.* (Bibliothèque de l'école des hautes études, 1010.) Paris, 1894.

The Feudal Monarchy in France and England from the Tenth to the Thirteenth Century. New York, 1964.

'Querimoniae Normannorum', *Essays presented to T. F. Tout*, ed. A. G. Little & F. M. Powicke. Manchester, 1925.

'Saint Louis', *Cambridge Medieval History* VI.

PHILOON, THURMAN E. *The Early Economic and Commercial Development of Aigues-Mortes, 1246–1314*, unpub. PhD. thesis. Yale, New Haven, 1940.

'William Boccanegra and Alphonse de Poitiers', *Medievalia et Humanistica* XV (1963).

POETE, MARCEL. *Une vie de cité, Paris de sa naissance à nos jours*, vol. I. Paris, 1924.

PONTAL, ODETTE. 'Le différend entre Louis IX et les évêques de Beauvais et ses incidences sur les Conciles (1232–1248)', *Bibliothèque de l'école des Chartes* CXXIII (1965).

POWELL, JAMES M. 'Frederick II and the Church, a Revisionist View', *Catholic Historical Review* XLVIII (1962–3).

POWER, EILEEN. 'The Opening of the Land Routes to Cathay',

Travel and Travellers in the Middle Ages, ed. A. P. Newton. London, 1949.

RENOUARD, YVES. 'Le rôle de l'empire Angevine dans la formation de la France et de la civilisation française aux XIIe et XIIIe siècles', *Revue Historique* CXCV (1945).

ROME. 'Henri II de Braisne, archévêque de Reims (1227–40), Blanche de Castille, et Saint Louis', *Travaux de l'Académie Nationale de Reims*, vol. 154 (1956).

ROUQUETTE, J. 'Saint Louis et le comté de Melgueil', *Revue de l'histoire de l'église de France* V (1914).

RUNCIMAN, STEVEN. *A History of the Crusades*, vol. III: The kingdom of Acre. Cambridge, 1955.

The Medieval Manichee. Cambridge, 1947, New York, 1961.

The Sicilian Vespers. Cambridge, 1958.

Saint Louis à la Sainte-Chapelle. Catalogue of exhibition, May to August, 1960.

SAYOUS, A. E. 'Les mandats de Saint Louis sur son trésor', *Revue Historique* CLXVII (1931).

SERVOIS, G. 'Emprunts de Saint Louis en Palestine et en Afrique', *Bibliothèque de l'école des Chartes* XIX (1857).

SETTON, K. M., general editor. *A History of the Crusades*, vol. II: The Later Crusades, 1180–1311. ed. R. L. Wolff & H. W. Hazard. Oxford, 1962; Philadelphia, 1962.

SOUTHERN, R. W. *Western Views of Islam in the Middle Ages*. Oxford, 1962; Cambridge, Mass., 1962.

STEPHENSON, CARL. 'Les "Aides" des ville françaises aux XIIe et XIIIe siècles', *Moyen Age* XXXIII (1922).

STRAYER, J. R. *The Administration of Normandy under Saint Louis*. Cambridge, Mass., 1932.

'Crusades of Louis IX' and 'Political Crusades of the Thirteenth Century' in Setton, *A History of the Crusades*, vol. II: The Later Crusades, 1180–1311, ed. Wolff and Hazard. Oxford, 1962; Philadelphia, 1962.

'The Laicization of French and English Society in the Thirteenth Century', *Speculum* XV (1940). (Also available in *Change in Medieval Society*, ed. Sylvia Thrupp. New York, 1964.)

TARDIF, J. 'Le procès d'Enguerrand de Coucy', *Bibliothèque de l'école des Chartes* LXXXIX (1918).

THOMPSON, J. W. *The Literacy of the Laity in the Middle Ages.* new ed. New York, 1963.

THROOP, PALMER A. *Criticism of the Crusade: a Study of Public Opinion and Crusade Propaganda.* Amsterdam, 1940.

TRABUT-CUSSAC, J. P. 'Le financement de la croisade anglaise de 1270', *Bibliothèque de l'école des Chartes* CXIX (1961).

WALLON, H. *Saint Louis et son temps*, 2 vols, 2nd ed. Paris, 1876.

WALNE, P. 'The Barons' Argument at Amiens 1264', *English Historical Review* LXIX (1954), 418–25; LXXIV (1958), 453–9.

WAQUET, HENRI. *Le Bailliage de Vermandois aux XIIIe et XIVe siècles.* (Bibliothèque de l'école des hautes études, 213.) Paris, 1919.

WEBB, C. C. J. 'Roger Bacon on Alphonse of Poitiers', *Esays in History presented to Reginald Lane Poole*, ed. H. W. C. Davis. Oxford, 1927.

WRIGHT, J. K. *The Geographical Lore of the Time of the Crusades.* (American Geographic Society Research Series, 15.) New York, 1925.

TABLE OF DATES

	France	*England*	*Spain and Portugal*	*The Empire and Italy*	*Papacy*	*Crusades*	*General*
1210	Philip Augustus 1180–1223 French victory at Bouvines 1214 attempted invasion of England	John 1199–1216 loss of French lands Magna Carta 1215 Henry III 1216–72	Ferdinand III of Castile 1213–52 James I of Aragon 1213–76	Frederic II (King of Sicily from 1197), King of Germany 1212–20	Innocent III 1198–1216 Lateran Council 1215 Honorius III 1216–27	The Fourth Crusade; capture of Constantinople 1204 Albigensian Crusade 1208–27 Fifth Crusade; capture of Damietta 1219	Foundation of Franciscans and Dominicans Growth of University of Paris and of Oxford
1220	Louis VIII 1223–26 Louis IX 1226–70 Treaty of Paris with Raymond VII 1229		Sancho II of Portugal 1223–46 success against the Moors by Castile, Aragon and Portugal	Frederic II emperor 1220–50	Gregory IX 1229–41 Founding of papal inquisition	Surrender of Damietta 1221 Frederic II recovers Jerusalem 1229	Building of cathedrals of Amiens and Rheims Founding of Royaumont 1228 Founding of University of Toulouse
1230	Blanche of Castile regent till 1234 Campaign in Brittany 1230 majority of Louis 1234 m. of Louis to Marguerite of Provence 1234 m. of Alphonse of Poitiers to Jeanne of Toulouse 1237	Campaign in Brittany 1230 m. of Henry to Eleanor of Provence 1236	Castile and Leon united 1230 Theobald c. of Champagne K. of Navarre 1234–53	Defeat of Lombard League at Cortenuova 1237	1235 Preaching of the Crusade	Mongol conquests in east and Europe 1230 on Sixth crusade: Richard of Cornwall and Theobald of Champagne, 1239–41	Royal dispute with University of Paris 1229–31 Louis acquires relics of the Passion 1239

1240	Campaign in Poitou 1242 Peace of Lorris with Raymond VII 1243 Louis arbitrates Flanders inheritance 1246 Louis on Crusade 1248–57	Henry III lands at Royar 1242	Alfonso III of Portugal 1246–77	Continual conflict of pope with Frederic II	Innocent IV 1243–57 1st Council of Lyons 1245	Fall of Jerusalem 1244 Seventh Crusade; capture of Damietta 1249	Sainte Chapelle built to house relics Consecrated 1248
1250	Death of Blanche of Castile 1252 Louis arbitrates succession of Flanders 1255–6 Grande Ordonnance Treaty of Corbeil with Aragon 1258 Treaty of Paris 1259	Henry in Gascony 1253–4 Provisions of Oxford 1258	Alfonso X of Castile 1252–84 Theobald Vc. of Champagne K. of Navarre 1253–70	Conrad IV K. 1250–4 kingship of Germany disputed between Richard of Cornwall and Alfonso of Castile Manfred ruler of Sicily 1254–66	Alexander IV 1254–61	Defeat of Mansourah 1250 Louis leaves Acre 1254	Well-known teachers in Paris Albert the Great
1260	Mise of Amiens 1264	Barons revolt: Lewes 1264 Evesham 1265 Statute of Marlborough 1267		Charles of Anjou K. of Sicily 1266–85 Benevento 1266 Tagliacozzo 1268 Execution of Conradin	Urban IV 1261–4 Clement IV 1265–8	Defeat of Mongols at Ain-Jalud 1260 Fall of Latin empire of Constantinople 1261 Fall of city of Antioch 1268	Thomas Aquinas d. 1279 Bonaventury
1270	Philip III 1270–85 Acquisition of Poitou and Toulouse by K. on death of Alphonse of Poitiers 1271	Edward I 1272–1307	Peter III of Aragon 1276–85	Rudolf I of Hapsburg, K. 1273–92	Gregory X 1271–6 2nd Council of Lyons 1274 Nicholas III 1277–80	Eighth Crusade: Death of Louis IX at Tunis 1270 Edward of England at Acre	First efforts for canonization of Louis 1273
1280	Philip IV the Fair 1285–1314		Peter of Aragon becomes ruler of island of Sicily	Sicilian Vespers 1282	Martin IV 1281–5 Honorius IV 1285–7	Fall of (Tyre 1287) (Tripoli 1289) (Acre 1291)	Enquiry for canonization of Louis 1282 Bull of canonization 1297

INDEX